Praise for

The Leadership Equation:
Strategies for
Are Champions for Ch... ...lies

S0-AKL-423

"Developing leaders is critical to the transformation of mental health care systems and particularly important to improving the lives of children, youth, and families in America. Leaders make decisions, guide practice, inform peers, galvanize change, and promote quality. As an eternal student of leadership, I have studied multiple strategies, tactics, tasks, and competencies of leadership. This book is an outstanding resource to anyone interested in becoming a champion in the field."

—A. Kathryn Power, M.Ed.
Director, Center for Mental Health Services
Substance Abuse and Mental Health Services Administration

"As former Surgeon General of the United States and the Director of the Satcher Health Leadership Institute, I can attest to the importance of leadership qualities to address the mental health needs of children and youth in America. This book provides valuable insights, real-world examples, and practical tools and is an excellent resource for all leaders in the field."

—David Satcher, M.D., Ph.D.
16th Surgeon General of the United States

"*The Leadership Equation* is a must-read for leaders, regardless of where you are on your leadership journey. It will reconnect you with the vitality that brought you into this field in the first place, at a time when vitality is very much needed. The book is nothing short of inspiring, brilliant, passionate, and mobilizing. Gary Blau and Phyllis Magrab have created the perfect how-to leadership book for anyone who wants to improve their leadership abilities. *The Leadership Equation* gives leaders, organizations, systems, and communities a model in which to move forward no matter how daunting the leadership challenge. We in the non-profit world have been waiting for this book for a very long time."

—Kathryn Shea, L.C.S.W.
President and CEO
The Florida Center for Child and Family Development
Georgetown University Leadership Academy Graduate

"While the field of children's mental health often focuses on services and strategies for improving the lives of children and their families, it is easy to forget the most important ingredient to making mental health services in the community successful—leadership! This book attends to the necessary ingredient that I believe is associated with the success of local systems of care. I recommend this book to anyone who dreams of leading community transformations aimed at improving the lives of children."

—Mario Hernandez, Ph.D.
Professor and Chair
Department of Child and Family Studies
Louis de la Parte Florida Mental Health Institute
University of South Florida
Georgetown University Leadership Academy Graduate

"*The Leadership Equation* provides a framework for understanding and implementing the complex set of variables necessary to develop a successful system of care initiative. Leadership bridges the values and philosophy of systems of care with on-the-ground pragmatism. I appreciate *The Leadership Equation* as a valuable new support for the wide range of potential leaders in communities like ours that are committed to this difficult and rewarding work."

—Matt Wojack, M.S.W.
Project Director, System of Care Initiative
Impact-Ingham County, Michigan
Georgetown University Leadership Academy Graduate

"Whether you're a new leader or a more seasoned one, this book will get you motivated to want to try a new way of thinking about leadership! You will be encouraged to step onto the balcony for a better view and not be hesitant to step into your power as a visionary to lead others. I highly recommend it!"

—Gwen Palmer
National Federation of Families for Children's Mental Health
Georgetown University Leadership Academy Graduate

"I thoroughly enjoyed reading this book. It is inspirational and practical, and it describes the art and the science of leadership. While written for emerging leaders, it is a valuable tool for experienced leaders as well. This book is for everyone who aspires to or finds themselves in a leadership role. Readers should be prepared to learn about leadership and children's mental health and to learn about themselves as leaders. Thanks to the many excellent contributors to this book. Those of us in the field have been waiting a long time for *The Leadership Equation*."

—Linda Roebuck, M.S.S.W.
CEO, New Mexico Behavioral Health Collaborative
Georgetown University Leadership Academy Graduate

"The concept of leadership as presented in this book is incredibly valuable because the material is presented in a manner that is easy to use and allows for learning, no matter your position or status. I would recommend *The Leadership Equation* as an excellent resource that can help leaders assess, plan and recast the direction of services for children and their families."

—Lenora Reid-Rose, M.B.A.
Director, Cultural Competence and Diversity Initiatives
Georgetown University Leadership Academy Graduate

**Systems of Care for
Children's Mental Health**

Series Editors:
Beth A. Stroul, M.Ed.
Robert M. Friedman, Ph.D.

The
Leadership
Equation

Other Volumes in This Series

THE LEADERSHIP EQUATION

Strategies for Individuals Who Are Champions for Children, Youth, and Families

edited by

Gary M. Blau, Ph.D.
Child, Adolescent and Family Branch
Center for Mental Health Services
Substance Abuse and Mental Health
Services Administration

and

Phyllis R. Magrab, Ph.D.
Center for Child and Human Development
Department of Pediatrics
Georgetown University

·PAUL·H·
BROOKES
PUBLISHING Co. ®

Baltimore • London • Sydney

Paul H. Brookes Publishing Co.
Post Office Box 10624
Baltimore, Maryland 21285-0624
USA

www.brookespublishing.com

Copyright © 2010 by Paul H. Brookes Publishing Co., Inc.
All rights reserved.

"Paul H. Brookes Publishing Co." is a registered trademark of
Paul H. Brookes Publishing Co., Inc.

Typeset by Aptara, Inc., Falls Church, Virginia.
Manufactured in the United States of America by
Versa Press, Inc., East Peoria, Illinois.

Library of Congress Cataloging-in-Publication Data
The leadership equation : strategies for individuals who are champions for children,
youth, and families / [edited] by Gary M. Blau and Phyllis R. Magrab.
p.   cm. — (Systems of care for children's mental health)
Includes bibliographical references and index.
ISBN-13: 978-1-59857-092-2
ISBN-10: 1-59857-092-7
1. Social work administration.   2. Leadership.   I. Blau, Gary M.   II. Magrab, Phyllis R.
III. Series: Systems of care for children's mental health.
[DNLM: 1. Leadership   2. Mental Health Services—organization & administration.
3. Adolescent.   4. Child   5. Family.   6. Professional–Patient Relations.   WM 30 L4335 2010]
HV40.54.L43 2010
362.2'04250684—dc22   2010015741

British Library Cataloguing in Publication data are available from the British Library.

2014   2013   2012   2011   2010
10   9   8   7   6   5   4   3   2   1

Contents

IV   Aspiration, Inspiration, and Survival

V   Leadership within a Cultural and Organizational Context

Series Preface

With the publication of this book, the series called *Systems of Care for Children's Mental Health* has now reached 10 volumes. This series, under the auspices of Paul H. Brookes Publishing Co., produced its first book in 1995. The anchors for this series are two large volumes addressing a wide range of issues on developing effective systems of care—*Children's Mental Health: Creating Systems of Care in a Changing Society* and the *The System of Care Handbook: Transforming Mental Health Services for Children, Youth, and Families.* Other volumes have covered topics such as service coordination, early childhood, cultural competence, services for youth and young adults in transition, outcome strategies, the effectiveness of services, and the challenge of integrating work into the lives of families with a child with mental health challenges.

The book series is designed to provide practical information to assist in the implementation of systems of care for children and adolescents with or at risk for mental health challenges and their families. The audience for the series includes policy makers, planners, administrators, program managers, practitioners, care managers, families, youth, advocates, educators, evaluators, researchers, and others concerned with improving services for children and families. The series is also targeted at university faculty in an effort to promote greater exposure to the system of care philosophy and approach within undergraduate and graduate programs across mental health disciplines.

The series, while seeking to provide practical information, also strives to capture the complexity and challenges involved in bringing about the type of system change needed to improve services and outcomes for children and families. Efforts to develop effective systems of care are enormously important not only to the well-being of children and families with special needs, but also to the health of entire communities. Such large-scale system reform efforts are difficult and multifaceted and call for a strong value base; clear conceptual and strategic thinking; effective partnerships and coalitions; the use of data for ongoing system improvement; strong leadership at multiple levels; and passion, dedication, and commitment.

We are pleased that through this book series we are able to capture the voice of professionals in the field and also of families and youth. The book called *Transition to Adulthood: A Resource for Assisting Young People with Emotional or*

Behavioral Difficulties, published in 2000, was particularly significant in this regard, with every chapter including a young adult as a co-author. We believe that it is essential that efforts to develop effective systems of care give voice to diverse perspectives, and we take pride in the diversity that is represented among the authors of the books in the series and the chapters within the books.

Systems of care are clearly at a different place now than they were in 1995 when the first book in the series was published. The concept is better understood, federal funding has helped support the development of systems in many communities around the country, and there is increased understanding of the mental health needs of children, youth, and families. The challenge now is to sustain the progress that has been made since 1982 when Jane Knitzer published *Unclaimed Children* (Children's Defense Fund, 1982), which systematically exposed the lack of services for youth with mental health challenges and the lack of "ownership" of this population at state and local levels. Now, the field must build on the knowledge and experience that has been achieved in order to enhance the effectiveness of systems of care and to expand them so that all children, youth, and families in need have access to effective services and supports consistent with system of care values and principles.

Dedicated and talented leadership at all levels within states, tribes, territories, communities, and service systems is required to meet this challenge. Such dedication, knowledge and skills must not be restricted to formal leaders, but also is needed among families, youth, service providers, and other stakeholders. The task ahead is to enhance the capabilities of individuals in formal leadership roles, as well as to build the leadership capacities of entire organizations, communities, systems, and consumers.

It is highly appropriate, therefore, that this 10th volume in the series is focused on the important topic of leadership. We hope that this volume will offer both important information and inspiration and will help to build the leadership that is essential to enhancing the effectiveness of systems of care and expanding them throughout the country.

As co-editors of this book series, it is our privilege to bring to you the voices of so many individuals whose work we admire and who have made such important contributions on behalf of children, youth, and families. We thank all of the contributors to this volume and to the prior nine volumes both for their contribution to the books and for their important work for many years. We also thank Paul H. Brookes Publishing Co. for the support that it has provided for this series, and we look forward to continued publication of important volumes to help advance the children's mental health field.

Gary M. Blau and Phyllis R. Magrab

Editorial Advisory Board

About the Editors

Gary M. Blau, Ph.D., Chief, Child, Adolescent and Family Branch, Center for Mental Health Services, Substance Abuse and Mental Health Services Administration, 1 Choke Cherry Road, Room 6-1045, Rockville, Maryland 20857. Dr. Blau is a clinical psychologist and is currently Chief of the Child, Adolescent and Family Branch of the Center for Mental Health Services. In this role he provides national leadership for children's mental health and for creating systems of care across the country. Prior to this, Dr. Blau was Bureau Chief of Quality Management and Director of Mental Health at the Connecticut Department of Children and Families and Director of Clinical Services at the Child and Family Agency of Southeastern Connecticut. He also holds a clinical faculty appointment at the Yale Child Study Center.

Dr. Blau was formerly a member of the National Association of State Mental Health Program Directors' Division of Children, Youth and Families, and from July 1, 1998, through June 30, 2000, he was the division's Chairperson. Dr. Blau has received several awards, including the prestigious Pro Humanitate Literary Award for "literary works that best exemplify the intellectual integrity and moral courage required to transcend political and social barriers to promote best practice in the field of child welfare," the Connecticut Governor's Service Award, the Phoebe Bennet Award for outstanding contribution to children's mental health in Connecticut, and the Making a Difference Award presented by Connecticut's Federation of Families for Children's Mental Health. Most recently, he was the recipient of the 2009 Health and Human Services Secretary's Award for Meritorious Service for his national leadership in children's mental health.

Dr. Blau has numerous journal publications and has been the editor of several books, including the recently published *Handbook of Childhood Behavioral Issues: Evidence-Based Approaches to Prevention and Treatment* (Routledge/Taylor and Francis, 2008), *Family Influences on Childhood Behavior and Development* (Routledge/Taylor and Francis, 2008), and *The System of Care Handbook: Transforming Mental Health Services for Children, Youth, and Families* (Paul H. Brookes Publishing Co., 2008). He received his Ph.D. from Auburn University (Auburn, Alabama) in 1988.

Phyllis R. Magrab, Ph.D., Director, Center for Child and Human Development; Professor, Department of Pediatrics, Georgetown University, 3300 Whitehaven

Street, NW, Washington, DC 20007. Dr. Magrab has dedicated her career to improving the quality of life for vulnerable children and their families. For the past 40 years, she has provided service, conducted research, and trained future professionals in the care of children with chronic illnesses, disabilities, and mental health needs and their families. She has been Director of the Center for Child and Human Development, a major research, training, and public policy program since 1975 and also has been Chief of Pediatric Psychology since 1969. Dr. Magrab has written/edited 12 major books as well as numerous research articles and chapters that reflect her personal and professional commitment to improving the quality of life for vulnerable children.

Over the past 3 decades Dr. Magrab has been actively involved in developing public policy to ensure society's commitment to children and youth with special needs and mental health challenges. She was one of the pioneers in the field of maternal and child health and children's mental health to establish community-based, family-centered systems of care for children and youth with disabilities, chronic medical conditions, and mental health needs. For this work, she has received numerous awards, including the U.S. Surgeon General's Award and, most recently, the U.S. Secretary of Health Award for Pioneer in Developmental Disabilities. At Georgetown University, there is an Endowed Chair, the Phyllis R. Magrab Chair, dedicated to the continuation of this work. Currently, Dr. Magrab is deeply engaged in global issues related to social justice, health, and education, guiding and developing policy and practice. In particular, she is working closely with the United Nations Educational, Scientific and Cultural Organization (UNESCO) on its Education for All (EFA) agenda with an emphasis on disability and literacy issues. In 2006, Dr. Magrab was named to a UNESCO Chair to honor this work and to establish her continuing role in implementing EFA, and this year she began her term on the United States National UNESCO Commission.

About the Contributors

Cathy Ciano, Parent Support Network of Rhode Island, 1395 Atwood Avenue, Suite 114, Johnston, Rhode Island 02919. Ms. Ciano is Executive Director of the Parent Support Network of Rhode Island, a statewide family organization that advocates for the needs of families who have children, youth, and/or young adults at risk for, or experiencing, mental health and related challenges. As a family leader, Ms. Ciano has been an active partner in changing state policy as it relates to children's mental health, provides ongoing training in developing family driven practices, and continues to develop and empower a strong cadre of family leaders to be actively engaged in reducing stigma associated with mental health issues. She is also a member of the Georgetown University Leadership Academy faculty. Cathy is a strong advocate for the Public Health Approach to Children's Mental Health, which emphasizes promotion and prevention. Ms. Ciano has over 20 years of experience raising five children, two with very significant mental health needs.

Shannon CrossBear, Post Office Box 214, Hovland, Minnesota 55605. Ms. CrossBear is an Ojibwe/Irish mother and grandmother, storyteller, and leader in traditional healing methodologies. She has demonstrated her lifelong commitment through 30 years of leadership in human services fields.

King E. Davis, Ph.D., School of Social Work, The University of Texas at Austin, Mail Drop 3500, 1 University Station, Austin, Texas 78712. Dr. Davis has held the Robert Lee Sutherland Chair in Mental Health and Social Policy since 2000. He served as director of the Hogg Foundation for Mental Health from 2003 to 2008 and was Commissioner of the Virginia Department of Mental Health, Mental Retardation, and Substance Abuse Services during the Governor Wilder administration, 1990–1995.

W. Henry Gregory, Jr., Ph.D., 9985 Village Green Drive, Woodstock, Maryland 21163. Dr. Gregory is a clinical psychologist whose expertise as a clinician, administrator, trainer, and consultant has included work in substance abuse, HIV/AIDS, juvenile justice, child welfare, school-based mental health, and behavioral health. Dr. Gregory's primary orientation is family systems. He is on the faculty at the University of Maryland, Baltimore County, and through his own organization, Rafiki Consortium, LLC, he consults and trains for public and private human services organizations.

Vivian Hopkins Jackson, Ph.D., National Center for Cultural Competence and National Technical Assistance Center for Children's Mental Health, Georgetown University Center for Child and Human Development, 3300 Whitehaven Street, NW, Suite 3300, Washington, DC 20057. Dr. Jackson is member of the faculty for the National Center for Cultural Competence at the Georgetown University Center for Child and Human Development, where she provides technical assistance and consultation for the Substance Abuse and Mental Health Services Administration's Children's Mental Health Initiative. Throughout her 30-plus years as a clinical social worker, Dr. Jackson introduced Stress Management programming as an integral part of client and family services in various health and mental health settings.

Ellen B. Kagen, M.S.W., Georgetown University Center for Child and Human Development, Suite 3300, Whitehaven Street, NW, Washington, DC 20007. Ms. Kagen is Director of the Georgetown Leadership Initiatives and one of the developers of the Leadership Academy Training Curriculum, a national leadership training and development program for professionals and families focusing on the leadership role within collaborative systems change and community transformation. Ms. Kagen is an experienced facilitator, trainer, and consultant and has more than 25 years experience working at the national, state, and local levels of government and nonprofits on leadership development, strategic planning, managing change processes, and community development.

Coretta Mallery, M.A., Center for Mental Health Services, Substance Abuse and Mental Health Services Administration, 1 Choke Cherry Road, Room 6-1032, Rockville, Maryland 20857. Ms. Mallery is currently Research Assistant for the American Institute of Research and is working at the Child, Adolescent, and Family Branch in the Center for Mental Health Services of the Substance Abuse and Mental Health Services Administration. She is a doctoral candidate and adjunct faculty member in Counseling at the George Washington University. Ms. Mallery's primary research and clinical interests are contextual influences on adolescent mental health.

Marlene Penn, 617 Stokes Road, Suite 4-315, Medford, New Jersey 08055. Ms. Penn began to navigate the children's mental health system through efforts to care for her own son and subsequently became an advocate for other families. She was the founding executive director of the Family Support Organization of Burlington County, and currently serves as a consultant on building family leadership within child-serving systems to communities and universities throughout the country.

Jessica Raper, J.D., Georgetown University, 37th and O Streets, NW, Washington, DC 20007. Dr. Raper is Senior Assistant to the President for Initiatives at Georgetown University, where she incubates strategic initiatives that require the development of collaborations within and outside the university community. Her priority areas of focus include health systems development and conflict resolution.

Knute Rotto, M.S.W., Chief Executive Officer, Choices, Inc., 4701 N. Keystone, Suite 150, Indianapolis, Indiana 46205. Mr. Rotto is Chief Executive Officer of Choices, Inc., a nonprofit organization that has developed cost-effective, comprehensive systems of care in Indiana, Ohio, and Maryland. Mr. Rotto is a nationally recognized expert in creating high-fidelity wraparound programs, managing provider networks of strength-based, community-based services, and developing braided and flexible funding streams.

Suganya Sockalingam, Ph.D., 2721 Breakers Creek Drive, Las Vegas, Nevada 89134. Dr. Sockalingam assists agencies by addressing systems transformation focusing on leadership, cultural competence, health disparities, and cross-cultural communication. She conducts focused dialogues, consensus development, strategic planning, and implementation workshops for public health, including behavioral health, social services, and education organizations.

Sandra A. Spencer, Executive Director, National Federation of Families for Children's Mental Health, 9605 Medical Center Drive, Suite 280, Rockville, Maryland 20850. Ms. Spencer has navigated a highly visible career path through local family organizing, state level systems of care development, advocacy, national meeting planning for both the Federation of Families for Children's Mental Health and the Technical Assistance Partnership, and providing training and technical assistance to family-run organizations. Ms. Spencer has become a much sought after public speaker on the subject of children's mental health from a national as well as a parent's perspective. Her combination of passion and experience validates her message.

Dnika J. Travis, Ph.D., The University of Texas School of Social Work, 1 University Station D3500, Austin, Texas 78712. Dr. Travis is an assistant professor at the University of Texas at Austin School of Social Work. Dr. Travis specializes in employee voice, leadership, and organizational behavior in nonprofit, public, and corporate settings. Her research and project management experience has specifically focused on employee engagement and retention, organizational change and effectiveness, and global workplace diversity and inclusion.

Elizabeth (Liz) Z. Waetzig, J.D., 485 Maylin Street, Pasadena, California 91105. Dr. Waetzig specializes in organizational behavior with an emphasis on leadership. She has been managing conflict as a lawyer, mediator, facilitator, and trainer for more than 15 years. She focuses her efforts in the areas of health care, mental health, child welfare, education, and other human services.

Jane A. Walker, M.S.W., Maryland Coalition of Families for Children's Mental Health, 10632 Little Patuxent Parkway, Suite 119, Columbia, Maryland 21044. Ms. Walker is a social worker and the mother of five children. She was a founding member of the National Federation of Families for Children's Mental Health, and since 1999 has been Executive Director of the Maryland Coalition of Families for Children's Mental Health.

James R. Wotring, A.C.S.W., Department of Pediatrics, Georgetown University Center for Child and Human Development, 3300 Whitehaven Street, NW, Suite 3300, Box 571485, Washington, DC 20057. Mr. Wotring is Assistant Professor and Director of the National Technical Assistance Center for Children's Mental Health at Georgetown University Center for Child and Human Development. In this role, he consults with states and communities on a variety of topics and supports a faculty and staff who provide training and technical assistance throughout the country. Prior to this, he served as Director of Programs for Children with a Serious Emotional Disturbance with the Michigan Department of Community Health.

Albert Zachik, M.D., State of Maryland Mental Hygiene Administration, Spring Grove Hospital Center, 55 Wade Avenue, Dix Building, Catonsville, Maryland 21228. Dr. Zachik is Director, Office of Child and Adolescent Services, Mental Hygiene Administration, Maryland State Department of Health and Mental Hygiene. He is a child and adolescent psychiatrist and a member of the American Academy of Child and Adolescent Psychiatry's Workgroup on Community Systems of Care. He is a member of the clinical faculty in psychiatry at the Johns Hopkins University School of Medicine and the Georgetown University School of Medicine. Dr. Zachik has a special interest in developing a statewide system of care in Maryland for children and adolescents with mental health needs. This system integrates mental health services into all existing programs that serve children and youth, including schools, early childhood programs, juvenile justice services, and social services.

Acknowledgments

Leadership is a journey that requires collaboration and teamwork. And, in fact, the journey of completing this book would not have happened were it not for our partners who embodied these qualities. First, we thank and acknowledge the work and commitment of our authors. They had to withstand and navigate the editorial process, with its multiple deadlines, and it is their collective experience and expertise that makes this volume spring to life in meaningful ways. We also acknowledge the assistance of our Consulting Editor, Cliff Davis. Cliff helped organize the details of the project and provided review of content and structure. We deeply appreciate his efforts. Similarly, we thank Coretta Mallery for her stewardship of the copyediting process, especially her work to make sure that everyone stayed on task and on schedule.

Many thanks to Series Editors Beth Stroul and Bob Friedman and Paul H. Brookes Publishing Co. for believing in the idea to produce a volume on leadership. Beth and Bob have provided leadership in systems of care for over 25 years, and it was a privilege to work with them and Brookes to produce this book. An extra thanks goes to Beth for providing the original inspiration to make this volume a reality. In addition, we pay tribute to the Harvard Kennedy School, where Phyllis and so many others were first inspired to embrace themselves as leaders, and to the leadership academy faculty who created the foundation for the curriculum that has become the Georgetown Leadership Academy.

We also do not want to let this opportunity go by without saying thank you to our families. Gary wants to specifically acknowledge his amazing wife of 26 years, Gwenn, and their two fabulous children, Jennifer and Andrew. All of them bring him tremendous pride in the people they are and have become. For him, they have been a source of inspiration and support, and he loves them more than simple words can express. Gary also acknowledges his parents, Burt and Louise Blau, and his mother-in-law, Elaine Brittner. The unconditional love of caring parents is the foundation for success, and he was blessed from birth and through marriage.

Phyllis wants first to acknowledge her lifelong love, Grant, who is ever patient and whose dedication to serve adolescents with the toughest behavioral challenges has been an enduring inspiration. Her three children Brendan (a very competent leader), Ryan (a successful entrepreneur), and Kylee (a born talent) have been the wellspring of her devotion to the well-being of the most vulnerable children. And they have brought their partners and children, Phyllis' grandchildren—Ryan, Carson, Justin, Quinn, Andrew, and Nate, who have enriched her life and brought perspective on the challenges for future leaders.

Finally, we want to acknowledge the leaders and future leaders of our field. We can think of no greater calling than to create a life and career dedicated to children and to improving services, supports, and systems. If this is your calling, this book is dedicated to your journey.

THE
LEADERSHIP
EQUATION

Introduction

A Philosophy and Framework for Leadership in Children's Services

This book, *The Leadership Equation: Strategies for Individuals Who Are Champions for Children, Youth, and Families* stakes out important, new territory in the leadership field by articulating the role and characteristics of leadership needed to develop effective human service delivery systems, particularly systems of care for children and youth with mental health challenges. Combining literature from various leadership perspectives, the authors of each chapter explore new dimensions of leadership, from mental models to culture, from old-style leadership to new, from a fundamental values base to resiliency, and from community organization to innovation. All of this is accomplished under the umbrella of the "leadership equation," a strategic approach from which individuals can chart their own leadership journey. More important, *The Leadership Equation* is more than the title of this book or a simple catchphrase; it is a deliberate and planned methodology that anchors and guides leadership work. For all leadership challenges, no matter how large or small and no matter the strategies used, *The Leadership Equation* provides a foundation from which to base decisions and actions.

Although the information and examples used in this book draw heavily from leadership lessons learned in the building of systems of care in the field of children's mental health, the content has broad application across all human service delivery systems. As is true in all areas of human service delivery, the complexity of providing effective services and supports, in this instance to children, youth, and their families who are faced with mental health challenges, requires dedicated leadership and commitment from multiple stakeholders, including parents, providers, program developers, policy planners, and others. For example, without a broad range of individuals who champion the needs and desires of children and families, little progress will occur to achieve improved mental health outcomes in the United States. Yet, all too often these needed leaders are thrust into leadership roles with little training, experience, or opportunity to reflect on their skills and impact. By combining theory and research with practical applications, this book brings together existing literature, examples from real-world situations, and personal tools readers may use to better understand and realize their leadership roles.

Because the context of this book is human service delivery leadership, it is important to reflect on the specific challenges to achieve effective coordinated systems of care and services at all levels, particularly the aligning of values and goals across the many partners. This systemization requires a special kind of leadership—a change from top-down, patriarchal dominance to alliances spread out across many equal partners. Alliance leadership depends on those who can help broker differences, lead the group to common ground, and think differently today than they did yesterday. This is a particular focus of this book.

Each author contributing to this book has followed a unique leadership journey, most spanning decades, and each brings that experience to bear in critical leadership areas. Most have led components of local or state systems of care or have played a leadership role in evolving effective human service delivery systems; all share a commitment to the development of broader, deeper leadership at the community, state, and national levels. Also of importance, the authors share a deep commitment to young people, especially those who experience a variety of life challenges, and the families who love them. This volume is based on a vast experience of providing a leadership-development program at Georgetown University to more than 1,000 leaders to date, which serves as a forum to stimulate thinking, create commitment, and inspire actions that will undoubtedly improve services and systems across America.

Because the context for this book is systems of care for children's mental health, the reader can benefit from an understanding of this concept and how it stands as an effective example for the broader field of human service delivery. A system of care

Is a coordinated network of community-based services and supports that are organized to meet the challenges of children and youth with serious mental health needs and their families. Families and youth work in partnership with public and private organizations to design mental health services and supports that are effective, that build on the strengths of individuals, and that address each person's cultural and linguistic needs. A system of care helps children, youth, and families function better at home, in school, in the community, and throughout life. (Stroul, Blau, & Sondheimer, 2008, p. 4)

The term *system of care* is handy because it has acquired deep meaning to the field of children's mental health.

Most broadly, systems of care are about the creation of effective collaborations across many partners within every community. Leaders within systems of care strive to ensure that every child in the community has a chance to grow to

maturity, irrespective of obstacles that might be placed in their way, and participate in society in ways meaningful to them. Systems of care bring together many
people to share a parent's pride as a young adult graduates, having overcome those
obstacles, and goes on to reach his or her full potential and a productive life in
the community.

The Core Values and Guiding Principles for systems of care call for least
restrictive, individualized, strengths-based, community-based, and culturally
diverse care for all children with needs in the community and their families
(Stroul & Blau, 2008). These principles have been codified in over half of the
states across the country and drive organizations in hundreds of communities
across the country, each using locally crafted language to express the shared values. In all iterations those consistent themes emerge—"keep them at home";
"keep them in their community"; "keep them in school"; "keep them out of jail";
"respect the family background."

The Core Values and Guiding Principles allow groups in communities across
the country to come together and commit to this values-driven approach on behalf
of the children and youth with mental health challenges and their families. The
foundation of shared values has allowed partnerships to flourish among community service agencies and among helpers and those helped in ways that could not
have been imagined half a century ago. Most important, care that is built upon
that foundation of shared values has proven to be more effective than older models of care, and none of this system building can take place without leadership.

The book is organized into five sections, linked together by content themes.
The first section, The Call to Lead, explores the personal realms of leadership
with a focus on personal vision and an exploration of personal values. Through
exploration of the relevant literature, examples from the leadership journeys of
authors, and instructional tools, readers will develop insight into leadership skills
and obstacles they may be required to address. This section will challenge the
reader to engage in self-exploration to answer the question "How am I a leader?"

The second section, Leading in the Context of Human Service Delivery,
presents a framework for addressing the critical issues of leadership in systems of
care. The framework is built on understanding the intersection between mental
models (how the leader perceives the work and the world) and adaptive challenges
(shifts in attitudes, practices, and beliefs) that must occur to create sustainable
reform. It is critically important to rethink or reframe the basic concepts of leadership to adapt to a philosophy that is driven by individualization and innovation.
The shift from a traditional, top-down, power-based leadership model to flatter
and more broadly distributed ownership and power is not easy. The strong
emphasis on partnerships in systems of care requires leaders to adapt and acquire
new skills, many of which are presented in this section.

The third section, The Leader in Action, builds on previous sections to present the key work of leaders. As the text explains, philosophies, values, strategic
plans, and individual skills only carry the work so far; it is action that creates the

changes that improve the lives of children and their families. Three intertwined action areas are necessary for system development: building and nurturing strategic relationships, facilitating groups to build shared vision and address differences, and implementing adaptive and innovative strategies to navigate challenges.

In the fourth section, Aspiration, Inspiration, and Survival, the authors provide an infusion of ideas for managing several types of pitfalls and personal stress. Many obstacles are predictable, and leaders can learn to recognize and navigate around them. Resiliency and stress management are critical for surviving the leadership experience. Systems of care leaders may come from anywhere, across a range of stakeholder groups, and system leadership will change over time as individual skill sets develop. The system of care approach thrives on this change and the influx of new ideas and perspectives it promotes.

And finally, the fifth section, Leadership within a Cultural and Organizational Context, examines the challenges presented by cultural diversity and racial and ethnic disparities in leaders' efforts to answer the call to lead. In doing so, the authors focus on how leadership can foster inclusion among collaborative organizations with different racial and ethnic histories and experiences.

We, the editors and authors of this book, are not alone in this leadership process, as we have seen countless examples of courageous leadership all across America. What this volume seeks to accomplish is to expand this cadre of leaders by encouraging and supporting leadership in as many people and systems as possible. Each reader's leadership journey is his or her own. What we seek to offer are guideposts along the way that support one's evolving leadership wherever it lives. This book encourages leaders to understand themselves and to seek inspiration in their own lives and from those around them. It encourages emerging leaders to purposefully create their own vision, looking to models in their own lives for guidance, wisdom, and mentorship. Systems of care leaders seeking to improve the lives of children, adolescents, and families must work to develop new skills, new perspectives, and new roles in this ever-changing world. In doing so, leaders can realize their own visions, dreams, and aspirations. We hope this volume helps inspire each reader to create his or her own path toward becoming an effective leader.

REFERENCES

Stroul, B.A., & G.M. Blau (Vol. Eds.). (2008). *Systems of care for children's mental health. The system of care handbook: Transforming mental health services for children, youth, and families.* Baltimore: Paul H. Brookes Publishing Co.

Stroul, B.A., Blau, G.M., & Sondheimer, D.L. (2008). Systems of care: A strategy to transform children's mental health care. In B.A. Stroul & R.M. Friedman (Series Eds.) & B.A. Stroul & G.M. Blau (Vol. Eds.), *Systems of care for children's mental health. The system of care handbook: Transforming mental health services for children, youth, and families* (pp. 3–23). Baltimore: Paul H. Brookes Publishing Co.

I

The Call to Lead

1

Personal Vision and Leadership

GARY M. BLAU AND CORETTA MALLERY

Much has been written about the principles and qualities of leadership (e.g., Kaiser, Hogan, & Craig, 2008). In fact, most people have preconceived notions of what leadership is and have their own ideas about people who demonstrate the characteristics of a leader. When asked, the vast majority point to political figures such as John F. Kennedy or activists such as Martin Luther King, Jr., or Mahatma Gandhi. More often than not, people equate leadership with the ability to inspire or motivate or to demonstrate courage in the face of adversity. Although these are certainly positive qualities, these notions suggest that leaders, or those demonstrating leadership qualities, are placed on a pedestal, some lofty place to which only a select few can aspire.

What has become increasingly understood after all of the writing and research is synthesized is that the field of leadership research still has no universally accepted definitions about leadership and very little agreement about how to develop leaders (Hackman & Wageman, 2007). There is even less agreement when it comes to addressing leadership issues in the mental health or human service fields (Anthony & Huckshorn, 2008). There is also the continued debate about whether leaders are born or whether leadership traits can be taught and modified (Sternberg, 2007). Sternberg (2003, 2007) wrote that leadership is the sum total of wisdom, creativity, and intelligence, all of which can be enhanced through skill development. Other models of leadership suggest that a complex interaction of factors is at play, including individual, environmental, and cultural indices along with situational and contextual components (Avolio, 2007).

In this chapter, the authors argue that everyone has the capacity to demonstrate and exhibit leadership. This does not mean that one must command a brigade, supervise hundreds of employees, or give speeches to an audience of thousands. Rather, it means that, in everyday activities, every person has the ability to act and behave in ways that are goal oriented and can encourage others to do the same. Every person can be purposeful in the direction he or she is heading, whether it is with family, one's own sphere of influence (e.g., at work or in the community), or in the broader context of society. For individuals involved with children and children's service delivery, this has often meant that it is important to find a way, every day, to value the importance of children and their families, to focus on helping every parent become a better parent, and to find a way to help others recognize the roles that health and social and emotional functioning play in development.

Becoming a leader—or perhaps, more important, recognizing ways to exhibit leadership qualities—starts with a personal philosophy. Leadership is personal, and each person must create his or her own leadership journey. This book is intended for current and emerging leaders who have an interest in personal development as a leader, and it is important to recognize that leadership is more than a simple list of qualities to aspire to or a set of behaviors to emulate. Each person's leadership approach and journey may change depending on circumstances and may differ at different life stages. A new social worker or nurse will undoubtedly have a different style and voice than will a Native American elder who sits on a tribal council. Context is also important. Leadership style will depend on sociocultural conditions, historical background, and the relationship between the leader and the follower. Each leadership journey is filled with choices, different paths, ups and downs, and ambiguity. What should remain constant is the guiding philosophy that transcends the twists and turns that occur across the leadership journey.

THE LEADERSHIP EQUATION

To chart the course for a leadership journey, the authors propose a strategic approach called the Leadership Equation. This approach is more than the title of a book or a simple catchphrase. It reflects a deliberate and planned methodology that anchors and guides a person as he or she seeks to have an impact in an area that matters—in this case, improving the lives of children, youth, and families. For all leadership challenges, no matter how large or small and no matter the strategies used, the Leadership Equation can provide a foundation from which to base decisions and actions.

$$L = (V + B + A) \times (CQI)^2$$

In this equation, Leadership is a function of Vision, Beliefs, and Actions, multiplied by Continuous Quality Improvement (squared). The vision provides the direction for leaders, in this case to transform children's health and mental health services so that all children experience joy, love, health, and hope and grow to reach their full potential and live full and productive lives. Beliefs are the values and principles that guide decision making—rooted in culture, morality, integrity, and spirituality—and serve as the guidepost from which actions are derived. Actions are the actual strategies used to apply the vision and beliefs to create impact. CQI represents the importance of obtaining frequent feedback so leaders can continue to grow and focus on being better tomorrow than they are today. CQI is squared to highlight the critical nature of feedback and input in effective leadership of system change.

Identifying a personal vision, recognizing and acknowledging one's beliefs, developing strategies to affect and improve lives, and obtaining regular feedback serve as the bases for the leadership journey. Depending on personal style, the development of a leadership approach and philosophy can be accomplished in a variety of ways, such as through self-reflection, in conversations with others, through a modeling and mentoring relationship, and perhaps through some form of journal or blog. Irrespective of personal style, what is important and crucial to the leadership journey is the process reflected in the Leadership Equation.

PERSONAL VISION

The journey to leadership begins with a personal vision, which reflects an individual's view of the world and framework for how she wishes to affect those around her. An example of this is the personal vision of Martin Luther King, Jr. He spoke of his vision of a "beloved community" in which all people are treated equally with compassion and justice (Baldwin, 1995). This vision guided his ideas and work. Personal vision is shaped by values, beliefs, culture, and the sum of one's life experiences. These things form the lens by which leaders view the world, and it inevitably drives every decision that they make.

A personal vision is often part of a greater shared vision within a community. The shared vision is an overarching theme that serves as the propeller for change and progress within the system. A vision can bring about pride in community members and serve as a beacon for the mission the community is working to accomplish. The vision at the Child, Adolescent and Family Branch of the Center for Mental Health Services in the Substance Abuse and Mental Health Services Administration is that "all children and their families live, learn, work and participate fully in communities where they experience joy, health, love and hope" (SAMHSA, n.d.-a, Vision section). This guides all of the branch's work and sets the stage for communication. Just as organizations and entities can have a vision, so, too, can individuals. Often, people do not consider the idea of creating their own personal vision, but the authors believe that a personal vision and the development of a personal vision statement are paramount to one's development as a leader.

To reflect on the importance of personal vision, take a moment to complete Worksheet 1.1 (My Personal Vision) at the end of this chapter. Write down your personal vision for yourself as a leader. What do you want to accomplish, and how can this be transformed into a statement that articulates your vision? Once you have completed Worksheet 1.1, take a moment to complete Worksheet 1.2 (The Call to Lead) at the end of this chapter. This worksheet is intended to help you think about yourself and your leadership qualities and characteristics. Where do you gain your inspiration, and what attributes do you possess that will help you on your leadership journey? Such introspection is important to the process and can often be the impetus for understanding and future action.

SYSTEMS OF CARE: A VISION FOR CHILDREN'S SERVICES

In children's services, the system of care movement was born from a shared vision to transform children's mental health services (Stroul & Friedman, 1986, 1996). From the shared vision, the following sets of core values and guiding principals arose: The core values are that children's mental health care should be community based, family-driven, youth-guided, and culturally and linguistically competent. The guiding principles call for individualized services that are comprehensive, including a range of services tailored to the particular consumer. Children, youth, and their families are included as full partners, and services are provided in the least restrictive environment appropriate. Services are coordinated at the system and service delivery levels and give emphasis to early identification and intervention (Stroul & Blau, 2008).

The success of the system of care concept is evidenced by the positive outcomes identified across many studies and evaluations (Manteuffel, Stephens, Brashears, Krivelyova, & Fisher, 2008) and by the recommendations of the President's Commission on Mental Health report (2003), *Achieving the Promise: Transforming Mental Health Care in America*. The system of care philosophy provided the foundation for the recommendations in the commission report and demonstrates how a vision can be transformed into action. The shared vision is not a prescription for how to implement this practice in a community but is a set of values that drives the way that infrastructure is created and emphasizes the importance of local control and community decision making. *System of care* was defined in 2005 by a group of stakeholders, including mental health professionals, family members, and youth:

> A system of care is a coordinated network of community-based services and supports that are organized to meet the challenges of children and youth with serious mental health needs and their families. Families and youth work in partnership with public and private organizations to design mental health services and supports that are effective, that build on the strengths of individuals, and that address each person's cultural and linguistic needs. A system of care helps children, youth, and families function better at home, in school, in the community, and throughout life. (SAMHSA, n.d.-b, para. 1)

Although a leader's personal vision needs to be aligned with the shared vision, the vision might not originate with the leader. It may be the leader's role to observe and organize an emerging vision shared by a group of employees or consumers, as was the case with the creation of the definition of *system of care*. The definition was born from the needs of the communities and stakeholders. It is then the leader's responsibility to become an advocate of the shared vision (Anthony & Huckshorn, 2008).

Along these lines, a leader's personal life cannot contradict this mission. If there is a perceived dissonance between the leader's purported vision and his or her actions, it will be difficult to spread the vision throughout an organization or a community. Furthermore, dissonance between the leader and the group regarding mission or vision, which becomes reflected in the leader's actions, makes it difficult to effectively implement the vision. Take, for example, the political leader who espouses the importance of morality and family values only to be discovered as an adulterer or an athlete who criticizes the use of substances and then tests positive for steroids. Such dissonance clearly impedes these leaders' credibility and ability.

THE LEADERSHIP JOURNEY

The leadership journey begins by taking a step outside of one's current schema to open up to new ways of thinking. This is a journey of self-exploration during which leaders become more thoughtful about themselves and more perceptive to their surrounding environments. People often make the mistake of trying to force a static way of doing things onto a dynamic and changing world and to create expectations that are rooted in traditional ways of doing business. Stepping outside of conventional methods allows a leader to see the best way to meet the changes. Karl Dennis, a wise and experienced founder of the wraparound service process and former head of the Kaleidoscope Project in Chicago, often says that "we can no longer think outside the box, but rather we must throw the damn box away" (personal communication, September 15, 2008).

Leaders who insist on giant changes are often missing the point, as small changes may ultimately lead to larger changes, often through a cascading effect. Letting go of the preconceived idea of serving people in an office setting, for example, allows the freedom to meet the needs of children, youth, and families in a different manner, taking into account a broader cultural context. For example, an intervention may be more effective when implemented in the home, school, or community than in traditional therapeutic settings because the work is done in the child's natural environment. This thinking is aligned with the system of care philosophy of being youth-guided and family-driven. Systems of care leaders must be willing to step out of their comfort zones and allow the needs of their communities to guide their work.

Systems of care leaders must also recognize that small changes can grow exponentially. The author of Chapter 10, King Davis, shares a story as follows:

The story comes from the tales of Kwame Nkrumah, the sage African lion, in a conversation with the youthful and arrogant Stokely Carmichael, an outspoken civil rights leader who coined the term "black power." According to the tale, Kwame and Stokely were discussing social change and the relative impact that one (Stokely, of course) assumed he would have in his lifetime. Kwame remarked that if Stokely assumed that he could move world affairs by an inch in his lifetime, he was a fool; if he assumed that he could move world affairs by even a quarter of an inch in his lifetime, he was an incurable egotist. The most that one could expect to move any social change effort was 1/16,000 of an inch, but the overall impact would be so great as to mark one's name forever in the annals of history. Quite a sobering and yet telling anecdote. (K. Davis, personal communication, January 23, 2009)

Just as leadership can result in change, it is often necessary for leaders to adjust and change as well. Leadership behaviors and one's leadership journey will change as a function of learning and feedback. As an example, the first chapter author had a personal vision that reflected the importance of family-driven care in mental health service delivery. Several years ago, this vision was modified to add the importance of youth-guided care. After meeting with groups of young people from across the country, it became clear that these young people, many of whom had significant experiences with child-serving systems, had unique perspectives and much to say about their own treatment and the treatment of other young people. From these discussions, a new policy direction was developed in which youth were empowered to have more voice and more involvement. Starting small with a national youth board, this idea has now transformed into a national organization (Youth MOVE National, Inc., which stands for Youth Motivating Others through Voices of Experience) that is creating chapters across America. This story also reflects how one small shift in thinking can spiral into a much larger systemic change. Indeed, the phenomenal results already accomplished by Youth MOVE were never imagined when the initial decision was made to begin including youth in the decision making. Youth leaders are emerging all over the country who are helping shape policy and practice.

Altering one's internal vision not only affects the community or organization, but it also has a significant impact on the leader. It allows a leader to transform his or her external reality instead of simply reacting to changes. This is the very change that leaders of systems of care are called to make. Some leaders adapt as little as possible so they do not disrupt the current system too drastically, yet other leaders choose to go through a major systemic overhaul guided by the system of care philosophy. Systems of care leaders exist in a reciprocal environment with the community they serve. Although they work to change the systems to best serve children, youth, and families, they themselves are profoundly changed by the children, youth, and families with whom they interact.

TRANSFORMING LEADERSHIP

Robert Quinn (1996) identified steps for leaders who wish to transform their leadership practice, the first of which is finding vitality. Young professionals in the mental health field are often drawn to the field by this vitality. They begin the arduous journey of graduate school and pursuing certification or licensure because of this vitality. It is not uncommon to hear young professionals talk of their passion for helping people. Leaders are continually challenged to reconnect with the vitality that initially brought them to the field.

The next step is to break old patterns of task pursuit and become open to new perspectives. All humans have certain ways that they have completed tasks in the past that have been reinforced either positively or negatively. When successful, these become rooted in one's mind as effective processes. Thus, someone who has been successful professionally as a children's social worker has this professional identity reinforced, and certain patterns become more and more firmly cemented as bringing success. This may prove challenging when the same social worker makes the transition to a different role that requires a new skill set. Leaders in the mental health field often have the vitality and enthusiasm for the work yet may lack management training; hence, they fall into the familiar pattern of using the skills that have worked for them in the past on a different set of tasks. It is then their challenge to set old patterns aside and to develop the new skills needed.

Being open to new perspectives is critical in a leader. Although one's core vision may be somewhat fixed, the external world is constantly changing and evolving. A community may have shifting populations that require new skills and new training. To meaningfully interact with this community, it may be necessary to be open to continuous self-evaluation and the possibility of restructuring.

As part of the leadership journey, it is also important to not be overly concerned with having the authority to provide leadership. Although this concept is covered extensively in Chapter 3, Leadership Functions and Styles, for the purposes of this chapter, one must consider and appreciate that leadership can occur at all levels. Zander and Zander referred to this as "leading from any chair" (2000, p. 66). Their insights go both ways, related to the leader and related to one who may be called upon to lead.

At the time their book was published, Benjamin Zander was the conductor of the Boston Philharmonic Orchestra. He tells the story of how he created "white sheets," which were simply blank pieces of paper left on every stand during rehearsals. The musicians could write down observations or ideas as feedback to the conductor (notice the similarity to the CQI component of the leadership equation) and, not surprisingly, once trust was developed, the blanks were often filled with creative and thoughtful comments, thereby improving the conductor's ability to lead. On the other side of the equation is the impact on the musician. Every person, regardless of the chair he or she occupied, began to recognize that each individual could have an impact on the whole, that leadership could occur from any location and any level.

A favorite story of the first chapter author comes from an interview for admission to graduate school. A group of prospective graduate school candidates were participating in a group interview. The professor conducting the interview asked, "Who in the psychology department should you get to know?" The interviewee thought he had the answer pegged and answered quickly with "the chairman of the department." The other candidates followed suit and identified the clinical director and the dean. The professor laughed at all of the answers and responded that in reality the most important person in the department, and the person who wielded extraordinary power and leadership, was the secretary. The secretary may not have had the same academic credentials as the faculty and certainly did not make as much money, but she knew how to make things happen and how to get the job done. That lesson not only turned out to be true, but it also has guided the author's personal vision from that moment on.

THE PATH TO DEVELOPING A VISION

The process of developing a vision over time and through experience involves internal commitment to the public good, recognition of individual worth, shared vision development (with mentors, peers, and consumers), and orientation to change. There are many steps along this path, the first being to engage with critical issues. In the case of systems of care, there was extensive documentation of the need to reform children's mental health care. This need drove the vision of reform.

This is also a process of self-discovery. Leaders must look within and clarify personal vision and individual worth. Quinn (1996) discussed the dangers of pursuing an end that is not aligned with one's vision. This process may begin by making a small trade-off that the leader feels is justifiable for the greater good. These trade-offs begin to make a cumulative impact on group vitality and zeal for the work.

Successful leaders often watch and evaluate other leaders. It is important to learn from peers and mentors how they develop and maintain their visions. People learn through vicarious reinforcement; thus, observing someone who has successfully navigated this path can assist with one's own journey. On the flip side, this can also help avoid the mistakes and roadblocks of others.

As current and future leaders go about creating, modifying, and evolving a personal vision for work in the children's services field, the authors offer six areas for alignment of personal vision, system vision, and leadership:

1. The quality of life experienced by children, youth, and their families

2. The individualization of care

3. Service flexibility and the incorporation of natural supports

4. The distribution of power through collaboration

5. The diversity of experience, viewpoint, belief, and possible solutions among stakeholders in the community system

6. The bridge between the state of the art and the state of the science

The quality of life experienced by children, youth, and their families: Perhaps the most common response when one is asked to explain one's call to lead within children's services is that the person cares about improving the lives of children, youth, and families. Within one's personal vision there is typically a passion and commitment to this endeavor. A person's path in life is often predicated on this concept, and leaders strive to create purpose. Quinn wrote about the heroic journey and the need to recognize that we must have a "continual search for meaning and direction in our lives" (1996, p. 46). A commitment to improving the lives of children is commonly expressed by systems of care leaders about their leadership.

The individualization of care: Emphasizing the uniqueness of individuals and creating and sharing a vision that allows for individual differences and adaptability is an important component of a personal vision. Each child and family is unique and requires flexible and individualized responses. Likewise, each community is unique and requires different resources and delivery styles. Systems of care leaders must remain cognizant of the need for this continuous flexibility in the implementation of effective systems, always remaining grounded in the shared community vision.

Service flexibility and the incorporation of natural supports: Leaders need to explore their own recognition of the importance of offering care across the full range of natural settings in which real families live and spend their lives. For example, office-based services may not be accessible or effective for some families, and strategies should be developed to create services that are adaptable. Leaders also need to push the system to recognize the importance of natural supports, of finding them and nurturing those ongoing relationships for every family. Leaders need to be open to the reality that anyone—literally anyone—could be the person who becomes important in life improvements for a child with mental illness and his or her family.

The distribution of power through collaboration: Systems of care leaders need to recognize that they do not control the group or the system they lead. Leaders understand that every group controls its own actions and decisions. A leader relishes helping the group find and wield its power by articulating the areas of agreement and shared commitment. This power has been amply demonstrated as families and youth have increased their direct involvement in system of care planning, decision making, and implementation. Some of the best decisions can be made when a leader turns over control to consumers. A testament to this is the strides the systems of care movement has made by turning over some of the power to the youth and families. There is an emerging body of literature showing that this practice improves outcomes (Osher, Osher, & Blau, 2008).

The diversity of experience, viewpoint, belief, and possible solutions among stakeholders in the community system: A personal vision must incorporate culturally competent services to address the needs of diverse populations. Moreover, the vision should move a step beyond simply accommodating diversity and value what diversity brings to the community. Leaders need to become very aware of their own cultural traditions and beliefs and recognize differences between their own culture and the diverse cultures represented in the group. Leaders who try to impose their own culture on a group quickly find resistance; leaders who listen for and articulate the group's culture find respect and progress.

The bridge between the state of the art and the state of the science: CQI, the last component in the leadership equation, should not simply be a necessary evil. Leaders should see value in it and incorporate CQI into their vision. This includes incorporating evidenced-informed practices, meaning practices that are based on evidence from research and clinical expertise that is consistent with the client and community values. To do this, one must first face any frustration or biases against accountability and evaluation. These terms are often used negatively in the mental health field because they can be taxing on time and valuable resources. Leaders must look to see how research and evaluation can actually strengthen their work and use it in a way that meets the needs of the systems they serve. Leaders must be willing to hear the feedback in response to system actions and make adjustments and improvements that reflect this feedback. This is a key strength of systems of care—the designed ability to continue to be responsive to today's needs, irrespective of what has happened before.

This chapter focused on the importance of developing a personal vision as a first step on one's leadership journey and for developing a foundation for one's call to lead. Although there will likely be forks in the leadership road, and changing decisions and strategies, there remains a need to maintain a vision for what one wants to accomplish. The remainder of this section addresses how values must also be considered.

REFERENCES

Anthony, W.A., & Huckshorn, K.A. (2008). *Principled leadership in mental health systems and programs.* Boston: Center for Psychiatric Rehabilitation.

Avolio, B.J. (2007). Promoting more integrative strategies for leadership theory building. *American Psychologist, 62,* 25–33.

Baldwin, L.V. (1995). *Toward the beloved community: Martin Luther King, Jr., and South America.* Cleveland, OH: Pilgrim.

Hackman, J.R., & Wageman, R. (2007). Asking the right questions about leadership. *American Psychologist, 63*(2), 43–47.

Kagen, E.B., & Hepburn, K.S. (Eds.). (2006). *Leadership in systems of care: An unpublished training curriculum.* Washington, DC: Georgetown University Center for Child and Human Development, National Technical Assistance Center for Children's Mental Health. Washington, DC.

Kaiser, R.B., Hogan, R., & Craig, S.B. (2008). Leadership and the fate of organizations. *American Psychologist, 63*(2), 96–110.

Manteuffel, B., Stephens, R.L., Brashears, F., Krivelyova, A., & Fisher, S.K. (2008). Evaluation results and systems of care: A review. In B.A. Stroul & R.M. Friedman (Series Eds.) & B.A. Stroul & G.M. Blau (Vol. Eds.), *Systems of care for children's mental health.*

The system of care handbook: Transforming mental health services for children, youth, and families (pp. 25–69). Baltimore: Paul H. Brookes Publishing Co.

Osher, T.W., Osher, D., & Blau, G.M. (2008). Families matter. In T.P. Gullotta & G.M. Blau (Eds.) *Family influences on childhood behavior and development* (pp. 39–62). New York: Routledge.

President's Commission on Mental Health. (2003). *Achieving the promise: Transforming mental health care in America. Final report* (DHHS Publication No. SMA-03-3832). Rockville, MD: Author.

Quinn, R.E. (1996). *Deep change: Discovering the leader within.* San Francisco: Jossey-Bass.

Sternberg, R.J. (2003). *Wisdom, intelligence, and creativity synthesized.* New York: Cambridge University Press.

Sternberg, R.J. (2007). A system model of leadership. *American Psychologist, 63*(2), 34–42.

Stroul, B.A., & G.M. Blau (Vol. Eds.). (2008). *Systems of care for children's mental health. The system of care handbook: Transforming mental health services for children, youth, and families.* Baltimore: Paul H. Brookes Publishing Co.

Stroul, B.A., & Friedman, R.M. (1986). *A system of care for children and youth with severe emotional disturbances* (Rev. ed.). Washington, DC: Georgetown University Child Development Center, National Technical Assistance Center for Children's Mental Health.

Stroul, B.A., & Friedman, R.M. (1996). The system of care concept and philosophy. In B.A. Stroul & R.M. Friedman (Series Eds.) & B.A. Stroul (Vol. Ed.), *Systems of care for children's mental health. Children's mental health: Creating systems of care in a changing society* (pp. 1–22). Baltimore: Paul H. Brookes Publishing Co.

Substance Abuse and Mental Health Services Administration. (n.d.-a). *CMHS Child, Adolescent and Family Branch logic model.* Retrieved from http://download.ncadi.samhsa.gov/ken/ppt/ChildrensCampaign/logicmodel.ppt

Substance Abuse and Mental Health Services Administration. (n.d.-b). *Systems of care.* Retrieved from http://www.systemsofcare.samhsa.gov/

Zander, B., & Zander, R.S. (2000). *The art of possibility: Transforming professional and personal life.* New York: Penguin.

Worksheet 1.1

My Personal Vision

Describe your personal vision statement for yourself as a leader who:

- Makes things happen
- Makes a difference
- Moves a community forward

My Personal Vision for Myself as a Leader...

From Kagen, E.B., & Hepburn, K.S. (Eds.). (2006). *Leadership in systems of care: An unpublished training curriculum.* Washington, DC: Georgetown University Center for Child and Human Development, National Technical Assistance Center for Children's Mental Health; reprinted by permission.

In *The Leadership Equation: Strategies for Individuals Who Are Champions for Children, Youth, and Families* edited by Gary M. Blau & Phyllis R. Magrab (2010; Paul H. Brookes Publishing Co., Inc.)

 **Worksheet 1.2**

The Call to Lead

1. What inspired you to lead?

_____

_____

_____

_____

2. What has prepared you for the leadership?

_____

_____

_____

_____

3. How well do your attributes serve you as a leader?

_____

_____

_____

_____

4. How does your character affect your leadership?

_____

_____

_____

_____

From Kagen, E.B., & Hepburn, K.S. (Eds.). (2006). *Leadership in systems of care: An unpublished training curriculum.* Washington, DC: Georgetown University Center for Child and Human Development, National Technical Assistance Center for Children's Mental Health; reprinted by permission.

In *The Leadership Equation: Strategies for Individuals Who Are Champions for Children, Youth, and Families* edited by Gary M. Blau & Phyllis R. Magrab (2010; Paul H. Brookes Publishing Co., Inc.)

2

Personal Values and Leadership

MARLENE PENN AND KNUTE ROTTO

Personal values—those emotionally charged beliefs about right and wrong—infiltrate every relationship, every decision, and every element of one's being. Everyone brings to each situation his or her own set of personal values, some known to them and some yet to be discovered. Likewise, leaders (and everyone they lead) come to service in a system of care with their own values, unique and personal, deeply honed by their own life experiences and cultural worldviews. In developing systems of care, leaders who emerge or are appointed to leadership roles need to examine the compatibility between their own values and the philosophies required to lead system transformation. This means that leaders must first gain clarity on their own values, actively seeking an increased awareness of those values that are entirely personal, not imposed by anyone else. Subsequently, leaders must examine how compatible these personal values are with those driving the missions of their organizations. Further, when leading transformation, skillful leaders must be able to recognize and appreciate the values base that other community members and stakeholders bring to the collaborative relationship and honor those values while remaining vigilant around core systems of care values. Jim Collins wrote the following in his book *Good to Great and the Social Sectors:*

> Level 5 leaders . . . are ambitious first and foremost for the cause, the movement, the mission, the work—not themselves—and they have the will to do whatever it takes (whatever *it* takes) to make good on that ambition. (2005, p. 11)

In the social sectors, the Level 5s' compelling combination of personal humility and professional will is a key factor in creating legitimacy and influence. Collins said, "True leadership only exists if people follow when they have the freedom not to." (p. 13) A leader with personal values aligned to the organizational mission will have people partnering with him or her for the cause.

PERSONAL VALUES

Everyone brings to each situation his or her own set of personal values, some known to them and some yet to be discovered.

Values can be defined thusly: 1) a collection of guiding, usually positive, principles; 2) what one deems to be correct and desirable in life, especially regarding personal conduct; and 3) beliefs in which one has an emotional attachment.

The core of a leader's personal values, those concepts around which emotions surface and defense is automatic, are of utmost importance in a developing system of care. These core values serve as a personal guide, setting standards of belief from which decisions are made and actions taken.

Kouzes and Posner described research in which responders, when asked to name a greatly admired historical leader, most frequently chose men and women who demonstrated one quality in particular: strong beliefs about matters of principle an "unwavering commitment to a strong set of values" (2007, p. 46). It is not enough for a leader to espouse lofty principles. Rather, the heart of the leader must be imbued with these principles. A "value-driven commitment" is a characteristic "critical to SOC [system of care] leadership" (Ferreira, Hodges, Israel, & Mazza, 2007, p. 4).

At times, the personal values of different system leaders may be in conflict, and the manner in which that dissonance is handled reflects the quality of system leadership. For example, leaders in a community system of care in a small Midwestern community felt that their decisions on discretionary spending were continually being challenged by a long-time juvenile court judge. The judge had long been an advocate of parental responsibility for the behavior and well-being of their children and clearly possessed personal values around those issues. He also possessed strong personal values around the use of public funds and often challenged some discretionary spending (e.g., new tennis shoes, battery for a parents' car, trips to a nearby amusement park) as inappropriate expenditures of public funds entrusted to the local system of care management entity. When a new administration appointed this judge to the position of statewide director of child services, system of care leaders were concerned that the judge was now in a position of authority to mandate additional controls over discretionary spending. Soon after appointment, the director publicly stated that he now understood that discretionary expenses, in and of themselves, did not always reflect an appropriate use of public funds but that he now realized that they were appropriate if managed carefully. He had come to realize that the skill of the care managers to help families separate needs from wants and the flexibility to meet the needs of a family through discretionary funds when all other sources of assistance had been exhausted were instrumental to the positive outcomes for families.

The director had not changed his personal values but had made exceptions as he realized the accomplishments of the greater good hinged on the flexible use of public funds. As Heifetz stated, "Values are shaped and defined by rubbing against *real* [*italics added*] problems" (1999, p. 22). Clarifying one's personal values is vital to effective leadership.

VALUES CLARITY

Leaders must gain clarity on their own values, actively seeking an increased awareness of those values that are entirely personal, not imposed by anyone else.

Effective system leaders must understand their own values and how they relate to system issues, and that clarity inspires others to follow, to build a vision, to join a cause. "If you don't burn with desire to be true to something you hold passionately, how can you expect commitment from others?" (Kouzes & Posner, 2007, p. 50). Leaders must reflect on their own personal values as a means to establishing a foundation for understanding their own leadership. Leaders must recognize and clarify within themselves those beliefs they hold dear based on their life experiences and view of morality. John Maxwell wrote in *Developing the Leader Within* that the most important ingredient of leadership is integrity—the "state of being complete, unified" (1993, p. 35). This can be equated to having leaders' personal values aligned and in sync with the organizations they are leading. He continued,

> A person with integrity does not have divided loyalties, nor is he or she merely pretending. People with integrity are "whole" people; they can be identified by their single-mindedness. People with integrity have nothing to hide and nothing to fear. Their lives are open books. (p. 36)

Maxwell quoted V. Gilbert Beers, who said, "A person of integrity is one who has established a system of values against which all life is judged" (p. 36). Maxwell further wrote,

> Integrity is not what we do so much as who we are. And who we are, in turn, determines what we do. Our system of values is so much a part of us we cannot separate it from ourselves. It becomes the navigating system that guides us. It establishes priorities in our lives and judges what we will accept or reject. (p. 36)

Often clarity in one's own values comes from "rubbing against real problems" as illustrated in the previous section. At other times clarity comes from listening to those one respects. "When you listen carefully to the voices of your mentors and role models, you learn a lot about yourself" (Kouzes & Posner, 2002, p. 54). Eric Bruns, a researcher at the University of Washington and co-director of the National Wraparound Initiative, discussed how he learned by listening to his mentor, the late John Burchard, a pioneer of the wraparound philosophy and a long-time advocate for community-based models of care for children with mental health needs. Dr. Bruns reflected,

> When I came to the University of Vermont in 1992 to work as John's graduate student, I came with a desire to help kids and families but with no idea what it meant to do rigorous research. When I left in 1996 I was still trying to figure out the research part, but I definitely learned the most important of those two things: how to help kids and families. By working with John, I learned what it looks like when a researcher rises to the level of being a leader. I learned from watching John what some people have written volumes trying to communicate—that being a researcher is not about the number of papers you publish or the amount of grant money you get but about making sure your work is relevant and useful to the families you're trying to serve and to the people who are actually doing the hard work out there with them. The amazing thing is that John was able to be *both* an advocate and a researcher; most people in our field can be one or the other, but not both—John could. He could do all these amazing, creative things and say the way he thought things should be and yet never lose his objectivity. But more than anything, what I really wanted to emulate about John is the way he lived his life. John's research was on a method of helping children and families that was based on the radical notion that services should be based on the strengths of the family, be creative and flexible, and on the notion that teams of people will accomplish more than people working alone. And that we should have unconditional commitment and positive regard for the families we work with. So it was natural that John would be a leader on this model, because these were principles he lived his life by. He was never too busy for anyone who needed his attention. Just the way he greeted people made them feel of value. If something needed to get done, he'd find some creative way to do it, one that built relationships and friendships and community. Over time, I learned that this was a rare gift and that John was unique in the way that he did things. Other researchers didn't really work that way, didn't truly lead. But it came naturally to John. It was just the way he did things. (E. Bruns, 2009, personal communication)

Values clarity also includes differentiating between values that leaders hold as their own and the values that are imposed upon them. It is far too easy to confuse corporate values with one's own personal values. For example, many organizations say that they value family-driven care, but one can quickly tell the difference between the individuals in the organization who truly embrace family-driven care and those who are trained to *understand* it. Although both may accept the *importance* of family-driven care, those whose personal values include the belief that families are the experts about themselves and must be primary decision makers about the services and supports they need for optimal outcomes live this out in a way that does not feel contrived or forced. Personal values always come out, irrespective of the corporate values one may support. An important understanding for leaders is that such authenticity has a way of attracting people who are true to themselves, and the unwavering passion with which one lives out his or her personal values often sets the stage for others to clarify their own values. This concept is illustrated by the experience of TaWanda.

TaWanda joined the Dawn Project, the system of care management entity in Marion County, Indiana, from juvenile probation. She eagerly shared the story about how, as a new Dawn staffer, she quickly became annoyed that every meeting began with successes. She knew that the organization placed great value on the strengths of individuals and families and even acknowledged that this is one thing that initially attracted her to the Dawn Project. Nonetheless, as a long-time probation officer, she was used to getting on with business—jumping right in to issues that needed to be discussed or problems to be solved. Before long, though, TaWanda noticed the positive dynamics that so regularly follow the discussion of successes. She learned that families often contact their care coordinators to remind them of the successes they want to share at their next team meetings. She saw the pride of the youth and family upon reporting even the smallest success. Dawn's mantra, "Incremental, not instantaneous," took on real meaning. She began to see celebration of successes in staff meetings as a way of recognizing and building on staff successes, not just an opportunity to publicly pat each other on the back. Over time, the corporate value of embracing individual and family strengths was transformed into a personal value.

External partners new to the child and family team process sometimes express frustration with how long it takes to get to the "important" stuff. But most—families and system partners alike—eventually gain clarity. Like TaWanda, many probably do not even realize when valuing of individual and family strengths transforms from a purely organizational to a personal value. Those that never make the shift, never embrace individual and family strengths—a key component in system of care work—continue to experience frustration because of the incompatibility of organizational and personal values.

VALUES CONGRUENCE

Leaders must examine how compatible personal values are with those driving the missions of their organizations.

Leaders in system development, from early to current, drew and still draw deeply on their own personal values to articulate a vision of community-based care that provides the energy and ignites the passion to create a family-driven, youth-guided, community-based, and culturally sensitive child- and family-serving system. Effective leaders bring to the service system a deep and abiding dedication to values consistent with core values of a system of care, creating the possibility of synergy for individuals, organizations, and systems. Evidence of that dedication is found in policies; in treatment of staff, family members, children, and youth; and in organizational integration into the community.

A team of new system of care community representatives, from the Burlington Partnership in New Jersey, had the opportunity to meet with leadership, staff, and families from Wraparound Milwaukee, the first government-operated managed-care program to utilize the principles of system of care and practice model of wraparound to serve families with children and youth with emotional and behavioral needs. When the director and clinical supervisor spoke about family-driven work, the visitors experienced that as an expression of values that were sincere and to be expected from management. As the visitors met with budget personnel and information technology representatives, they heard the same message—that the decisions that people make every day were centered on the needs of families, whom the staff genuinely cared about. This was a great lesson for the emerging system leaders. System of care core values, when truly internalized, are experienced not as "brochure language" or a mandated requirement but as a value that touches people throughout the organization personally and is congruent with their own beliefs (M. Dallahan, personal communication, 2009).

Values congruence is difficult to quantify because it happens along a continuum. Individuals and organizations will never experience 100% congruence. Other than rejecting an organization or a system because of an overriding personal value, such as not wanting to work for a pharmaceutical company that uses animals for testing, one generally does not make initial decisions based on organizational values. Indeed, even leaders often have only a vague idea of what an organization's or system's values are, because values are determined by intentions and actions, not by words, and they do not clearly understand intention or see the full impact of actions until they are well indoctrinated into the organization or system. This is why leaders in systems of care may not recognize the core system of care values as reflective of their personal values from the onset.

Determining values congruence is a journey that a person and an organization take together. Leaders, whether leading system of care efforts as a care coordinator or a system partner, may come to embrace these core system of care values as TaWanda did with learning to value individual and family strengths. It serves both the leader and the system well for leaders to proactively examine how compatible their personal values are with the values driving the missions of their system of care-involved organizations. Fullan (2009), in *The Six Secrets of Change,* wrote that developing leaders at all levels operating within the same values structure create a culture that reinforces each other as they grow and develop. After studying Toyota for several years, Pfeffer and Sutton concluded that such a culture, developed over time, produces an effect on an organization that equates to having no leadership effect. "In other words, no individual leader is indispensable, but leaders from all corners of the organization continue to move the organization forward because the *culture* [*italics added*]—actions embedded in the norms, competencies, and practices of the organization—ensures it" (2006, p. 126).

A system of care organization has a values framework already built in that assists the individuals, both leaders and participants, and partners in strengthening the culture. Incongruent values portrayed by staff or leaders are quickly spotted/observed and addressed by the organizational culture as a whole, if the system of care culture has been defined. There are numerous examples of new system of care organizations seeking a strong leader to help start up the organization, and so they hire an individual with strong credentials who appears to be a fit. But values incongruence often appears rather quickly, and when difficult decisions need to be made, they are often in direct conflict with the system of care values. Examples include when the leader does not acknowledge the practice of looking at the strengths of the child/youth and family, instead examining only the problems and needs; when the leader does not create the place where families are listened to and given a voice but rather told what to do or what will be done to them; and when leaders align too closely with the child welfare and/or juvenile justice mandates, which can seem to be in direct conflict with system of care values. Individual and organizational congruent values are critical elements that require continuous work on all levels.

Values congruence does not mean the absence of conflict. Diversity of thought is vital to any healthy organization. Both personal values and those of the organization are shaped and defined by rubbing against real problems. In the same way that the internal conflict between an individual's values is important to values clarity for the individual; the conflict between individual and organizational values is important for values clarity for organizations.

In strong system of care communities, one often sees a domino effect as individuals' personal values are tempered. This affects the personal values of staff in system partners and, over time, the corporate values of those system partners. As Dawn Project leadership was seeking ways to further develop champions for system of care in their community, a staff member who had recently been in the audience for *The Late Late Show with Craig Ferguson* explained how prior to the taping, one of the show's writers addressed the audience and explained that his job as a writer depended on the audience's welcome of Chuck, the show opener, who then would introduce Craig Ferguson. The writer said when Chuck walks out on stage the audience must welcome him with everything they have. When Chuck took the stage, Chuck thanked the audience for their warm welcome and said that his job depended on how well they enhance the show. Chuck said they were no longer audience members but "show enhancers," and that although the welcome was great for him, it needed to be twice as big for Craig. In addition, Chuck said, as a show enhancer, we know you will not appreciate all of the humor. If you cannot laugh at a joke, you must be silent and let the other enhancers laugh and be heard. The show enhancer's response to Craig Ferguson is what makes the show. Chuck made it clear that the job of the show enhancers was as important as anyone else's job that night and that the success of the televised show depended on them.

This story led to a discussion on how Dawn Project staff might develop "Dawn enhancers"—partners who understand that the success of not only the individual families but of the whole system of care depends on them. Over the past 2 years, the Dawn Project has developed a cadre of Dawn enhancers by choosing staff members of system partners who embrace as their own the system of care core values and who, in turn, have shared these values with others in their organizations. Local system of care leadership is beginning to see corporate/organizational values align more with system of care values throughout the community.

VALUES CONTINUUM

Skillful leaders must be able to recognize and appreciate the values base that other community members and stakeholders bring to the collaborative relationship.

As people come together with varying cultural experiences, beliefs and understanding of the environment are expressed in a multitude of ways. Where collaboration and diversity are honored and encouraged, diverse beliefs are welcome and indeed bring a greater truth to the environment.

Leadership is easy when others have the same core values or when the decisions faced are simple. Within a system of care community, although one typically finds common values that are easily shared, such as honesty or integrity, there are other common values that people present along a continuum. For example, some people thrive on change, whereas others feel a deep commitment to stability or tradition.

System building in partnership with others who do not share the same core values can be frustrating and requires finesse by a leader. The consortium that provides direction to the system of care that includes the Dawn Project includes representatives from mental health, residential treatment services, juvenile justice, education, and child welfare. A diffuse power structure exists, as is common in system of care communities around the country, with what Jim Collins called legislative leadership. As Collins explained,

> No individual leader—not even the nominal chief executive—has enough structural power to make the most important decisions by him- or herself. Legislative leadership relies more upon persuasion, political currency, and shared interests to create the conditions for the right decisions to happen. (2005, p. 11)

A great visual of legislative leadership also comes from Collins:

> When Frances Hesselbein became CEO of the Girls Scouts of the USA, a *New York Times* columnist asked what it felt like to be on top of such a large organization. With patience, such as a teacher pausing to impart an important lesson, Hesselbein proceeded to rearrange the lunch table, creating a set of concentric circles radiating outward—plates, cups, saucers—connected by knives, forks, and spoons. Hesselbein pointed to a glass in the middle of the table. "I'm here," she said. Hesselbein may have had the title of Chief Executive Officer, but her message was clear: I'm not on top of anything. (2005, p. 9)

Although the primary goal of the Dawn consortium is to further develop an integrated system to keep children at home, in school, and out of trouble, the personal values of individual members of the consortium make it difficult at times to come to consensus on a plan to reach that goal. The juvenile court representatives feel strongly that "tough love" is needed. The community mental health representatives maintain that therapy and pharmacological interventions are key to stabilizing the child and thus the family situation. Residential treatment providers contend that the typical child served in a system of care will benefit greatly from intensive services that can only be delivered in an inpatient setting. Education representatives . . . well, the picture is clear. Many work in the arenas they do because of their strong belief in those systems and the values they espouse. Their personal values reflect those system values from the onset. The diversity of thought and the breadth of perspective represented in this consortium—and, yes, even the tensions that those elements produce—are a big part of why this consortium has been able to consistently move the Marion County (Indiana) system of care forward for more than 12 years. This is a testament to the consortium's leadership and to the leaders' appreciation of the values base that all stakeholders bring to the collaborative relationship.

VALUES DISSONANCE/VALUES CONFLICT

Skillful leaders must honor the personal values of system of care colleagues while remaining vigilant around core system of care values.

Leaders committed to a values-based approach must be alert to possible conflicts between their personal values, the personal values of other leaders, and the community values shared with other leaders and constituents. As people who have been engaged with countless systems, including those seeking to move toward a comprehensive system of care, the authors have found that honoring the personal values of colleagues is a key element to a successful collaborative relationship. This does not mean, however, that all competing personal values are equally important or valid in a system of care. As noted in the preceding section, those whose personal values are in direct conflict with the core values of systems of care can have detrimental effects on the collaborative efforts focused on system transformation.

It is challenging to lead change under the best of circumstances. When leaders find that their personal values or those of other system leaders do not easily correspond with the family-driven, community-oriented, or culturally based philosophies, there can be serious discord. When leaders do not, from a personal value base, embrace these core philosophies, they will not be able to engage the families, the staff, or the community in the type of shared vision needed to propel transformation. Failure is often a result of different values among the organizations that must collaborate in a system of care.

> As Ohio was building its system of county family- and children-first councils in the 1990s, county-level councils were required by statute to include family members of children who had received, or were still receiving, services to ensure family voice in all decision making. At the same time, the state-level cabinet council refused to consider including a family member or advocate in its deliberations, citing the confidentiality and proprietary responsibilities held by system leaders. The appointed system leaders appeared to others to act on one set of values while expecting local leaders to follow another set, which undermined local belief in the potential for council success. (C. Davis, personal communication, November 5, 2009)

Families with multiple public-serving systems involved in their lives often experience conflict because the public systems have different mandates and competing values within their agency cultures. Juvenile justice holds a statutory mandate to protect community safety and that too often translates into an institutional intervention before a community-based plan is tried. If the system of care's primary referral source is juvenile justice, the leaders will have to figure out how to identify and work through the possible system–values conflicts so that individual families can get their needs met. Identifying and understanding the impact of values, even at the risk of conflict, does not mean leaders or stakeholders must give up their values. Effective system of care leadership promotes a common understanding of shared concerns and commitments. Jointly developed core values are the touchstone to which leaders ground their efforts.

Family leaders also have to carefully examine their own personal values and culture to determine if the collaboration, or nonadversarial advocacy and teamwork interactional style typical of systems of care, is the best fit for them. To illustrate, one family leader recalls that to get what she needed for her son's education, she always felt it necessary to be armed with a tape recorder, an advocate, and whatever else she needed to "do battle." As a family leader within a statewide system of care, she realized the adversarial style she had used successfully in the past would not work, as it was in conflict with the system of care values of partnership and collaboration. Now, as a family leader, she works hard to uphold the values of collaboration and working in teams with a nonadversarial spirit.

Making the shift from an adversarial to collaborative mode of advocacy, and knowing when each style is the most appropriate and effective, is a challenge that many family leaders have to face. (See Leadership Styles in Chapter 3.) Huffine and Anderson (2003) described the sometimes rapid trajectory of emerging family leaders, both on an individual family team and within the organized family movement, as being a chief factor contributing to conflicts that occur between family organizations and their leaders and other system of care partners. They indicated that struggles may ensue unless family leaders and their professional partners have the opportunity to go through necessary developmental stages, during which they are given time and support to examine their beliefs on advocacy, power, the sharing of resources, and other values-based dynamics. In *Learning from Colleagues, Family/Professional Partnerships, Moving Forward Together,* the authors concluded that, before attempting any strategy to create a collaborative process between the professional community and family members, participants must be "excruciatingly honest about personal values" (National Peer Technical Assistance Network, 2000, p. 53). In so doing, parent leaders and their professional partners are well advised to engage in a guided discussion of their personal beliefs about critical topics and thereby come to an understanding of how each perspective may differ and identify what values they share. By preparing the community in this manner, fertilizing the ground, and preparing parents and providers through personal reflection and discussion of the core values, a more authentic and sustaining partnership is likely to develop.

When personal privacy is key in a family's culture, family leadership within a system of care is likely to present a values conflict. Telling personal stories to each other is one way families develop supportive and trusting relationships that bind them together into an extended family or family-run organization. Within this "family," the confidentiality of personal stories is valued, respected, and protected. As individual family members take on system leadership roles, they step into a public arena. Here privacy may not be protected when they tell stories about their children and family. All family leaders can expect that some things about their families will be publicly exposed. Indeed, their credibility as a system family leader depends, in part, on their being identified with an authentic story. System of care family leaders (and those aspiring to leadership roles) should examine how much they value their privacy. They should discuss the implications of public disclosure with their children and other family members. They should agree on how much of their story to tell and what to protect. Not everyone or every family feels comfortable with the public disclosure generally expected of a family leader within a system of care. The challenge in such cases is to forge a leadership role and develop an advocacy voice that is not dependent on their personal experiences.

As an advocate for system reform, I, as one of the authors of this chapter, was delighted to have the opportunity to personally speak with then Governor Christie Whitman of New Jersey at a public forum. What a shock to wake up the next morning and see my picture with the governor in the newspaper with the caption beginning "Marlene Penn, mother of a troubled child. . . ." I had to really examine my own cultural value of privacy and the potential conflicts that public leadership with expectations of personal disclosure might pose for my family and me.

LEADERSHIP DEVELOPMENT

The following reflective exercise offer an opportunity to examine one's personal value base and consider how it is consistent with leadership in a strengths-based, family-centered, and culturally competent system of care.

1. My values. Who am I in the workplace?

From the following list select 10 items that are reflective of what is most important to you—that serve as guides for how to behave or as components of a valued way of life. Feel free to add to the list.

Achievement	Competence	Ethical Practice
Advancement	Competition	Excellence
Adventure	Creativity	Excitement
Affection (love and caring)	Decisiveness	Expertise
Arts	Democracy	Fame
Challenging Problems	Ecological Awareness	Fast Living
Change and Variety	Economic Security	Fast-Paced Work
Close Relationships	Education	Financial Gain
Community	Efficiency	Freedom

(continued)

(continued)

Friendships	My Country	Responsibility and Accountability
Getting Along with People	Money	Security
Having a Family	Nature	Self-Respect
Helping Other People	Order (Stability)	Serenity
Helping Society	Personal Development	Sophistication
Honesty	Physical Challenge	Stability
Independence	Pleasure	Status
Influencing Others	Power and Authority	Time Freedom
Inner Harmony	Privacy	Truth
Integrity	Public Service	Wealth
Intellectual Status	Recognition from Others	Wisdom
Job Tranquility	Respect	Work Under Pressure
Leadership	Religion	Working Alone
Loyalty	Reputation	Working with Others
Meaningful Work		

From Kagen, E.B., & Hepburn, K.S. (Eds.). (2006). *Leadership in systems of care: An unpublished training curriculum.* Washington, DC: Georgetown University Center for Child and Human Development, National Technical Assistance Center for Children's Mental Health; adapted by permission.

2.   How do I know if I am in alignment with the organization?

Take a look at the 10 items that you have selected. Choose three that say the most about what is important to you, those that shape your values. Now think about the values or principles that your agency or workplace promotes. How consistent are your most personal values with those of your agency? Can a leader change his or her values when he or she sees that they are out of alignment with the organization or community? What changes you? How can a leader influence the core values of an organization or community?

3.   How well am I understanding others' values? How am I doing at that?

Individuals go about their daily lives with their own personal values framed by their cultural experience and mental models of the way the world works. When you perceive a conflict with a co-worker, system partner, or family member, can you identify when personal values are creating the discord? Looking back at the three items you listed reflecting what is most important to you, choose the one that is so precious that you absolutely would never compromise. Think about people with whom you have worked. Can you remember a time when it was satisfying to collaborate with that person or group of people? Can you identify a critical value that both of you might have had in common? Think about someone with whom you simply cannot agree on anything or have had much difficulty collaborating with. Do you think that a conflict in personal values was at issue?

CONCLUSION

Personal values are an asset, a leadership tool in each leader's toolbox. Those who lead can and should deepen their self-awareness of the alignment between personal and shared system values. As Goffee and Jones said in *Why Should Anyone Be Led by You? What It Takes to Be an Authentic Leader,* "Effective leaders are authentic: They deploy individual strengths to engage followers' hearts, minds, and souls. They are skillful at consistently being themselves, even as they alter their behaviors to respond effectively in changing contexts" (2006, p. 161). This is the impact of leading from a set of core values. Who the leader is does not change from situation to situation, and yet he or she must adapt to appropriately influence the outcome of the situation. Leaders take their core values everywhere, so in any moment they can ask, "How can we ensure that we are guided from a values foundation and be more family-driven and youth-guided in this situation?"

Fullan stated,

> Leaders who thrive and survive are people who know they don't know everything. In fact this knowledge—knowing that you don't know—is crucial for enabling others. Pfeffer and Sutton conveyed the need to let go in the following words: The mindset . . . entails . . . being willing to let go and let other people perform, develop, learn and make mistakes. It is hard to build a system where others can succeed if the leader believes he or she needs to make every important decision and knows better than anyone else what to do and how to do it. It is in finding the balance between guidance and listening, between directing and learning, that those in leadership roles can make their most useful contributions to organizational performance and to the development of an individual's personal values as a system of care leader (2006, p. 126).

REFERENCES

Collins, J. (2005). *Good to great and the social sectors. A monograph to accompany* Good to Great. Boulder, CO: Author.

Ferreira, K., Hodges, S., Israel, N. & Mazza, J. (2007). *Lessons from successful systems: Leadership qualities in successful systems of care* (System implementation issue brief #3). Tampa: University of South Florida, Louis de la Parte Florida Mental Health Institute, Research and Training Center for Children's Mental Health.

Fullan, M. (2009). *The six secrets of change: What the best leaders do to help their organization survive and thrive.* San Francisco: Jossey-Bass.

Goffee, R., & Jones, G. (2006). *Why should anyone be led by you? What it takes to be an authentic leader.* Boston: Harvard Business Press.

Heifetz, R.A. (1994). *Leadership without easy answers.* Cambridge, MA: Belknap Press of Harvard University Press.

Huffine, C., & Anderson, D. (2003). *Family advocacy development in systems of care.* In A. Pumariega & N. Winter (Eds.), *The handbook of child and adolescent systems of care.* San Francisco: Jossey-Bass.

Kagen, E.B., & Hepburn, K.S. Eds. (2006). *Leadership in systems of care: An unpublished training curriculum.* Washington DC: Georgetown University Center for Child and Human Development, National Technical Assistance Center for Children's Mental Health.

Kouzes, J.M., & Posner, B.Z. (2002). *The leadership challenge* (3rd ed.). San Francisco: Jossey-Bass.

Kouzes, J.M., & Posner, B.Z. (2007). *The leadership challenge* (4th ed.). San Francisco: Jossey-Bass.

Maxwell, J.C. (1993). *Developing the leader within you.* Nashville, TN: Thomas Nelson.

National Peer Technical Assistance Network. (2000). *Learning from colleagues, family/ professional partnerships, moving forward together* (2nd ed.). Alexandria, VA: Federation of Families for Children's Mental Health.

Pfeffer, J., & Sutton, R.I. (2006). *Hard facts, dangerous half-truths and total nonsense: Profiting from evidence-based management.* Boston: Harvard Business School Press.

II

Leading in the Context of Human Service Delivery

3

Leadership Functions and Styles

ELLEN B. KAGEN AND CATHY CIANO

Leaders can count on change—systems are changing, funding patterns are changing, and politics are changing. There is always change and the changes leaders are asked to facilitate seem to come at an accelerated rate. Agencies and organizations are asked to do new and, perhaps, very different tasks to support new ways of serving children, youth, and families. Due to the scope and magnitude of all these changes, leaders need to adapt and learn new behaviors as well.

In his book *Deep Change, Discovering the Leader Within,* Robert Quinn (1996) told a story about working with senior executives at a successful organization in Asia. He was impressed with their efforts to design an organization that could make deep change more frequently and effectively. They told him that they were trying to become an "organic organization"—one that is "responsive, acts quickly and in a coordinated way, and can adjust, learn, and grow" (p. 6). Quinn noted that many organizations have similar statements, but the next thought really grabbed him: "Only organic individuals can create an organic organization" (p. 6). This concept can be taken one step further to say that, in times of change, only organic leaders can create and lead organic organizations. The ability to be flexible in practicing leadership functions and styles will be the hallmark of the 21st-century leader.

This flexibility in leadership styles and functions is intimately connected to the demands of our organizations and systems. The styles and functions needed emerge from the organization or system as it evolves—moving constantly from stability to change and back again. Leaders need to offer the right kind of function and style as the situation requires. The functions of both leadership and management are necessary in systems change, and they need to be recognized as two different things. Often leaders get these two functions confused or fail to recognize the difference. Assumptions about management and leadership can cloud the ability to see the two as distinct, and leaders must be mindful not to fall into that trap. For example, the assumption may exist that if one is a good manager, then one can be a good leader. However, these two roles require two different skill sets. Another assumption might be that leaders are born; individuals may not realize that the skills of leadership can be learned and developed, even though they may not seem to be automatically present.

Many come to the work of leadership by moving up through the ranks, perhaps gaining personal experience as clinicians, service providers, teachers, and/or family members. Those roles require an important set of specific skills and competencies. As leaders deepened their engagement with the field, new skills related to management and administration of organizations were required to become effective managers or supervisors. These skills are necessary yet not sufficient for the role of leadership in today's systems of care.

Though many believe that leaders are "born to lead," it is more realistic to understand that individuals can build on natural talents and, through focus and effort, create leadership capacity within themselves and within others. Leadership is more than acting the part. As earlier chapters describe, *everyone* has the capacity to demonstrate leadership. Leadership is driven by personal values and vision and is based on choices—decisions that are defined by values and thus determine behaviors. Leaders are individuals who reflect upon their personal vision and values, learn how to listen to their inner voice and the voices of others, act through conviction based on a set of core principles, facilitate shared vision, and have the ability to distinguish between the functions of leadership and choose when and how to lead. Leaders need to develop opportunities to learn multiple styles of leadership and utilize such styles to align their decisions and behaviors with the particular situation called for by the changing system.

This chapter identifies key attributes of management and leadership and supports the reader's ability to differentiate between the two. Also addressed are leadership styles, roles, and behaviors and matching the most effective style of leadership to the context and situation. Several styles of leadership are outlined, and readers are encouraged to expand their range of leadership styles. Readers will understand their choices in the application of various leadership styles and the need to focus attention on how to align the style and situational context to reach the goal or desired outcome within systems change.

MANAGEMENT AND LEADERSHIP

Management and leadership are both necessary skills and provide different and distinct functions within an organization or system. Leadership without management is nothing but a dream. Management without leadership may not be heading in the right direction. Leadership and management function as partners and can coexist in each leader. Understanding the difference between leadership and management enables leaders to examine themselves and their work, leading to the ability to differentiate leadership and management functions and behaviors.

Quote from the Field *My role in terms of management is ensuring that contract deliverables are met; my role in terms of leadership is mobilizing others to take on leadership functions that move the mission of the organization forward.* —Leader in children's mental health

Managing Is . . .

Management typically requires work within boundaries, such as following established job descriptions and work plans, staying within budgets, utilizing logic models, and collecting and analyzing data to drive decision making. Management includes:[1]

- Controlling resources
- Planning to reach goals
- Contracting how and when work will be done
- Emphasizing reason and logic supported by intuition
- Deciding present actions based on the past and precedent
- Waiting for all relevant data before deciding
- Measuring performance against plans

Leading Is . . .

Leading involves expanding boundaries and communicating in a way that influences others to create and sustain a shared vision for the possible future. Leading requires a commitment to getting the work done no matter what. Decisions regarding actions are often driven by intuition and feelings focused on the envisioned future. Accomplishments are measured against vision, which must be constantly revisited. Leadership practices such as the following are used with management practices to get the best out of people:[2]

- Expanding boundaries
- Influencing others

[1,2]From Bellman, G.M. (2001). Leading when you are not in a position of authority, *Getting things done when you are not in charge* (p. 14). San Francisco: Berrett-Koehler; adapted by permission.

- Creating a vision of a possible future

- Committing to get the work done no matter what

- Emphasizing intuition and feelings supported by reason

- Deciding present actions based on the envisioned future

- Pursuing enough data to decide now

- Assessing accomplishment against vision

As the concepts of the two functions have been outlined above, it is important to recognize that perceptions and practice of management and leadership are culturally based and are expressed within the context of personal worldview. In addition, both management and leadership are necessary skill sets, and both functions must be present for an organization or system to run smoothly and evolve through a changing environment. Though many managers are in leadership roles, the tasks and functions of jobs and job descriptions have a tendency to be much more managerial in nature. Therefore, leaders have the responsibility to be aware of the need to demonstrate *both* leadership and management and to understand that they are not mutually exclusive. Leaders may often be required to perform these functions sequentially or even simultaneously. Leaders are often driven toward one or the other role by forces both within organizations and systems and from outside the organization or system.

As an example, let's take Charlie. Charlie is a special education administrator within the local school district. He has been asked by his boss, the district superintendent, to develop a plan to cut the special education budget. At the same time, the county director of the Office of Children Youth and Families has asked Charlie to serve on a local collaborative with a mission to build a collective approach to serving the needs of school-age youth with mental health challenges. As a manager, Charlie needs to figure out how to work within his budget constraints, look at data, and develop a plan (managerial functions, internally driven) while strengthening relationships that support the development of a shared vision and working collectively to meet the needs of students with emotional and behavioral challenges (leadership functions, externally driven).

As stated above, job descriptions are often weighted toward managerial functions. To operate daily, managers regularly need to pay attention to management responsibilities. However, within all day-to-day demands, the opportunity to perform the leadership function can get easily get lost and overshadow the important long-term work of leadership. To counteract that tendency, leaders must first be aware of where they put their time and attention to expand and enhance their leadership practices. Developing concrete actions to raise awareness, such as those in the following list, is an important first step in strengthening leadership abilities.

Tools for Application

- *Keep a daily log for 2 weeks at a time.* Every day is full of action. Stopping to reflect on each day's activities supports the ability to see how precious time is spent. Categorizing activities into management functions and leadership functions will help leaders see where each day is weighted. Though the balance sheet does not have to be equal, such a log is likely to include surprises.

- *Commit to performing a behavior that offers significant challenge.* People tend to perform tasks that are the easiest and most comfortable. To develop new capabilities, try performing a leadership behavior that is difficult and outside of your usual comfort zone.

- *Keep a personal vision of leadership in mind at all times.* The personal vision of leadership emerges from core values and core purpose. Writing a personal leadership vision and then keeping it in mind provides constant reminders of personal leadership goals and capabilities along the path taken by the leadership journey.

- *Anchor a leadership timeline in your very earliest leadership experiences.* Think of the first time you or others recognized leadership. Plot the leadership journey through time. Reflect on the items highlighted by the timeline. Can patterns be identified? If so, what are they?

- *Keep a journal of the leadership journey.* Keeping a journal allows review of the leadership path over the long term. Leaders tend to fall into patterns of behavior. Documenting the journey will aid self-reflection on how time is spent and support the ability to recognize both management and leadership moments. Through reviewing timelines and journaling, the art of self-reflection will become routine.

- *Review a current job description.* What might look different in the job description if leadership responsibilities were infused into it? A meaningful job description would outline both managerial functions and leadership skills and activities, such as the responsibility to inspire a shared vision.

CONVENTIONAL LEADERSHIP AND FUSION LEADERSHIP

In their book *Fusion Leadership,* Richard Daft and Robert Lengel (1998) offered additional ways to review the variety of roles leaders perform within an organization or system. They defined the "conventional leader" as one who takes on more of the managerial functions and "fusion leaders" as those who move an organization or system forward within changing environments. They offered the idea that the characteristics of fusion leadership unlock the subtle forces that change people and organizations and posited six subtle forces that have a direct bearing on organizational effectiveness: mindfulness, vision, heart, communication, courage, and integrity. Each subtle force has elements of both conventional and fusion leadership. The conventional leadership function works well within stability; when an organization or system is in change, fusion leadership functions are also required.

Table 3.1. Vision: Functions of conventional leader and fusion leader

Conventional Leader	Fusion Leader
• Discover future	• Create future
• Analyze hard data	• Facilitate hopes and dreams
• Pursue goals and objectives	• Pursue higher purpose that touches the heart
• Direct people	• Inspire people
• Focus on measures, money	• Focus on values, yearnings
• Consider dreams fuzzy, unrealistic	• Consider dreams concrete, reliable
• Stick with the logical, doable	• Think big, do the impossible
• Scorn vision	• Cherish vision as motivating, energizing
• Live by tomorrow's deadlines	• Live by hope and personal experience

From Daft, R.L., & Lengel, R.H. (1998). *Fusion Leadership*. San Francisco: Barrett-Koehler; adapted by permission.

Table 3.1 presents an example of how conventional and fusion leadership apply to vision.

Tools for Application

- Reflect on the difference between conventional leadership and fusion leadership within vision in light of your current work activities, and think about how you spend your time.

- List the five items where you spend the most time *currently* (mark with a C).

- List the five items where you need to spend your time in the *future* to mobilize change (mark with an F).

- The Shifting Leadership Behaviors figure (Figure 3.1) describes three steps you will take to go from C to F.

Shifting Leadership Behaviors

Three steps I need to take to shift my leadership behavior from where I practice leadership in the present (C, currently) to where I need to be (F, future) to mobilize change.

1.

2.

3.

Figure 3.1. Leadership to mobilize change.

A Note About Advocacy and Leadership

Not much has been written about the relationship between advocacy and leadership. To move the conversation forward, a distinction needs to be made between advocacy and leadership. Advocacy puts an adaptive challenge (see Chapter 4) on the table, brings awareness to the issue, and can create distress, pressure, tension, and conflict. Where the leadership role takes over is in creating a process and opportunity for everyone to learn about the new values, attitudes, and behaviors and learn their way to new solutions. Often leaders say, "I raised the issue, but no one did anything about it." In this case, the function of advocacy has raised the issue and now needs the function of leadership to continue the movement toward changes in attitudes, values, and behaviors.

LEADERSHIP STYLES IN ADAPTIVE WORK

Each person comes to the work of leadership with a natural tendency toward one or more styles of leadership. One's established style may be dependent on personality, history, culture, experience, environment, or education. However, in the work of change, multiple styles of leadership are necessary to navigate and ultimately affect the outcomes in building healthy communities. Leaders are not always afforded the opportunity to act on how they are feeling at any given moment; instead, it is essential that leadership action be guided by what is needed to move the agenda of change forward, always with the best interest of the community in mind. It is critical for leaders to be intentional about their reactions and interactions in any given situation and manage their emotions toward the strategic selection of leadership-style response. In adaptive work, leadership style and behavior must be a conscious decision in response to the context and situation. Determining how to ensure that the most effective style of leadership is chosen is a critical skill of leaders in adaptive work.

LEADERSHIP STYLES

Leaders have the capacity to learn multiple styles of leadership and to utilize a variety of styles to align with any given situation. It is important for leaders to pay close attention to why a particular style of leadership is most appropriate and how it can be utilized to accomplish their goals within the process of change. Leadership styles are leadership tools, and utilizing only one style for every situation is like using only a screwdriver to build a roof. The right tool is necessary for each job! With an understanding that the work of change involves both adaptive and technical work, leaders are encouraged to expand their range of leadership styles.

Examples of Leadership Styles

For each style of leadership, note the following:

- Name of the style and the definition

- Situation/context where this style is most appropriate and effective

- Tasks/activities that leaders would implement

- An example/quote of what a leader might say utilizing this style

- Outcomes—What the leader is trying to accomplish or what the style might help avoid

Directive Style of Leadership   This is characterized by the use of authority or command and control. As an example, leaders utilizing this style would be clear about the parameters of any given project and describe the elements that are not negotiable. There is a time and place where leaders need to be clear and direct about a given reality and need to articulate (respectfully) that reality to their teams. The intended outcome is often alleviating confusion and clarifying expectations about roles and responsibilities. Using this style is also a way to respond to those who say, "We are ready. Just tell us what to do."

Example from the Field   Running a mental health agency requires the leader to learn how to most effectively utilize the various styles of leadership to achieve desired goals and outcomes. Rachael is the clinical coordinator and supervises the work of the large clinical staff. As the agency has been facing constant change, she has had to pay close attention to how the directive style of leadership is used, being careful not to create an environment that shuts people down and feels exclusive but instead continues to encourage the voices and ideas of the team. Rachael sees herself as much more of a fusion leader, as opposed to a conventional leader (one that inspires as opposed to directs), but she does understand the need for both. Over time, she has learned that there is an appropriate time and place to use a directive style of leadership. For example, when it comes to the safety of the youth and the staff, there must be clarity. Rachael has developed a set of rules and regulations that staff must follow in case of emergencies. There are regular briefings on the procedures and mock drills to give everyone a chance to practice. The staff may sometimes challenge why they are being given certain tasks, but one very important lesson she has learned is that when it comes to situations where quick decisions are necessary, her staff must feel as if they know who has the lead role and what each of them needs to do to ensure the safety and security of everyone. In this case, a directive style of leadership is necessary.

Quote from the Field   *I realize that we are all used to doing things a certain way. However, for you and the youth we serve to feel safe and secure, we have*

developed policies and procedures to be followed in the event of an emergency. Next week we will have staff drills to practice these skills and techniques. Please understand that the contract we have entered into with the state has committed us to the following procedures, and we are required to meet this obligation.
—Director at a large mental health agency

Other examples of where the directive style would be appropriate are as follows: a project director telling a team where and when to come together at a large conference so the participants from a state would feel as though they were a delegation, rather than a collection of individuals; closing a facility that is harming students; or providing procedures for students with special needs in the event of a disaster.

Motivational Style of Leadership   This style is characterized by the use of incentives or providing compelling reasons for action. As an example, leaders utilizing this style would inspire their teams to feel valued and connected to the vision of the organization or project. There is a time and place where leaders need to encourage and be passionate about the work. The intended outcome is often to discourage apathy and encourage enthusiasm, participation, and energy.

Example from the Field   The contributions of volunteers in any organization are invaluable to its growth, capacity, and sustainability. The ability to motivate others that share the same values and vision for building healthy communities is key to developing a strong and powerful collective of leaders who are "willing to do whatever it takes." Leslie, a project director from a system of care, sees that there is clearly a great deal of value in providing and supporting families to have ongoing opportunities to be involved in ways that are meaningful and embrace their strengths, cultures, and capacities. She understands that their work is often uncompensated, so valuing this participation through enthusiasm, appreciation, and gratitude will make or break how willing families are to stay involved. As an example, each year she passionately orchestrates an opportunity to recognize the outstanding contributions of family volunteers within the system of care. As she brings together families that have been involved, she makes a point to identify and honor the volunteer of the year with a special award and describes how his or her effort has moved the system forward.

Quotes from the Field   *One should never underestimate the impact of recognizing and celebrating the commitment, passion, time, and talent that each one of us brings to the constantly evolving and challenging work of system transformation.*
—Project director, system of care

Today we are celebrating your outstanding contribution and tireless advocacy to make the world a better place for our children and to remove the injustice of disparities in mental health care in our community.
—County executive

Other examples of where the motivational style would be appropriate are as follows: staff decided that for the holiday season they were going to raise money for the youth in the group home to have a special dinner; an agency will receive $1,000 as an incentive through their contract for every child brought back from out-of-state placement; the unique contributions of individuals are recognized through personal expressions of gratitude.

Participatory Style of Leadership   This is characterized by inclusion, providing encouragement, sharing, partnership, and equality. System change and system building require bringing together diverse groups of people, each bringing their unique perspectives, experiences, cultures, roles, values, and ideas. A leader must have the ability to facilitate communication, encourage inclusiveness, create environments where voices can be heard, and help to ensure that people feel valued in the process. As an example, leaders using this style would recognize that multiple voices need to be heard and bring together individuals and communities with distinct and dissimilar perspectives to join forces around an issue. There are times and places where leaders need to stop talking and spend more time listening and facilitating discussion. The intended outcome is to discourage siloed thinking and isolation, instead encouraging connection, a sense of ownership, and the feeling that each individual is part of something larger.

Example from the Field   The county child welfare, juvenile justice, and mental health departments have been at the forefront of developing and organizing the work of the Youth at Risk Coalition. The focus of the coalition is the prevention of truancy, particularly related to youth at risk or who have mental health and related challenges. As project coordinator, Tim's first step in the development of this coalition was to identify the membership, reach out to those with whom the organization had existing relationships, and build new relationship with others who would play an important role with this work. In addition to the three supporting agencies, Tim was successful in bringing together families and youth and representation from family court, child advocate's office, law clinic, community action agencies, the Department of Education, the Truant Officers Association, and family advocacy organizations. Tim facilitated the process of developing a shared mission and vision statement, was always welcoming, reinforced all of the ideas, and linked and connected ideas to each other. This coalition has been working together over the last 2 years and has continued to have the participation of the majority of the original membership. This is because Tim used the participatory style at the right time, a time when individuals could truly share their concerns and design solutions together to bring about change. Through the participatory style of leadership, the members felt ownership, increasing their ability to develop shared goals and enhancing their willingness to work together. In this case, fewer youth will experience truancy and more will stay in school and receive appropriate services and supports within the context of their home and community.

Quote from the Field   *I am so inspired to see how many of you are concerned about the issue of diverting youth from truancy and making sure they receive the appropriate services and supports so they have the opportunity to thrive in their homes and communities. It is amazing to see the diversity of perspectives and roles that have come together to address this issue. It is critical that we take the time to hear from each and every one of you. Your perspective and experience are needed to strategically develop actions that will help to ensure that youth are never denied an opportunity for graduation and removed from their homes and communities due to truancy. Without your participation we would not be able to move this important agenda forward.*
—Chair, steering committee to improve outcomes for students with emotional disabilities

Another example of where the participatory style would be appropriate is as follows: designing a blueprint that would drive the direction of an early childhood initiative around which multiple voices and perspectives are required. For future actions to be successful, participation from heath, mental health, child care, Head Start, primary care, early care and education, early intervention, families, local and state policy makers, and civic leaders would be needed.

Educational Style of Leadership   This style is characterized by the capacity to provide and facilitate learning opportunities that enhance the knowledge base. The intended outcome is to ensure that uninformed opinions do not drive decisions. Instead, data are used to drive decisions, thus alleviating confusion and preventing decision making based on the status quo. This also helps to deepen the understanding of issues and strengthens the ability of leaders to make well-informed decisions.

People who are in "expert" roles—such as researchers, academics, writers, surveyors, and evaluators—and who use data and knowledge to move an agenda forward, utilize this style of leadership. It is important to note that individuals who are in these roles also have a very important leadership function to play within systems change. It decreases guessing and supports data-driven decision making.

Example from the Field   Joe understands that every time he disseminates data he needs to link it to the policy agenda at hand. His expertise has a purpose beyond just the sharing of statistics. He has an ability to see the big picture and relates his findings to the need for systems change. Leaders with this style have two significant responsibilities. One is to provide factual information as a way to stop (or at least slow) the flow of anecdotal opinion masquerading as fact. Second is to provide a factual basis on which groups can confidently make well-informed decisions. Joe employs this type of leadership regularly in addressing the state legislature because he regularly links data to fiscal implications.

- -

Quote from the Field   *I am pleased to share data around the number of children with unmet mental health needs who drop out of school in comparison to all students and all students with disabilities: The dropout rate for students with unmet metal health needs is two times greater in comparison to all students with disabilities and ten times as much as all students. In communities where the 'wrap-around transition model' has been implemented through the system of care, that rate has been cut in half, thus saving the community thousands of school drop-out-prevention dollars.*
—Director of quality assurance, state department of children youth and families, division of children's mental health

Other examples of where the educational style would be appropriate are as follows: an evaluator makes sure that the process of data gathering reflects the values of the system reform (e.g., family-driven, youth-guided); a leader stops a conversation because additional information or data are needed to move forward and new facts need to be included in the discussion; and an evaluator provides a data presentation to the governing board, including startling facts around disparities. Prior to the data presentation, the governing board was unaware of the magnitude of the disparities issue and that the program was not reaching the population for which it was intended. The evaluator used the educational styles of leadership to present data to show the gap between the system of care values and the behaviors of service implementation.

Adaptive Style of Leadership (see Chapter 4)   This style is characterized by the ability to generate new ways of thinking and help teams discover and learn new solutions. Leaders who exemplify this style have an ability to observe and reflect on their own behavior and the behavior of others and do not fear confronting identified conflicts in values that will lead to major paradigm shifts within themselves, their organizations, or their systems. Their primary goal is to support the change in attitudes, behaviors, and values so progress can be made. They understand the need to work across sectors and boundaries and are keenly attuned to preventing resistance through the use of shared vision and the process of building common ground.

This style is most effective for leaders who are leading significant systems change that challenges the status quo and will require long-term focused attention. The outcome that this style is most likely to achieve is a successful change. This style will also help avoid the buildup of resistance to change.

Example from the Field   Directing a family advocacy organization presents unique leadership challenges due to the constant focus on promoting system change and transformation. It is essential to be aware of external changes and forces (e.g., political, socioeconomic, cultural, environmental) to ensure that decisions made internally are well informed and, most important, stay aligned with the organization's mission, vision and values. In a midwestern state involved in a significant redesign of its statewide system of care for children with mental health needs and their families, the system changes were so significant that it was incumbent upon the family organization to reexamine its model and understand what it would take to stay funded and continue the invaluable work that it had done with individual children and their families. In light of the state redesign of the system of care, a new set of state priorities for the family organization emerged, focusing on community development rather than on providing peer-to-peer support as a singular service within the system of care. The primary role of the organization was challenged. The new priority required changes in the values, attitudes and behaviors of the staff and required the family organization to focus more on community education and family leadership and advocacy, within the policy-making structures at the local and state levels.

After many months of negotiations, the family organization was successful in agreeing upon a new model that would no longer look like formal service delivery at a centralized level but instead would support the ongoing leadership and skill development of families and youth at a regional level. The newly designed model is now more in line with growing the capacities of families and youth in the new community-development paradigm.

The change in the model for the family organization was very significant. It was asked to give up a way of working that it knew well and that had served the community well for many years. The staff were comfortable in their abilities and had fallen into the routine of the status quo.

To build a new model, the organization's management team was driven to redefine the functions of the staff and reorganize the way in which staff needed to work with the community. Instead of providing support to families as its primary function, staff now were focused on building skilled family leaders across the state to develop a strong and sustainable cadre of family leaders who could work with policy makers to achieve systems change.

Staff were supported in strengthening and developing new skills and competencies such as community organizing, public speaking, curriculum development, training, and facilitation. This was, without a doubt, an adaptive challenge that would require the leader to use his or her ability to generate new ways of thinking and support the team in discovering and learning new values, attitudes, and behaviors together. The leader needs to make sure that the adaptive challenge is identified, the distress of the staff is regulated as he or she move away from the status quo, the focus is maintained over the long haul, and that the staff is exposed to ways they can incorporate the change into their day-to-day activities and behaviors.

Quote from the Field *Over the course of the last several months, we have been in negotiations with our funder so we can continue to be supported in doing the invaluable work we do. I know people have been feeling anxious and uneasy. Questioning if we would still have jobs and not having clarity has created some distress in all of us. I acknowledge that and want you to know that the next phase of our work is not going to be easy. I know many of you would like me to have all the answers up front for you; however, change and transformation does not work like that. Together we will define the new roles and responsibilities, and we will work together to further strengthen them going forward. We are changing from a*

model where we have expertise through our access to information and deliver it to the families to a model where we share our knowledge to build expertise and leadership with all of our families and youth. By shifting to this model we will support the ongoing development of family and youth leadership throughout the state to bring system transformation to the next level.
—Executive director, statewide family organization

Another example of where the adaptive style would be appropriate is as follows: a family leader is writing a letter to state policy makers to address the gap between expressed values and action. The leader needs to constantly reflect on how he or she is going to close the gap between expressed values and action and his or her ability to tolerate and live in the conflict. Leaders must also recognize their roles in surfacing tension, maintaining forced attention to the issue, and providing a context in which people can learn what the values shift would really mean in their day-to-day work.

DECISION MAKING IN LEADERSHIP STYLES

In choosing a leadership style for any given situation, key elements of the decision making process must be considered:

- What is the leadership decision to be made?

- What values are involved?

- What old information is available?

- What new information is needed?

- What outcome is needed?

- What level of risk is acceptable?

- Brainstorm response/action options. (Is it a moment to model or challenge?)

- Make the leadership decision.

- Check back; see how it feels; gain access to its impact.

Tool for Application

Personal learning in leadership involves reflection, taking stock, making choices, and practicing leadership styles that align with the situation/context. Leaders have choices in the application of various leadership styles and need to focus attention on how to match the situational context. Not only does the style need to be reflective of the situation, but leaders must be strategic in their selection of tasks and activities to ensure alignment with the style. The community relies on the leader knowing which style is appropriate; there can be negative implications when the leader chooses an inappropriate style.

For example, if there is a fire in a building (context), it is not the time to bring people together (participatory) for a retreat (activity) to come to shared vision (outcome) about what to do with regard to the fire (see Figure 3.2). Instead,

Style	Context/ Situation	Tasks and Activities	Accomplishes	Avoids
Directive	Fire	Procedure for evacuating the building and practice	Safety	Confusion

Figure 3.2. Aligning leadership styles with the needs of the situation example. (From Kagen, E.B., & Hepburn, K.S. [Eds.]. [2006]. *Leadership in systems of care: An unpublished training curriculum.* Washington, DC: Georgetown University Center for Child and Human Development, National Technical Assistance Center for Children's Mental Health; adapted by permission.)

leaders should define clearly (directive) the route people should take to evacuate the building (activity) and should previously have created opportunities to practice (activity) this response to ensure the safety of the building inhabitants (outcome).

Tool for Application

In Figure 3.3 identify for each style their situational applications, the appropriate tasks and activities, and what the style helps to accomplish or avoid (outcome).

PASSING THE BATON OF LEADERSHIP

Varied leadership styles are required to move an organization or system forward. A leader must assess his or her own strengths with various styles and recognize when the situation calls for styles that may not be present in his or her skill set. In these situations, sharing leadership and passing the baton of leadership is a valued option.

Style	Context/ Situation	Tasks and Activities	Accomplishes	Avoids
Directive				
Motivational				
Participatory				
Educational				
Adaptive				

Figure 3.3. Aligning leadership styles with the needs of the situation worksheet. (From Kagen, E.B., & Hepburn, K.S. [Eds.]. [2006]. *Leadership in systems of care: An unpublished training curriculum.* Washington, DC: Georgetown University Center for Child and Human Development, National Technical Assistance Center for Children's Mental Health; adapted by permission.)

As an example, let's use Ms. K. Ms. K is a civic leader in her community who cares about positive youth development. With the support of the United Way, she has pulled together leaders from various youth serving organizations to discuss and build a shared vision around improving the ability of youth to thrive in the community. Ms. K has excellent facilitation skills and is very comfortable with the participatory style. At some point, the group becomes deadlocked in its deliberations. Ms. K recognizes that new information about the current status of youth in the community is needed to move the group forward. She calls upon the leadership of Dr. G to do a survey of youth to expand the knowledge base of the group. Dr. G completes the survey and reports not only the outcomes but how these data will shape the group's recommendations (educational). As the group concludes their work, the county council has requested a briefing on their recommendations. Ms. K strategically recognizes that she needs to pass the baton of leadership again to others who will be more skilled and effective in taking the group to the next step. She asks businessman Jay and youth Emily to present. Jay is comfortable telling the county commissioners that without new programs, such as the ones the report recommends, there will not be a workforce available for companies such as his (directive), and Emily exudes her enthusiasm on how a program, such as the one recommended, changed her life (motivational).

CONCLUSION

The work of change requires leaders to take on many different roles and styles as they lead their organizations and systems through challenging times. This chapter identified key attributes of management and leadership and differentiated between the two. The chapter also described five styles of leadership to give the reader a sense of the range of styles that are needed for systems change. It also identified flexibility as a key leadership attribute, because leaders need to strategically shift between management and leadership functions and assume many varied leadership styles as situations demand. Leaders should try on different styles of leadership and expand their capacity to be competent in as many styles as possible. When a style of leadership is called for and not present in the leader's took kit, a leader must partner with other leaders to ensure that the full range of styles is available to the community system. System change is a complex task. Mastering the shift between multiple functions and expanding each leader's range of styles are foundational skills necessary to traverse the challenging waters of change over time.

REFERENCES

Bellman, G.M. (2001). *Getting things done when you are not in charge.* San Francisco: Berrett-Koehler.

Daft, R., & Lengel, R. (1998). *Fusion leadership.* San Francisco: Berrett-Koehler.

Kagen, E.B., & Hepburn, K.S. (Eds.). [2006]. *Leadership in systems of care: An unpublished training curriculum.* Washington, DC: Georgetown University Center for Child and Human Development, National Technical Assistance Center for Children's Mental Health. Washington, DC.

Quinn, R. (1996). *Deep change, discovering the leader within.* San Francisco: Jossey-Bass.

4

The Work of Leadership in Systems Change for Human Services and Education

Addressing the Adaptive Challenge

ELLEN B. KAGEN, SUGANYA SOCKALINGAM, JANE A. WALKER, AND ALBERT ZACHIK

L eading system change requires a specific set of leadership skills and the ability to change existing paradigms in others. Leaders are often confronted with organizational structures and a workforce that does not readily embrace such change. As a result, leaders must equip themselves with knowledge, a conceptual framework, and a set of competencies that will allow them to affect the system and effect change.

This chapter explores two key conceptual frameworks critical for leaders: mental models and adaptive work. Mental models are the perceptions one holds that influence one's thinking and behaviors. Mental models are derived from one's values and beliefs and relate to one's personal perspective. Adaptive work is the process by which one's mental model or worldview is changed to reflect a new way of thinking. It is how one's values and beliefs are shifted to form a new approach or model. In children's mental health, for example, traditional training emphasized individualized, office-based therapy, but over time and through a series of adaptations, many clinicians now provide home-based treatment and focus on families.

It is important that a leader recognize and understand his or her mental models and those of others to help the shift to new approaches. A successful leader works to uncover the values and beliefs that must shift to create change and then to identify the type of strategies necessary to ultimately shift the values, beliefs, attitudes, and behaviors of individuals, organizations, and systems.

MENTAL MODELS

Senge defined mental models as "deeply ingrained assumptions, generalizations, or even pictures or images that influence how we understand the world and how we take action" (1990, p. 8). Mental models are deeply held internal images of how the world works, images that limit us to familiar ways of thinking and acting. Senge stated, "Very often, we are not consciously aware of our mental models or the effects they have on our behavior" (1990, p. 8).

According to John Arango (1998), organizations have many mental models, such as nonprofit organizations with mental models about the population being served and the role of the organization in service delivery. Such views frame the way organizations and service providers relate to their clients and the communities they serve.

Mental models also create the frame from which leaders assess the issues, develop intervention strategies, and evaluate their success related to adaptive work. Mental models are like the filters in front of a camera lens that influence the color tones of a photo print. They influence the view of the environment and the circumstances that effect outcomes. It is precisely because of this impact that leaders must be aware of their own mental models and those of their constituencies, organizations, and systems.

Relationship Among Mental Models, Values and Beliefs, and Culture

Mental models are driven by deeply held personal beliefs and values (see Chapter 2) that are culturally driven. Culture (see Chapter 10) is a compilation of a society's beliefs, customs, habits, conventions, humanism, lore, arts, sciences, and more. Culture is shared by members of a group and is socially transmitted from generation to generation. It structures perceptions, shapes behaviors, and guides beliefs that affect behavior. Culture helps define an individual's mental model, and an institutional culture helps define the perspective and mental model of an organization. For example, if the organizational culture is to serve a population that is predominantly below the poverty threshold, then this will potentially give rise to assumptions about the clients and their families.

Family organizations within children's mental health and systems of care hold a strong mental model that children are best served within the context of the family environment through comprehensive community-based services. The child welfare system holds a mental model that children who come into care are in that situation due to parental neglect and abuse, and, as a result, they should be removed from their families. These opposing mental models may serve as a source of conflict and dissonance that requires resolution through building common ground (see Chapter 6).

To best understand one's own mental model requires self-reflection and an honest appraisal of one's attitudes, beliefs, and behaviors. To accomplish this, the reader is asked to complete Worksheet 4.1 (My Values, My Culture, My Behavior) at the end of this chapter. It is through this self-discovery that the leader will be in a position to address others' mental models and then engage in the adaptive work necessary to effect changes that are designed to improve the way services are delivered to children, youth, and families.

Evaluating Mental Models

Senge, Roberts, Ross, Smith, and Kleiner (1994) asserted that people operate according to mental models to make sense of the information they receive—mental models are necessary to manage the magnitude of information that people receive and to make sense of the world. The goal is not to eliminate mental models but to explore them and test them to ensure their validity. Importantly, mental models are beliefs or ideas that are held by people whether or not there is any evidence to support them. They guide assumptions and are the operating principles from which people think and behave (Kies, 2009). Everyone makes assumptions based on mental models. Some assumptions may have supporting evidence (warranted) and others may not (unwarranted). When a mental model interferes with the ability to think clearly about any particular issue, it may hinder effective decision making. It is therefore critical to test and evaluate these assumptions rigorously.

If we believe something to be true that is not tested or not true, we often act as if it is true.
—Daniel Kies (2009)

As Figure 4.1 implies, the process of inference first begins with all Observable "Data" and experiences (data that can be objectively observed akin to what could be captured with a movie camera). The second step is to Select "Data" from what is observed. This is the process of selecting data—whether people are aware or not that they are filtering the information. The next step is to Add Meanings (Cultural & Personal) to the selected data and experience. People continue on to Make Assumptions based on meanings, then Draw Conclusions from these assumptions and finally Adopt Beliefs about the world. The final step is to Take Actions based on beliefs which will then lead to more Observable "Data and experiences.

Argyris (1993) believes that people can be taught to see the flaws in their mental models, and the reader is directed to complete Worksheet 4.2 (Left Hand–Right Hand Column Exercise) at the end of this chapter. The idea is to create self-awareness of assumptions that influence conversations, interactions, and thought processes critical to adaptive work. Through this exercise the reader reflects on a

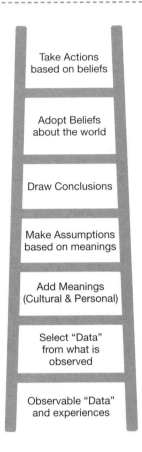

Figure 4.1. The ladder of inference.
(From THE FIFTH DISCIPLINE by Peter M.
Senge, copyright © 1990, 2006 by Peter M.
Senge. Used by permission of Doubleday, a
division of Random House, Inc.)

dialogue and records the detail in the form of a script (the right-hand column).
In the left-hand column, one records what he or she is really thinking during
the dialogue. Argyris believes that true learning occurs when the left-hand and
right-hand columns begin to truly assess and guide what is being said, felt, and
thought.

Mental models can potentially lead to wrong assumptions and perspectives.
They are the images and mental narratives that can wrongfully inform assumptions
and perspectives of the world. Misperceptions, misunderstanding, and even conflicts can arise out of the most mundane circumstances because of inaccurate
assumptions or misperceptions. Reflection, or turning inward to scrutinize these

internal images and narratives, is part of the process the leader must use to address issues and effect change. It is this process that is foundational to the "adaptive work" of leadership.

Mental Models of Leadership

Individuals also have powerful mental models regarding the concepts of leaders and leadership. One's internal self-view of leadership is informed by these mental models. In *Discovering the Leader Within* (Lee & King, 2001), seven views, or mental models, of leadership are proposed: genetic, learned, heroic, top-only, social, calling, and positional.

The genetic view is based on the philosophy that people are born to leadership, whereas the learned view is based on the notion that people can study leadership and practice to be effective leaders. Between these two views are several that range from the heroic view, which presumes that leadership is practiced by performing courageous acts, to the social script view, which is based on there being a time and place for taking on the mantle of leadership. In the top-only and positional views, leadership is assumed to occur when the individual is at the top of the agency or is conferred a position and title. Last is the calling view, where the move toward leading is compelling and involves a deep personal sense of mission, of purpose (see Table 4.1).

Holding on to any one of these views of leadership may stifle the ability of a leader to mobilize change. An inflexible view of leadership may not support the work of change that is required in communities, especially if the community's view says to wait for a leader who is born to lead them (heroic, social script, and genetic views), versus finding leaders in the community who have come to it through their own internally driven mission (calling view). Worksheet 4.3 (Views of Leadership) at the end of this chapter, offers an opportunity for self-examination on the views of leadership. You as the reader can identify on the worksheet the degree (%) to which each of these views corresponds with your mental models of leadership. After you have completed that, review how these leadership views provide benefits and/or hindrances to your leadership situation. For example, if you believe that leadership is assigned (social script) you could be waiting forever to apply leadership in a given situation, when, in fact, your leadership is needed. If a direct care staff member or family member believes in the top-only view of leadership, he or she may never realize his or her full leadership potential. In these cases and others, changes in one's own mental models of leadership may be required to advance the work in systems of care.

Understanding Mental Models

As indicated above, leaders must examine their own mental models as part of the process to determine whether they support or hinder the ability to mobilize and

Table 4.1. Seven views of leadership

The Genetic View
- Only some individuals are born with leadership talent.
- They are naturals—with inborn talent to be effective leaders.

The Learned View
- Individuals can study leadership carefully and practice to be effective leaders.
- This applies no matter who they are, no matter where they sit in the organization.

The Heroic View
- Good leaders are those who perform courageous, wise, and benevolent feats that the rest of us cannot.
- In this view, these leaders get the rest of us out of trouble.

The Top-Only View
- Leadership happens only at or close to the top of an organization.
- Everyone else "just follows the orders" or "helps implement the rules."
- In this view, if you are the boss, you have the power to make things happen.

The Social Script View
- When it is your proper time to be a leader, you will be asked.
- When asked, you should accept and be grateful. After all, not everyone is asked.
- Social scripts also create expectations about who is likely to be asked.

The Position View
- If you are in the job and have a title, you are a leader.
- If your title is phrased "director of" or "head of," then your leadership abilities and virtues are assumed.

The Calling View
- Although not necessarily a religious experience, a "call" to lead can be quite compelling.
- It involves a deeply felt sense of mission, of private purpose, of inevitability.
- It might be so powerful that one has little sense of control. This calling is not especially rational; it is extremely personal.

From Lee, R.J., & King, S.N. (2000). *Discovering the leader in you: A guide to realizing your personal leadership potential.* San Francisco: Jossey-Bass. Copyright © 2001 by Jossey-Bass. Reproduced with permission of John Wiley & Sons, Inc.

create change. Once better understood, an effective leader can use the knowledge about mental models to develop strategies and actions. As an example, consider the relationship between law enforcement and the community. Many individuals and communities hold a mental model about police. They may view police officers as authoritarian or even dangerous. The police officers may view community members as apathetic or disengaged. This may drastically affect the ability to implement community policing practices and create trust and cooperation. The need in this relationship is to recognize the underlying mental models from all perspectives, evaluate the historical context, and then develop strategies to improve collaboration and shift the way the police and community members view each other and interact.

Understanding mental models can lead to reframing. Reframing is the shift in perspective that can allow a change in meaning. It is a way of looking at something from a different point of view that thereby opens up new possibilities, which then has the potential of moving a situation from its current paradigm to seeing things in a new way, as illustrated by the following story of the new beach.

The New Beach

In a community along the coast, everyone was preparing for a pending hurricane. While out driving for some last-minute supplies, one resident overheard an interview between a newscaster and a geologist, the latter whose specialty was the impact of storms and climactic change on shorelines and beaches.

The interviewer and his guest were discussing the severity of the pending storm and the current warnings for local residents. They discussed the official notification that the storm would hit the immediate local community. As the driver felt the anxiety of protecting himself, his family, and his property from the storm, the interviewer asked the geologist what he would expect to see tomorrow after the storm. The geologist answered simply, "A new beach." (Adapted from Wheatley, M., *Leadership and The New Science: Discovering Order in a Chaotic World*, 1999, p. 137)

Reframing can only occur after mental models are recognized and understood, and it is an important leadership skill directly tied to the process of adaptive work. Again using the example of community policing, if the behavior of community members is reframed from being apathetic to feeling helpless, this may affect how police officers interact with them. If the police officers' behavior is reframed from aggressive to anxious, perhaps this would help to explain the appearance of having a "quick trigger" and a reluctance to reach out. Reframing offers alternative perspectives so mental models can shift toward a common understanding and the common good. (See Chapter 6 for strategies on reframing.)

In addressing mental models, it is important to understand the connection between a leader's beliefs and actions. Senge et al., in *The Fifth Discipline Fieldbook* (1994), offer an excellent model to explore this relationship. The circular reinforcement of behavior is explained though the B.A.R. (belief, action, results) template (Innovation Associates, Inc., 1992) (see Figure 4.2). For example, if leaders move toward change and new ways of doing business but continue to use old mental models of leadership (e.g., have all the answers, solve the problems), they may find others less ready and more conflicted about change in the work world in which they have been operating. Alternately, leaders may believe strongly in the need for change and, as leaders, will attempt to "lead" by asserting their view on others. They assume that others will listen to what they have to say. They speak emphatically, enthusiastically, and authoritatively about the need to change, and they work toward convincing others to share this view. This leads to reactions that may include questioning, withholding comments, or challenging by those whom they are trying to engage. This in turn reinforces the leaders' belief that they must be more convincing and stronger in their effort to get this new view across to others.

Because mental models "limit us to familiar ways of thinking and acting" Arango (1998) believes that organizations must, at some point, expose and challenge

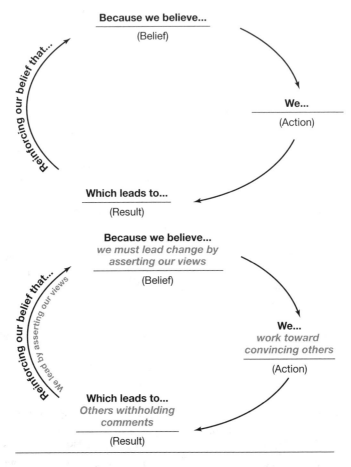

Figure 4.2. The belief, action, results template. (From Goodman, M.R. [1992]. *Systems thinking: A language for learning and acting.* Boston: Innovations Associates Organizational Learning; adapted by permission.)

the organization's mental models. He goes on to state that not all mental models need to be changed and, once exposed, may attest to the essence of these organizations. However, some of these organizational mental models will have to change to address the needs of the system. It is the leaders' job to help the group identify the mental models and then decide which ones need to be changed.

As noted previously, it is also the leaders' job to continually address their own mental models, especially those related to the function of leadership. Often the word *leader* is associated with authority. Typically, mental models of leadership have looked at these two concepts as being the same. As the work of a leader is discussed in this and other chapters, it is referred to as a function and set of behaviors that can be performed by many people in a system and is not linked to the position or title of any one person or individual. Worksheet 4.4 (The Impact of Existing Mental Models) at the end of this chapter is a useful self-reflective tool that will enable one to explore the impact of existing mental models.

Mental models influence the manner in which leaders assess programs and services, how they develop strategic and action plans, how they implement interventions, and how they evaluate programs and services. Mental models influence who will be served, the issues addressed, actions that will be undertaken, outcomes that are desirable, and standards that will be used to determine effectiveness of programs and services. Because leadership is a set of behaviors everyone must continually address the impact of mental models on themselves and individuals within systems. Leaders must use the knowledge about mental models to engage in adaptive work, which is truly the process to change mental models.

THE WORK OF LEADERSHIP AS A SET OF BEHAVIORS: TECHNICAL AND ADAPTIVE

The process of shifting values, attitudes, and behaviors within the leader—or within agencies, systems, and communities—is the process of adaptive work. Addressing mental models overtly and evolving strategies to create change is at the heart of this work. Technical work is task oriented and often occurs when perspectives are aligned. In technical work, the tasks are often clear, and the work of the leader is to manage the concrete strategies. Technical work is targeted and focused on tasks; adaptive work is more process oriented and focuses on attitudes and internal belief systems. Both have their place in leadership.

In this section, adaptive and technical work will be explored and the differences will be presented. Examples will be given to show how to apply technical and adaptive skills to human services and when each skill type is needed, as each approach has its place in leading change. Much of this work is based on the writings of Ron Heifetz (1994), who outlined the framework between technical and adaptive work in his book *Leadership Without Easy Answers*. In 2002, he collaborated with Marty Linsky on a book called *Leadership on the Line* and focused on the skill sets needed within the adaptive context. Recently, Heifetz and Linsky (2009) published *The Practice of Adaptive Leadership* with Alexander Grashow and solidified the term *adaptive leadership*. Leadership, as outlined by Heifetz (1994) and later Heifetz and Linsky (2002) and Heifetz, Linsky, and Grashow (2009), reinforce that leadership is a set of skills and behaviors performed by individuals with and without authority.

Technical Work

Technical work is often considered to reflect more of a management approach to leadership because of the focus on tasks. One key to successful leadership is determining whether a technical solution is likely to work or if the challenge is more adaptive (i.e., reflective of mental models) in nature.

The following example from child welfare allows the exploration of the characteristics of technical problem solving. Leaders in a child welfare agency learn that most of the maltreatment reports come in after 5 p.m. and that the office currently does not have coverage after hours. Calls are then directed to law enforcement. Law enforcement officials say they do not really know how to respond to maltreatment calls, and they want child protective services (CPS) to respond. The CPS workers want to be responsive to the calls and would prefer taking the lead in responding (with law enforcement as a backup, if and when needed, instead of having law enforcement respond alone).

Characteristics of Technical Work

Values, beliefs, and perspectives are aligned. In the example above, all agree that a change is needed and that child welfare should take the lead, with law enforcement backing up when necessary.

Definition of the problem is clear and understood by all in the same way. The child welfare leaders, child welfare staff, and law enforcement all agree that the problem is the lack of CPS response to maltreatment calls after 5 p.m. All agree that an interagency agreement between law enforcement and child welfare is needed.

Solution and implementation for the problem is clear and understood by all in the same way. All entities agree that CPS should respond to the reports after hours, with law enforcement as backup. All agree that an interagency agreement should be developed and implemented. The agreement should outline roles and responsibilities and the conditions under which backup will be requested.

Primary locus of responsibility for organizing and delegating the work and the responsibilities for planning and monitoring the progress is the leader (most likely an individual with formal authority having a management role). Needed changes can be handled by the CPS leader and whoever is authorized by the leader to move the work forward. Direction, activities, roles, and responsibilities can be delegated by the leader, and the leader has the overall responsibility for the work getting done.

In this instance, the ability of the child welfare agency and the law enforcement agency to work together was clear, and a technical solution (i.e., task focused) was not hard to create. Adaptive work is not so simple.

Adaptive Work

Peter Senge, in his seminal work, *The Fifth Discipline,* speaks to the challenge of adaptive work in his introduction:

> The changes required will be not only in our organizations but in ourselves as well. . . . Only by changing how we think can we change deeply embedded policies and practices. . . . Only by changing how we interact can shared vision, shared understandings and new capacities for coordinated action be established. (1990, p. xiv)

Table 4.2. Moving to adaptive work: The paradigm shift for leadership values, skills, and behaviors

Leaders having answers	to	Leaders asking questions
Leaders having control	to	Leaders seeking collaboration
Leader having solutions	to	Leader seeking solutions from diverse group of others
Leader making decisions	to	Leaders collating and synthesizing the process of decision making

To manage the process of adaptive work, a number of paradigm shifts must occur. These are fundamental shifts in the mental models leaders bring to the work that must be identified and addressed regularly in the work of change. For example, there may be a shift from controlling the situation to seeking the collaboration of others. In human service delivery systems, this may require giving up a certain amount of control and giving it to another agency or system. In the past, leaders have been seen as people who have command of a situation and provide solutions to the problems systems seek to reform. To do adaptive work, leaders will have to shift their roles in decision making (see Table 4.2). Leaders do not want to "let the people down," and they will need to seek solutions from a diverse range of other voices. Leaders in the past made the decisions; leaders today are those who can identify and foster varying perspectives and synthesize the process of decision making. The leader must address the roles of managing day-to-day tasks and creating technical solutions and must include moving to a bigger picture and fostering change.

Characteristics of Adaptive Work

Adaptive challenges have specific characteristics.

Values, beliefs, and attitudes are not aligned, and there are legitimate, yet competing, perspectives or forces. Families often have multiple risks or co-occurring needs, requiring child serving agencies to cooperate and collaborate with each other to provide services to vulnerable children and their families. As a result, leadership is not simple. There are new notions, new challenges, new roles, and more gray than black and white. The "typical" relationship between child welfare and mental health can be used as an example. These agencies have different perspectives and different resources. Mental health agencies may propose a system of care approach with wraparound services as the best way to respond to a particular family. The child welfare agency may be in agreement that services need to be individualized for children and families but may not have the capacity to offer wraparound processes and individualized services, or it may see the services being recommended by mental health as ineffective in addressing maltreatment issues. Child welfare agencies may provide families with the resources they have available, rather than responding more directly to what the families need in terms of treatment. This is a fundamental difference that relates to attitudes and beliefs.

Another example relates to substance abuse and child maltreatment. Families involved with the child welfare system may need substance abuse treatment focused on the adult's ability to see and address the impact of substance abuse on parenting. The substance abuse treatment program, however, may not focus on the parenting aspects of the adult's life.

Another example comes from the juvenile justice system. Aggressive youth regularly enter the juvenile justice system with past or current involvement with mental health. The mental health focus might be on treatment and medication, whereas the juvenile justice focus is on moving the youth through the court system. The perspective of each agency will influence the way in which services are provided. These are three examples where there are competing legitimate perspectives about providing services.

The definition of the problem is unclear. To respond effectively to multiple needs of families, it is necessary for human service agencies to collaborate with other entities. Building a collaborative approach brings different perspectives, solutions, and partners to the table. Mental health, child welfare, juvenile justice, domestic violence, health, education, child care, and others must be at the same table. Each agency brings a different perspective about the work, and therefore, within a collaborative approach, even the definition of the problem is not clear to all who are interacting with the family (e.g., child welfare may view the family situation as threats to safety, mental health may view the family situation as needing treatment).

The solution to the problem and its implementation requires new learning. Everyone around the table has a different idea about what words mean and what new ideas intend. Individuals need time to process, absorb, and understand the new paradigm. This requires opportunities to delve into new values, attitudes, and behaviors and learn what the paradigm shift is truly about.

For example, mental health proposes that a system of care is the most appropriate approach to dealing with child and family issues. This often means using a wraparound approach where the assessments and services are individualized to meet the specific needs of children and their families. Public health may ask what is happening in the environment/community that might be causing these challenges for children and their families. They will ask how many others are seeking support and how the community can build protective factors or eliminate risk factors within the population so that children and their families can thrive. New ways of looking at the solution and implementation must be found by exploring and understanding the various perspectives represented at a collaborative table. Leaders need to first find ways to maximize all of the resources that are available from various agencies, determine what gaps there are, and then find other needed resources.

The primary locus of responsibility is not the formal leader (the leader with authority). In technical solutions, a leader proposes the answer. In adaptive work, the leader cannot solve the problem alone. To continue with the public health example above, the move forward to develop and provide population-based interventions with communities requires shifts in values, attitudes, and ways of working. Public health perspectives will require a serious look at community data, whereas mental health and child welfare will be focusing their attention on the individual data of children and families within their spheres of interest. Everyone around the table will need to learn about the others' perspectives and be able to make shifts in values, attitudes, and beliefs. The formal leader cannot force or delegate "changes" but rather creates the environment for new learning to occur. In adaptive work, the responsibility of the leader is to mobilize adaptive work on the part of the group so that they can learn their way to new solutions—new ways for agencies to work together and new ways of working with children and their families.

DISTINGUISHING BETWEEN ADAPTIVE AND TECHNICAL WORK

Leaders must distinguish the difference between adaptive and technical work (Heifetz, 1994). Adaptive work is more complex than technical work. Adaptive work affects deeply held, culturally bound beliefs, values, and perspectives. Leaders in this new age of leadership must understand and be able to facilitate collaborative learning processes that lead groups of people to find new solutions for difficult challenges. Therefore, leaders must ultimately understand the framework of adaptive work, shift to the new paradigm for the role of leadership, and develop new skills to engage others and align perspectives in moving toward new solutions and mobilize people to change.

Adaptive work requires that leaders address the need for changes in values, behaviors, and attitudes and in learning new ways to respond to challenges. This harks back to the mental models that underlie the work. Without these changes, the technical fixes we might apply to problems will not work. At the very least, adaptive work requires that the gap between the values people stand for and the realities they face are diminished. For example, an agency director, a state legislature, or Congress may pass a new law or change a policy to deal with a particular challenge, thinking this activity will solve whatever problem is at hand. These approaches are technical solutions, but many of these challenges cannot be solved by answers from above. Such challenges require adaptive responses, including taking risks and experimentation, new discoveries, and adjustments from many places within an agency, system, or community. Without learning new ways, or changing attitudes, values, and behaviors, people cannot make the adaptive leap that is necessary to respond effectively to today's challenges.

Adaptive work requires learning to address conflicts in the values people hold or to close the gap between the values people stand for and the realities they face. To mobilize adaptive work, a leader has to engage people in adjusting their unrealistic expectations about the new paradigms and to address their mental models. Rather than satisfying people by trying to make the challenge seem easier than it is or applying a technical fix, leaders need to keep the focus on the challenges and not be dissuaded by the confusion or stress that people in the system exhibit.

At the beginning of the adaptive process, no leader can clearly see what the true benefits of change will be, compared to what the current policies or practices will yield. In fact, when leaders endeavor in systems change in the form of new polices or practices, many can view the changes as a loss. At a personal level, many involved in the change might try to avoid a painful adjustment to their lives, hoping that changes are postponed or that someone will come to the rescue. In fact, when fears or passions run high, people can become desperate and look to authorities to fix the problem so that change will not be necessary (i.e., technical solutions).

As an example, Paul's cholesterol is very high, he is gaining weight, and he is identified as having diabetes. Paul wants the doctor to prescribe medication that will bring the levels down. Paul does not want to change his sedentary lifestyle, so he will ask the doctor to solve the problem with a technical fix. Will that work? Probably not, because Paul needs to change his sedentary lifestyle, and that will require an adaptive response.

When characteristics of adaptive work are prevailing, it is clear that the function of leadership cannot be technical in nature. In these circumstances, leaders who pursue technical solutions may feel as though they are making progress, but, in the end, adaptive challenges are not amenable to technical fixes. A leader may have products in hand, such as needs assessments, strategic plans, budgets, or logic models, but the attitudes and values of the people will not have changed.

Decision making and solution finding are activities that demand interaction and dialogue between a diversity of people who care to develop mutually acceptable answers. Heifetz and Laurie (1997) defined this group of people as the "collective intelligence" and emphasized the importance of engaging others from many different sectors and levels of the work, utilizing the knowledge and experience from each in the process of discovery. Only by engaging this group to learn from each other will group members be able to recognize and do the adaptive work necessary in their own thinking, which will in turn lead to new and creative solutions. Mobilizing the collective intelligence in this process of alignment and discovery is at the heart of the leaders' role in adaptive work.

Ultimately, the role of leadership in adaptive work is to create a meaningful context for learning so that the collective intelligence can absorb and understand the change, align their perspectives, and ultimately act in concert with one another toward a vision they share. It is important for leaders to differentiate their role in adaptive work from their role in technical work. Leaders may have to shift their own mental model, and do their own adaptive work to be effective in mobilizing the work of change.

I really thought that in order to serve youth and young adults in transition, we had to extend the system of care to age 24. Now my mental model has shifted and I see that this population needs its own uniquely designed service delivery system. Now I understand my role in the change process.
—Leader, children's mental health system

To differentiate between technical and adaptive work, a leader needs to look out into the setting and ask the following important question: "Will we be able to make progress on this problem without a change in people's values, attitudes, and/or habits of behavior?" If the answer is no, then the leader must engage in adaptive work; new competencies, beyond technical solutions, will be required. There are many problems in human services that are not amenable to authoritative expertise. However, technical and adaptive work are not mutually exclusive— instead, they intersect and support one another. The key is to know when in the change process each is needed. To lead effectively, leaders assess the environment and select the appropriate response based on the needs of the system.

Job descriptions of most leaders focus on the roles most linked to technical work, so it is common for leaders to fail to identify adaptive work, leading to attempts to implement technical solutions for adaptive challenges. Choosing technical solutions for adaptive challenges happens with great frequency and takes place in all kinds of settings. This can be considered a great leadership mistake. Several examples may help illuminate this important concept.

Example One: Technology in the Workplace

A large training and technical assistance entity wanted to upgrade its technical presence in the field and asked its staff to begin utilizing new hardware and software. A simply technical approach would be to put the hardware on people's desks, give them the manual, and teach them how to use it. But what is the adaptive challenge? The adaptive challenge is to help new users understand how useful the new experiment can be in completing their work, to address uncertainties about technology and openness to changing the way they complete their work every day.

Example Two: Strengths-Based Assessments

A Midwest community decided that it would like its service delivery system to be strengths based. A technical approach might include a new intake form that uses strengths-based language and assessment strategies. But what is the adaptive challenge? The adaptive challenge is to help providers focus on the strengths of individuals and families, rather than their difficulties and problems. This shift in values can be facilitated by the technical support of a new intake form, but an opportunity for the values shift must accompany, or perhaps precede, the use of new forms.

Example Three: Family Involvement

A child welfare agency has seen the outcome data from the system of care in its community and has decided to take the concept of family involvement more seriously for the population it serves. The technical solution would be to make sure that family members receive information and notices of meetings and appointments and that child care and transportation are not barriers. But what is the adaptive challenge? The adaptive challenge is to affect the values and attitudes of the workforce so that they act inclusively of families, recognize that families drive the decision process, and design approaches that support the partnership between providers and families.

Example Four: Interagency Collaboration

A governor wants to raise the level of interagency collaboration in the state. A technical response would involve copying best practice agreements and asking the counties to alter them by inserting their own county's name. The adaptive solution is a 10-year adaptive process to reach the technical success of completing a multi-agency agreement. The governor's suggestion offered a technical solution without acknowledging and understanding the adaptive work required for success in each county. It is unlikely that one county's work can be replicated like a fast-food franchise in another county. The adaptive challenge is to get interested parties together to share ideas and agree to move forward together in a joint application. Then one moves to the technical challenge by developing a draft agreement and back again to the adaptive process to review, evaluate, and engage in further discussion. Editing and rewriting is then a technical challenge.

Example Five: Cultural and Linguistic Competence

A mental health agency leader decides to implement cultural and linguistic competence practices in the agency. A technical response is to translate brochures and materials into languages other than English and have interpretation available. But what is the adaptive challenge? The adaptive challenge is to integrate and accept diverse cultural beliefs and perspectives into everything the agency does. The adaptive work is to help the group recognize that truly meaningful communication requires all parties to understand and value each other's points of view.

Very often the distinction between technical and adaptive work is not made, and the urge to check items off a list is great. Adaptive and technical work differ in approach, so work done by a group can be one or the other, depending on the alignment of values, attitudes, beliefs, and behaviors over time. The new paradigm of leadership focuses on adaptive challenges. It is adaptive work that often gets overlooked and includes elements and actions that challenge basic values, attitudes, and beliefs. It is important that a leader prioritize the role of mobilizing people to do adaptive work.

Technical work is not the solution for an adaptive challenge. Resistance to change in a group can be met by meeting the adaptive work head-on. Although the process of change requires both technical and adaptive work, the key is knowing which to use at any given time to move the work of systems change forward.

SKILLS OF ADAPTIVE WORK

Adaptive work is difficult, can be stressful, and requires a cultural shift when it represents a different way of serving children, youth, and families and a collaborative approach to the work. Leaders can benefit from both the adaptive and the technical frameworks to understand the tasks in this new environment. The new role of the leader in adaptive work is to create a context for learning so that new concepts, such as family-driven and strengths-based concepts, can be understood, absorbed, and implemented by all. Leaders can practice specific skills and utilize tools to carry out the work associated with adaptive challenges. These practices, when applied consistently, can facilitate the process of building relationships across boundaries and levels, with people learning from one another, and, ultimately, help them expand their worldview and learn their way to new solutions.

Building on the work of Heifetz (1994) and Heifetz and Linsky (2002), this section explores the practice of adaptive leadership and outlines six leadership skill sets required to face adaptive challenges: Getting on the Balcony, Identifying the Adaptive Challenge, Regulating Distress, Maintaining Disciplined Attention, Giving the Work Back to the People, and Protecting All Voices (Heifetz, 1994).

Getting on the Balcony

Leaders must be able to step back and see patterns in struggles over values and power, recognizing patterns of work avoidance, resistance to change, and other signs of conflict. Leaders in each moment must understand the context within which they are operating. At any given moment, leaders need to be both active and reflective; one participates or leads and one observes what is going on at the same time. Heifetz (1994) compared the difference between active and reflective to the experience of dancing on the dance floor in contrast to standing on a balcony and watching other people dance. When you are dancing, it is not possible to see the patterns made by other people on the dance floor. Dancers are living in the moment and swept away by the music and the dancing.

To discern the larger pattern on the dance floor—who is dancing with whom, in what groups, in what location, who is sitting out, and who has walked out of the room—leaders have to stop moving and get to the balcony. Once they have been on the balcony and have seen patterns, they can go back to the dance floor. Leaders occasionally need to take themselves out of the action, if only for a moment, and distance themselves from the situation.

For example, a player learning a new team sport, such as basketball, who only focuses on his own actions will contribute less to the success of the team than a player who can keep the big picture in mind. Each player on a successful team needs to know where his teammates are and where an assist is needed and to recognize the best opportunities to move the ball forward. To do so, the player—or the adaptive leader—needs to step back from the game and see the larger pattern of play and then return to the game.

Example from the Field   For years in a large Midwestern state, youth and young adults in transition were not on the radar screen for mental health agencies as a population with special needs. The elements of the service system for youth and young adults in transition worked in silos and tried to hand off responsibility for working with this population to one another. Without the benefit of deep collaborative dialogue leaders thought the answer to better serving youth and young adults in transition rested on where services were located—the adult service system or the child service system—and the age of eligibility for these services. The leaders in each child-serving educational, vocational rehabilitation, and mental health agency advocated raising the eligibility for the children's system of care services and interventions to age 24, whereas the adult mental health leaders advocated maintaining the age of service eligibility for adult services at 18. Each system believed that what it had to offer was sufficient and that the eligibility was the problem. The delivery system was in gridlock, and youth and young adults were falling through the cracks, refusing to seek traditional services, such as day treatment programs, through the adult mental health system. Families were desperate and did not know where to turn for assistance.

Leaders who cared about this issue then got on the balcony and began to see the values conflicts between the systems and the mental models amongst themselves that were preventing forward momentum. The leaders had work to do to assess, evaluate, and diagnose the problem. They had to assess their assumptions and perceptions and make sure that they were not relying on ineffective mental models in place of careful analysis. They spoke directly to families and heard their frustrations in trying to get a job or housing for their sons or daughters with mental health needs. Most important, they spoke to youth and young adults who voiced their needs, their hopes, and their dreams. None of the youth spoke of wanting to be part of any system. On the contrary, they spoke of wanting independence and having a life like others their age.

The leaders looked at both the child- and adult-serving systems and tried to see if either met the vision of what the youth and families wanted and needed. While on the balcony, they recognized that this was a unique population with service needs that neither the child-serving system nor the adult-serving system could fully address. It would be as inappropriate to have youth and young adults in transition remain in the child-serving system through age 24 as it would be to have them enter the adult system at age 18. Only from the balcony could leaders clearly see that effectively serving youth and young adults in transition requires a different approach involving a new way of thinking and new, innovative approaches to serving young adults' need for independence. Until they got on the balcony, neither side could see that they did not have the full complement of skill sets needed for youth and young adults in transition and that no one system could take complete responsibility. A new system requiring a collaborative approach would need to be formed.

Identifying the Adaptive Challenge

Adaptive work toward change needs to be named, framed, and described. For the leader to do that work, it needs to be identified. A leader on the balcony can more clearly identify shifts in values, attitudes, and behaviors that will allow change to occur. Each member of a collaborative may perceive different aspects of the challenge and identify new solutions. The collective contribution of all the stakeholders and the willingness of each stakeholder to take new steps and learn new skills will produce a strategy for success. The leadership skill is to identify and understand underlying values conflicts and embedded attitudes that allow old practices to remain in place. Adaptive work addresses adaptive challenges. Without proper identification of the adaptive challenge, the leader might move forward with technical solutions and miss the real work of change. Once the adaptive challenge is identified to the group, it can be addressed directly. The adaptive challenge can also be called "putting the elephant that is in the room on the table!" Rest assured—putting the adaptive challenge on the table will create distress, conflict, and disequilibrium. For example, consider the initiative of family team meetings or conferencing. To develop an approach that would give families both a forum and the power and responsibility to make a plan for their child, the adaptive challenge has to be framed in a way that recognizes the various perspectives and feelings about viewing families as capable.

Example from the Field Identifying the adaptive challenge took time and occurred at different stages for state leaders in the field of youth and young adults in transition. The adult mental health system held a mental model that the system needed to prepare youth and young adults in transition to move into the adult service system, which had been created for individuals with chronic mental illness. This belief was reinforced by the fact that the adult system was highly regarded for evidence-based programs. Leaders in the adult system did not yet understand how the young people aging out of the child-serving systems did not fit the profile of an adult with chronic mental illness. Leaders in the child mental health system held onto their mental model, too. They held on to the value of family-driven care and were very protective of the young people. They thought that to better serve youth and young adults in transition, the system needed to extend child and adolescent services beyond age 18 up to age 24 years.

Education, which had a big role to play, felt that their job was done once the youth left school, whether by dropping out, graduating, or expulsion. They were not sure they had a role beyond certain criteria. Vocational rehabilitation had been more focused on youth and young adults in transition with developmental disabilities and was not sure what to do with these young people with mental health needs.

After getting on the balcony and listening to families and to the young people, leaders learned that the adaptive challenge was not changing age limits or shifting responsibility from one system to another; it was to create a new and unique system where the youth would transition into a yet-to-be-created array of services and opportunities that would have at its foundation the value of independence—a strongly held value for the young people. The adaptive challenge was that youth and young adults in transition did not want to make the transition into the adult system or any system; they wanted to make the transition to independence.

In this situation, no one leader could do it alone and they had to frame the challenge as a call for collective action. They began to ask the tough questions: What can we do together? How does each system need to shift to meet the needs of youth and young adults in transition? While on one hand these "ah-ha" moments were exciting, they created a tremendous amount of distress among all parties involved as the realization began to sink in that everyone would have to change.

Regulating Distress

Once a leader has the opportunity to get on the balcony and identify and articulate the adaptive challenge, the leader should expect a certain level of distress from individuals within the agency or system. The adaptive challenge is a call for change. People who are in comfortable habitual situations could very well be required to shift their values, attitudes, and beliefs, which might ultimately change their day-to-day activities. The distress leaders will encounter is primarily based on fear, complacency, skepticism, pessimism, and the difficulties of learning new ways to serve children, youth, and their families. Addressing adaptive challenges, coming to common ground (see Chapter 6), and creating new solutions generates distress as a natural part of the change process. The skill for the leader is to regulate the distress, not take it away or let it get out of control. Regulating distress means pacing the work and using distress as a creative tool in the adaptive process. The metaphor of a pressure cooker is often used to describe this phenomenon. It keeps the pressure on to cook the food but releases

Table 4.3.   How to regulate distress in a holding environment

Raise the Temperature
- Draw attention to the tough questions.
- Give people more responsibility than they are comfortable with.
- Bring conflicts to the surface.
- Don't let people explain away the problem.

Lower the Temperature
- Address the technical aspects of the problem.
- Establish a structure for the problem-solving process by breaking the problem into parts and creating time frames, decision rules, and clear role assignments.
- Temporarily reclaim responsibility for the tough issues.

From Heifetz, R.A., & Linsky, M. (2002). *Leadership on the line: Staying alive through the dangers of leading* (p. 11). Boston: Harvard Business School Press; adapted by permission.

the pressure so that the top does not blow off the pot. Leaders can increase the distress and orchestrate conflict by asking tough questions that cause the agency or system to explore longstanding attitudes and behaviors and help "unlearn" old expectations and break habits, but no one is well served if that distress gets out of control.

Whereas a leader's role in adaptive work is to keep the pressure up, he or she must also make sure that the distress and conflict does not become so intense that individuals in communities, agencies, and systems walk away from the change and rebel outright. Heifetz and Linsky (2002) offer a series of suggestions on how to decrease distress, such as inserting technical work in the midst of change. By using technical work, people may feel comforted by the structure of committees or task forces, planning processes, or needs assessments. The technical work might be a part of the process, and it can be utilized as a strategy for diminishing the distress felt by an organization as it moves through adaptation and innovation. (See Table 4.3 for strategies to regulate distress.)

The skill of regulating distress is supported when leaders create what Heifetz (1994) called a "holding environment"—a safe space where difficult adaptive challenges can be discussed; diversity of opinion is welcomed; experiences, values, and assumptions can be challenged; and stress is expected and tolerated. In holding environments, leaders keep their composure and do not get into the action. They manage their own stress by recognizing that the group needs to go through some serious and often difficult conversations to vent frustration; relieve tensions; unlearn old values, attitudes, and habits; and define new methods and strategies to meet the new paradigms of serving children and their families. In adaptive work, the role of the leader is not to fix the problem or make the decision. Instead, using presence and poise, the leader's adaptive work is to create and maintain the holding environment.

Table 4.4. Where everyone is safe to speak: tips for creating a holding environment to regulate distress

Create an Inclusive Process:
- Make sure that everyone has an opportunity to tell his or her story.
- Share the stories of those not able to be in the room.

Communicate to Understand:
- Be patient and listen with intent—not just to respond with an answer.
- Differentiate between positions and interests and help others do the same.
- Look for opportunities to change "or/but" conversations to "and" conversations.
- Use the following for effective communication:
  —Restate—listen for factual content.
  —Reflect—listen for emotional content.
  —Reframe.
  —Ask open-ended questions.
  —Use "I" statements.
  —Summarize.

Manage the Communication:
- Give everyone at the table time to tell his or her story—spend time equitably drawing out everyone's story.
- Be careful and precise when setting up expectations and ground rules/norms.
- Do not feel like you always have to compromise; on the other hand, be flexible.
- Support others to be problem solvers rather than just jumping in (give the work to the people).

Maintain Focus for the Communication:
- Separate the person from the problem.
- If necessary, encourage the use of a "parking lot" to table conversation not relevant to the current conversation.
- Make sure there will be no retribution from you or from others.

Personal Management:
- Slow yourself down.
- Work through your own defensiveness.
- Defer your own immediate emotional response and ask for clarification.
- Take risks to slow things down.
- Empower others through listening.

From Kagen, E. B., & Hepburn, K. S. (Eds.). (2006). *Leadership in systems of care: An unpublished training curriculum.* Washington DC: Georgetown University Center for Child and Human Development, National Technical Assistance Center for Children's Mental Health; reprinted by permission.

Creating a holding environment requires a variety of skills and techniques. A list of practices that leaders can employ to create and maintain a holding environment and tips on how to manage the leader's stress are outlined in Table 4.4. (Note: A neutral facilitator often has the skills to support holding environments. Leaders, however, are challenged to hold themselves back from the action lest they lose their capacity to maintain a safe space for all voices to be heard.)

Example from the Field   Creating a safe environment was critical as leaders continued to work together on creating systems change for youth and young adults in transition. Within a safe environment, each system leader had his or her own "ah-has" about the shift in values, attitudes, and beliefs each had to make. Personal feelings entered the picture, too. Some feared losing control of a program or funding; others felt that holding on to their systems service philosophy was a personal reflection of their professional success or failure.

The adult mental health and child mental health leaders started a process to dialogue with each other about their different approaches to serving youth and young adults in transition. They realized that they had much to learn about each other to remove longstanding mental models. As they continued to dialogue, each leader recognized that he or she was rooted in his or her own paradigm. The adult system leaders recognized that their system served a narrow population of individuals with chronic mental illness and may not have the necessary experience with the youth and young adults in transition population, whereas the child system leaders realized that they had to help their system shift from its longstanding family-driven and youth-guided values to a paradigm that put the youth first—youth-driven and family-centered care. During one of a series of retreats (holding environments), the vocational rehabilitation leader realized that her system did not have the expertise needed and that they were not equipped to support the youth and young adults in transition population. She realized that for them to be a full partner, she was going to have to lead her system to change. Vocational rehabilitation had been nationally recognized for serving adults with chronic mental illness. Their mental model suggested that they were doing great. Adult mental health felt the same. The fact that their success with adults with chronic mental illness did not translate to the youth and young adults in transition population created enormous distress.

The leaders regulated distress by keeping focus on the issue and providing safe spaces for the work of change to occur, such as hosting a series of facilitated retreats and opportunities for dialogue where leaders did not feel pressured to make decisions and had the chance to explore new ideas and discuss opportunities for risk taking. In addition, a child leader reached out across the aisle to an adult leader and began a relationship so that, in the event of increased pressure to change and amplified heat as a result of distress, perhaps the relationship could help them both get through it and maintain their collaborative approach. One way of building a strong relationship was finding opportunities to publicly recognize the work that each had done. Another way was to make sure that any time the youth and young adults in transition issue was discussed all the parties were at the table. Another child system leader built a holding environment by consistently reaching out and sending messages that she would not give up on working together and showed determination and optimism that they were all going to figure this out together. Leaders from the various systems also spent time doing technical work by writing a white paper, which was a way to raise the adaptive issues and keep the heat up while conversely lowering the heat by focusing on a technical task. In that paper, they agreed that youth, their families, and collaboration would be the foundational values of their work.

Maintaining Disciplined Attention

The leader of change has an important role in maintaining focus on the issues at hand. As resistance to change emerges, the leader will notice a variety of work-avoidance behaviors. Leaders will hear phrases like "It's not in my job description" or "Let's give this issue to a task force to study" as ways to deflect attention from the hard adaptive work to be confronted. One of the most challenging examples of work avoidance is denial that the adaptive issue even exists. Sometimes the stress of change is too difficult and some will want to sweep it under the rug and simply make it go away. The leader recognizes that the issue will not go away because the underlying values conflicts are still in operation. The leader's role is to identify distractions and take actions to regain focus.

During this phase of a change process, it is important to continue reflection on the balcony to identify and correctly diagnose the distractions from the process of change. Leaders can lose credibility if people are, in fact, working hard to change and the leader cannot see it.

If a leader is in a position of authority, it is not risky for him or her to move forward with actions that ensure proper attention to the adaptive challenge. However, it is quite another case when a leader operates outside the realm of his or her authority. Leaders need to be aware that they can become the focal point for work avoidance, with scapegoating or attempts at eliminating their presence within the structure or process. Leaders without authority will want to build strategic alliances with authority figures (see Chapter 5) or employ strategies to gain informal authority as the issue of change ripens.

It is natural to avoid the work of change. As known by anyone who has been on a diet or tried to quit smoking, change is hard and requires effort and support. In systems change, that support comes from the leader through maintaining focused attention. As the work of change progresses and distress occurs, stakeholders may be tempted to blame others for lack of progress. The adaptive leader "holds steady" (Heifetz & Linsky, 2002) when distractions arise, clarifies the real issue, redirects the people, and brings focus back to the work at hand.

Example from the Field   Adaptive leaders recognize that this work is long and complex and that they must keep their eye on maintaining the work of change. In addition, they must be aware of all the forces (political and fiscal; internal and external) that could derail and delay the change at any moment. In this youth and young adults in transition example, a new federal grant program was announced and, in response, some leaders independently called a meeting to bring together a small group of system leaders to take action on the grant announcement. Another stakeholder found out about the meeting and insisted that it was not reflecting the values that had been agreed to in the white paper and retreats. The leaders put the adaptive challenge back on the table by showing how the values of the agreement were out of alignment with their behavior. The meeting was cancelled, and a new, more inclusive collaborative group emerged to respond to the proposal.

Another holding environment was created and a negotiated solution that stayed true to the values emerged.

Giving the Work Back to the People

As change progresses, each individual within an organization or system has to go through his or her own process of adaptive work. It is not something that the leader can do for him or her—it is something each individual has to go through him or herself. Leaders provide support, not control. They make sure that there are opportunities for people to learn new ways of doing things and to collaborate and learn from each other. Leadership failures occur when leaders think they can make people change their values, attitudes, or beliefs by virtue of their authority or by virtue of the rightness of their stance. Change happens when everyone involved carries responsibility for the problem and the solution, and the leader's role is to give him or her every opportunity to confront, struggle, and dialogue about how to address the adaptive challenge and work into the future. Leaders easily take on too much responsibility for change and fail to give the work of change back to the appropriate levels, where change will actually occur. Many leaders need to break their longstanding habit of providing technical fixes, which can bring credibility and success but not address the true underlying adaptive challenge. Any unaddressed adaptive challenge will inevitably rise again until leaders place the work of change where it belongs.

Example from the Field   There was tension when some leaders created a separate group to respond to the proposal. Most of the leaders felt it was up to the entire group to make sure they were creating change together. They used the opportunity of the grant writing to rebuild their relationships and reinforce the value of collaboration. The leaders who created a separate group had to work hard to change their own mental models of how things are done and shift to a collaborative stance. The group worked hard to reinforce this value and make it stick. The leaders showed by their actions that no one leader could simply write the proposal because it needed to reflect shifts in each of their systems, changes that each system would need to accept. The work of change had to be given back to each system as they moved forward.

Protecting All Voices

The leader must be open to voices of leadership from all sectors of a collaborative group, including voices that may conflict with a prevailing view or with individuals from the group. All voices have the potential to set the direction for a community or initiative. Leaders must learn to expect that solutions can come from anywhere and remain open to and embracing of all the voices.

Some of the best solutions may come from individuals who have sat on the sidelines in the change process, such as the youth and young adults, or people without formal training. Adaptive leaders protect all voices by providing an opportunity for all stakeholders to give input, no matter what roles they held in the past. The adaptive leader also manages the behaviors of others who may attempt to quash these new voices though careful facilitation and active listening.

Examples from the Field   Throughout the systems-change process for TAY, the leaders' work had to ensure that the youth and young adult voice was clearly heard and not censored. They created opportunities for the youth voice to be heard, and they fostered a spirit of truth telling by encouraging and reinforcing the validity of their story. There were times when the youth voice was shrill, telling the systems to stop spending money on fancy forms and documents that were not youth friendly. Although their words made some bristle, the leaders provided positive feedback and protection that allowed their voices to continue to be heard.

As the adaptive leader becomes more comfortable with this role, these six skill sets will become a fluid part of their repertoire. Although they have been written in a way that shows how they may flow in a logical progression, the work of change can be messy, and these skills will be called upon in varying degrees, frequency, and order, depending on each adaptive challenge.

CONCLUSION

Changes in today's world of diverse communities involve youth and families, in collaboration with multiple systems and stakeholders, and demand new ways of working. Many transformation efforts take longer and require more resources than necessary or even fail because leaders have not recognized their role as adaptive leaders. Leaders in this new world must meet the challenge of moving from technical to adaptive work, which involves a multidimensional paradigm shift. The leader must recognize the role of mental models and move away from a management role to get on the balcony and see the bigger picture. Adaptive work affects deeply held culturally bound beliefs, values, and perspectives and can take a very long time to complete.

Leaders in this new age must understand and be able to facilitate collaborative learning processes that lead groups of people to find new solutions for difficult challenges. Leaders who understand the difference between adaptive and technical work and who put the skills of adaptive work into practice will promote the discovery of new solutions and new ways of doing business. Therefore, leaders must understand the framework of adaptive work, shift to the new paradigm for the role of leadership, and develop new skills and use tools to engage others to mobilize toward new solutions.

REFERENCES

Arango, J.B. (1998). *Mental models.* Algodones, NM: Algodones Associates. Retrieved January 7, 2010, from http://www.algodonesassociates.com/planning/Mental%20models.pdf

Argyris, C. (1993). *Knowledge for action. A guide to overcoming barriers to organizational change.* San Francisco: Jossey-Bass.

Goodman, M.R. (1992). *Systems thinking: A language for learning and acting.* Boston: Innovations Associates Organizational Learning.

Heifetz, R.A. (1994). *Leadership without easy answers.* Cambridge, MA: The Belknap Press of Harvard University Press.

Heifetz, R.A., & Laurie, D. (1997, January–February). The work of leadership. *Harvard Business Review 75(1),* 124–134.

Heifetz, R.A., & Linsky, M. (2002). *Leadership on the line: Staying alive through the dangers of leading.* Boston: Harvard Business School Press.

Heifetz, R.A., Linsky, M., & Grashow, A. (2009). *Practices of adaptive leadership: tools and tactics for changing your organization and the world.* Boston: Harvard Business Publishing.

Innovation Associates, Inc. (1992). *Systems thinking: A language for learning and acting: The Innovation Associates systems thinking course workbook.* Framingham, MA: Innovation Associates.

Kagen, E. B., & Hepburn, K. S. (Eds.). (2006). *Leadership in systems of care: An unpublished training curriculum.* Washington D.C.: Georgetown University Center for Child and Human Development, National Technical Assistance Center for Children's Mental Health. Washington, DC.

Kies, D. (2009). *Underlying assumptions.* Retrieved January 8, 2010, from http://papyr.com/hypertextbooks/comp2/assume.htm

Lee, R.J., & King, S.N. (2000). *Discovering the leader in you: A guide to realizing your personal leadership potential.* San Francisco: Jossey-Bass.

Senge, P. (1990). *The fifth discipline: The art and practice of the learning organization.* New York: Doubleday.

Senge, P.M., Roberts, C., Ross, R.B., Smith, B.J., & Kleiner, A. (1994). *The fifth discipline fieldbook: Strategies and tools for building a learning organization.* New York: Doubleday.

Wheatley, M. (1999). *Leadership and the new science: Discovering order in a chaotic world.* San Francisco: Berrett-Koehler.

 **Worksheet 4.1**

My Values, My Culture, My Behavior

Value Based on Cultural Worldview	Cultural Messages Derived from Value	Impact on Beliefs and Behaviors

From Kagen, E.B., & Hepburn, K.S. (Eds.). (2006). *Leadership in systems of care: An unpublished training curriculum.* Washington, DC: Georgetown University Center for Child and Human Development, National Technical Assistance Center for Children's Mental Health; reprinted by permission.

In *The Leadership Equation: Strategies for Individuals Who Are Champions for Children, Youth, and Families* edited by Gary M. Blau & Phyllis R. Magrab (2010; Paul H. Brookes Publishing Co., Inc.)

Worksheet 4.2

Left Hand–Right Hand Column Exercise

- Think of an incident where you experienced conflict.
- Select an interaction that had a great effect on you or an interaction on an issue about which you felt passionately.
- Use the right-hand column to write the script of the incident.
- Use the left-hand column to write unsaid thoughts and feelings.

Unsaid Thoughts and Feelings	What Was Said—The Script

Source: Senge (1994).

From Kagen, E.B., & Hepburn, K.S. (Eds.). (2006). *Leadership in systems of care: An unpublished training curriculum.* Washington, DC: Georgetown University Center for Child and Human Development, National Technical Assistance Center for Children's Mental Health; adapted by permission.

Worksheet 4.3

Views of Leadership

1. How much do you think your view of leadership is represented by each of the seven views? Make sure the total is 100%.

    _____

    _____

    _____

    _____

2. Determine how and when each particular view as either been a benefit or a hindrance.

View	%	Benefits	Hindrances
The Genetic View			
The Learned View			
The Heroic View			
The Top-Only View			
The Social Script View			
The Position View			
The Calling View			
TOTAL	100%		

From Kagen, E.B., & Hepburn, K.S. (Eds.). (2006). *Leadership in systems of care: An unpublished training curriculum.* Washington, DC: Georgetown University Center for Child and Human Development, National Technical Assistance Center for Children's Mental Health; reprinted by permission.

In *The Leadership Equation: Strategies for Individuals Who Are Champions for Children, Youth, and Families* edited by Gary M. Blau & Phyllis R. Magrab (2010; Paul H. Brookes Publishing Co., Inc.)

Worksheet 4.4

The Impact of Existing Mental Models

Mental Models About People and Professions

Teenager:

What is your existing mental model?

_____

Does this mental model support or hinder effective interaction/involvement?

_____

Consumer/Client:

What is your existing mental model?

_____

Does this mental model support or hinder effective interaction/involvement?

_____

Physician:

What is your existing mental model?

_____

Does this mental model support or hinder effective interaction/involvement?

_____

Police:

What is your existing mental model?

_____

Does this mental model support or hinder effective interaction/involvement?

_____

(continued)

From Kagen, E.B., & Hepburn, K.S. (Eds.). (2006). *Leadership in systems of care: An unpublished training curriculum.* Washington, DC: Georgetown University Center for Child and Human Development, National Technical Assistance Center for Children's Mental Health; adapted by permission.

In *The Leadership Equation: Strategies for Individuals Who Are Champions for Children, Youth, and Families* edited by Gary M. Blau & Phyllis R. Magrab (2010; Paul H. Brookes Publishing Co., Inc.)

Mental Models About Concepts

Leadership:

What is your existing mental model?

_____

Does this mental model support or hinder effective interaction/involvement?

_____

Religion:

What is your existing mental model?

_____

Does this mental model support or hinder effective interaction/involvement?

_____

Cultural Competence:

What is your existing mental model?

_____

Does this mental model support or hinder effective interaction/involvement?

_____

From Kagen, E.B., & Hepburn, K.S. (Eds.). (2006). *Leadership in systems of care: An unpublished training curriculum.* Washington, DC: Georgetown University Center for Child and Human Development, National Technical Assistance Center for Children's Mental Health; adapted by permission.

III

The Leader in Action

5

Building Strategic Relationships

PHYLLIS R. MAGRAB AND JESSICA RAPER

Supporting children and youth who have a complexity of behavioral needs and their families requires engaging multiple service sectors as well as an array of providers, consultants, case managers, and community agencies. Leading in the complex environment that evolves requires multiple partners including mental health, child welfare, juvenile justice, education, and primary health care agencies and providers. Importantly, these partners, at both the community and state level, may well have differing philosophies, mandates, structures, policies, and levels of resource that pose a challenge for creating a cohesive and collaborative approach to care. The compelling leadership challenge is to build productive relationships and interactions with these partners and allies to achieve a system that is adaptable, dynamic, and responsive to the needs of families.

The science of complexity theory, how dynamic systems adapt to their contexts and how order emerges from chaos, informs leaders on how to transform the landscape. In addressing this "new science," Wheatley (1992) underscored that systems are not machines to be regulated through planning, procedures, power, or control but, rather, are living organisms that can creatively adapt to changing times. She emphasized that the patterns of relationships in these living systems, not their hierarchies, tasks, and functions, are critical. In applying this thinking to the human service delivery system, as leaders attempt to foster the requisite adaptations and change, the greatest barrier is their mental model of leadership—command-and-control rather than facilitation (Plsek & Wilson, 2001). To implement creative, fluid systems where information and ideas are exchanged freely, a new style of leadership must be embraced, a style that is dependent upon building relationships and engaging the voices of all the key stakeholders.

THE FACILITATIVE LEADER

The call for a different frame for leadership is best expressed in the notion of the facilitative leader—a leader who develops trust, secures commitment, and respectfully elicits the perspective, wisdom, and creativity of all partners. The possibility of diverse partners with divergent points of view is welcomed rather than suppressed; the power of diversity is fully embraced. An underlying assumption is that collaboration and collective decision making produce better results. Whether in individual or group situations, the facilitative leader strives to achieve constructive dialogue, balancing inquiry with advocacy. A value and goal is to increase involvement of all stakeholders.

A key to facilitative leadership is having transparency and effective communication. Leaders employ techniques to encourage participation, sustain engagement, provide explanations, and set expectations—the four E's of facilitative leadership in a problem-solving process. Because much of facilitative leadership is about shepherding this process of problem solving and decision making with partners and collaborators, it is critical for leaders to recognize the unique value of each partner, leverage internal commitment, and create opportunities for informed choice.

Facilitative leadership is a value-based, systemic approach moving beyond self-interest and focusing on common goals. Through constructive dialogue, deep engagement of partners and collaborators, and creative management of conflict, facilitative leadership typically generates positive long-term results. The facilitative leader checklist (Figure 5.1) that follows is a useful tool for a leader to assess his or her status as a facilitative leader.

- Sets as a goal the engagement of key stakeholders
- Reaches out to diverse potential partners
- Encourages active engagement of all partners
- Creates a sense of community
- Values collective decision making
- Has the tools to engage in constructive dialogue
- Creatively manages conflict situations
- Values "joining forces"
- Looks for commonalities emphasizing mutuality

Figure 5.1. The facilitative leadership checklist.

EFFECTIVE LEADERSHIP
THROUGH BUILDING CONNECTIONS

The connective leadership model of Lipman-Blumen (1996) provides an excellent framework for understanding effective facilitative leadership in systems of care. Recognizing that in this decade there are new challenges for systems of care leaders— shorter time frames, fewer second chances, need for innovative solutions, goals that must reach beyond the initial problems, thinking for the long term despite short-term pressures—systems of care leaders must draw on a broad range of behaviors. Leadership has to emphasize mutuality and common interests as well as inclusiveness through addressing the issues of diversity. Lipman-Blumen asserted that connective leaders join their dreams to the dreams of others, strive to overcome common problems, create a sense of community, encourage active constituents, join with other leaders, nurture potential leaders, and demonstrate authenticity through dedication. They prefer the "politics of commonality" and take the widest view of what is needed.

The connective leadership model (see Figure 5.2) consists of three major sets of behavioral styles: direct, relational, and instrumental. The *direct style* is to

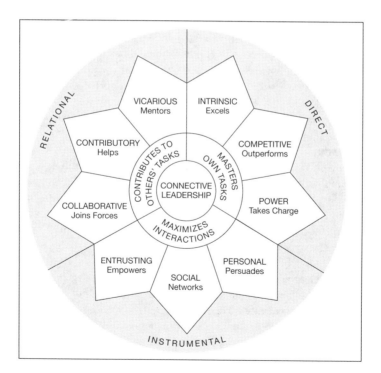

Figure 5.2. Connective leadership model. (From Lipman-Blumen, J. [1996]. *The connective edge* [p. 112]. San Francisco: Jossey-Bass. Reprinted by permission of the Denise Marcil Literary Agency © 1996 by Jean Lipman-Blumen.)

confront tasks individually using mastery, competition, and power. It typically is an expression of individualism. The relational style represents a preference to work in groups to attain a goal. It speaks to interdependence through joining forces, helping, and mentoring. The instrumental style implies using oneself and others as instruments toward community goals through networking, empowering, and persuasion. The latter two frame a strong basis for relationship building and collaboration.

Leaders have access to all these behaviors. Through their instrumental style they act as brokers and matchmakers. They use relationships in multiple ways to carry out their task, but they can also lead the charge. The connective leadership model gives leaders diverse ways to take action and to identify the leadership strategy they might apply to a given situation.

Case Example   Let us take a moment to apply this model, particularly the relational and instrumental style behaviors of the leader, to a familiar example of a leadership challenge in systems of care work.

A 15-year-old youth with complex behavioral needs is known to the juvenile justice, child welfare, substance abuse, and mental health agencies in his community. Over time, the single mother of this young man has become increasingly frustrated by the absence of a coordinated treatment plan for her son and now has sent repeated e-mails of complaint to the governor's office. The governor's office has asked you, the state director for children's mental health, to respond. In many ways, this young man represents a larger group of youth with complex behavioral needs in your state who are not receiving effective supports for very similar reasons. Your challenge is not only to respond to this family but to address the underlying leadership challenge of implementing an effective system of coordinated care for all youth like this young man.

Clearly this is not a problem your agency or you can solve alone. It will require the engagement of all the agencies noted above with possible additions such as the education and health agencies. The state director for juvenile justice is an old friend of yours, so you call him first for advice and ideas on how to proceed (instrumental behavior). In thinking through this challenge, together you identify some common-ground issues for the two of you, including the financing of care and supports, and note that these may well be common-ground concerns for all the agencies potentially involved. You both conclude that this broader group of agencies must be brought together to address the larger issues and to find strategies to implement solutions at the local level (relational behavior). Together you put together an invitation list, including a representative from the governor's office and from a statewide family advocacy organization. You frame the invitation around discussing common issues for serving youth with multiple behavioral needs and cite the current urgent request from the governor's office. This is the beginning of a process you plan to put in place for ongoing dialogue among these agencies.

In this scenario, the state director for children's mental health applies both instrumental and relational behaviors to address the leadership challenge, critical to long-term success. By engaging others to collaborate both around this specific situation and the larger, more systemic issue, the possibilities for creative solutions are multiplied and the chances for creating a coordinated system of services is enhanced, not only for this family but statewide.

Connective leaders recognize that leadership embraces all varieties of behavior, and they combine many strategies to achieve their goals. They use themselves as versatile leadership instruments. As shown in this example, critical to the model are the issues of timing, choosing the appropriate behavior for the specific moment, and building connections.

As the leadership paradigm has shifted from independence to interdependence and from competition to collaboration, it is obvious why leadership models focus less on the individual leader and more on building relationships.

STRATEGIC RELATIONSHIP BUILDING

Strategic relationships include all of the various relationships into which an individual *or* organization can enter, each bringing different benefits and requiring different types of investments.

The natural extension of forming strategic relationships is the implementation of collaborative work. The word *collaboration* comes from the Latin root *collaborare,* which means "to work together." For people to work collaboratively, the leader must focus on process and problem solving, address the interests of all the stakeholders, identify and take action on issues that are ripe for collaboration, and understand the group's capacity for change. This section describes how to analyze strategic relationships to support this process of collaborative work in human service organizations. There are several steps involved in looking deliberately at the building of strategic relationships, including the following:

- Mapping current relationships

- Setting goals for developing new relationships

- Developing skills to create, foster, and expand strategic alliances

This chapter includes a number of tools to help assess the nature of potential partners. The next chapter, Building Common Ground, focuses on the process of working together and how leaders develop these relationships.

Confidants and Allies

A leader needs different kinds of strategic partners to support different personal and professional needs. Heifetz and Linsky (2002) provided a helpful distinction between these two types of partners: confidants and allies. In building strategic relationships, it is important not to confuse the role of a confidant with the role of an ally; although these types of relationships are complementary, they serve different functions.

A confidant is someone with whom one can be completely open and trust. A confidant is a source of feedback and a person who often has no investment in the work per se; in fact, it may be even better if a confidant has no ties to the work, bringing uncontested loyalty to the relationship. Typically, a confidant has an investment in the growth of the leader as a person. Confidants provide the emotional support to do challenging adaptive work and often provide a sounding board for analytical or intellectual explorations. The importance of these relationships cannot be overstated in a diverse and complex working environment.

An ally provides a different sort of support. An ally operates across an organizational boundary but nonetheless shares common interests or values, or at least some common strategy. Because allies operate across a boundary, they are not always able to be loyal to the leader. The benefit of allies is that they bring a different perspective, a complementary set of resources, and missing ingredients to the strategic alliance.

Mission-Driven Strategic Alliances

Choosing allies is a strategic process. Bailey and Koney (2000) defined a number of environmental and organizational forces that motivate a leader to create and maintain strategic alliances, including the following:

- Resource interdependence, which allows partners greater access to and opportunity for necessary resources

- Social responsibility, where leaders desire to address a certain community issue or public concern

- Strategic enhancement, when alliances strengthen capacity for service delivery

- Operational efficiency, which improves productivity relative to the available resources in service delivery and/or ongoing operations

- Environmental validity, when alliance members bolster their legitimacy of external partners

- Domain influence, including motives of power and control

As Bailey and Koney (2000) described, leaders can use strategic alliances to increase their resources in areas such as physical facilities, technological systems, information sharing and human resources, access to funding sources, and more efficient resource allocation. Alliances also can allow leaders to address broader issues that might otherwise be outside the scope of an individual's or organization's skill or capabilities, even promoting system reform. Alliances can provide safety in numbers; stimulate new creative ideas for service delivery, including co-location of services; and encourage innovation, quality, and access.

Although any of these benefits might seem reason enough to engage in a strategic alliance, a leader must also be cognizant that any strategic alliance will consume resources. Alliances can cause both real and perceived organizational resource diversion from the organization to the partnership—including tangibles such as funding, priorities, services, information, and time spent on consensus building and negotiating multiple organizational hierarchies and intangibles such as identity, flexibility, values, and ideas. Accordingly, leaders must consider the appropriate use of resources in deciding how to participate in strategic relationships.

CONNECTING WITH PARTNERS

The literature on strategic alliances has developed a broad vocabulary where terms such as *communication, coordination, collaboration,* and *integration* have different definitions; however, one commonality shared among the literature is that the processes for developing strategic alliances form a continuum of interaction that moves from lesser to greater intensity based on the outcomes sought (Bailey & Koney, 2000; Mattessich & Monsey, 1992; Winer & Ray, 1994).

Unfortunately, alliances do not always work out the way the partners expect, leading to tensions that drain partners' time and energy, threaten alliance cohesiveness, and decrease the likelihood that organizations will achieve their desired outcomes. These situations happen frequently because of a basic underlying issue: At the beginning of relationship development, leaders are not sufficiently clear with one another, or with themselves, about what they want from, and want to contribute to, a strategic alliance. In fact, many leaders rush into relationships without having seriously considered—much less shared and gained mutual understanding on—issues such as how they perceive the alliance, the resources they are offering, and their core interests at stake.

To address this issue, leaders must approach the task of strategic relationship building analytically and with deliberation, no matter what sort of relationship is contemplated. In other words, the skill of relationship building requires approaching each type of relationship—whether of "communication," "integration," or anything in between—with the same analysis of the partner, the desired outcomes, and the process. This method allows each relationship to develop with maximum honesty and efficiency.

Considering Natural and Unnatural Partners

The human services context provides opportunity for strategic relationship development with both natural and unnatural partners. Natural partners are those who are commonly thought of as necessary to advancing the tasks of one's work and are those upon whom we call to address technical and adaptive challenges, as in the earlier example of the agencies engaged in addressing the issue of providing a coordinated system of services to youth with complex behavioral problems. Unnatural partners can provide new and innovative ideas based on their positions, which may be thought of as "outside" the scope of typical relationships for the work at hand. For example, in addition to the traditional agencies serving the single mother and her son with serious behavioral problems in the previous example, one might include the director of a local motorcycle club because of the youth's special interest in riding a motorcycle and the club director's past experience working with the juvenile justice agency.

Strategic alliances have the potential to positively affect individuals, agencies, organizations, and communities in ways never before seen. Whether these partnerships focus on expanding programs, shaping policy, providing education, or conducting research, both natural and unnatural partners are joining forces and learning from and with each other. This trend will only continue, given the increasingly complex demands of legislative reform, the push toward greater community-based and integrated services, and funder and accountability requirements.

Level and Intensity of Potential Relationships

Different relationships yield different types of benefits and have different associated costs (Bailey & Koney, 2000; Strimling, 2006). Within the categories of strategic relationships for communication, coordination, collaboration, and integration, there are a number of different strategic alliance models from among which leaders can choose. Models can include affiliations, federations, coalitions, consortia, networks, and joint ventures or joint projects. These models vary in the level of organizational integration and formalization, as well as in the amount of investment required for the relationship to be successful. Less formalized relationships include affiliations and federations, whereas more formalized configurations of these strategic relationships include relationships such as networks and joint ventures.

Case Example   The earlier example of agencies addressing the issue of providing a coordinated system of services to youth with complex behavioral problems provides a helpful look at the continuum of level and intensity of alliances that both exist and develop out of a shared response to an adaptive challenge.

The state director for children's mental health was very pleased with the response to the invitation he and the state director for juvenile justice sent. The invitation was framed around discussing common issues for serving youth with multiple behavioral needs and cited the current urgent request from the governor's office (communication). The initial discussion went well, which led to a process of ongoing dialogue among these agencies and an attempt to look for ways to work together to provide services for the 15-year-old youth who was the subject of the governor's office request (coordination). Over time, several core members of the team developed an interest in responding at the system level, given that the young man represented a larger group of youth with complex behavioral needs in the state who were not receiving effective supports for very similar reasons. The agencies engaged together in developing an effective system of coordinated care for all youth such as this young man, with each team member (all from various organizations) looking for resources to support the work that they were most suited to provide (collaboration). Eventually, this work became so intensive that the various team members involved decided to develop a memorandum of understanding to describe how they would conduct the planning, handle the collaboration development, and manage the funding for this new system of care (integration).

Mapping Strategic Alliances

Table 5.1, adapted from a diagram developed by Andrea Strimling (2006), provides the opportunity to look at all of one's relationships in light of the continuum of possibilities. This table can be used to map linkages focused on one task or all of the linkages that make up the spectrum of a leader's strategic alliances.

As a leader assesses whether to enter into a new strategic alliance or to expand a strategic alliance on the basis of new information or opportunity, ensuring that the potential benefits outweigh the costs of the relationship is key. One

Table 5.1.   Alliance opportunity mapping for a specific leadership challenge

	Low intensity *Greater autonomy* *Less interdependence* *Less formalization*		*High intensity* *Less autonomy* *Greater interdependence* *Greater formalization*	
Strategy	**Communication**	**Coordination**	**Collaboration**	**Integration**
Activities	Information sharing; idea sharing (e.g., joint analysis of situation, joint assessment of outcomes)	Synchronizing timing, sharing resources, coordinating contacts, and so forth	Joint design and/or implementation of specific activities; active partnership on an *ad hoc* or sustained basis	Strategic integration of personnel, resources, strategies, operations, and identity, up to the combination of two or more organizations into a single organization
Types of Relationships	Affiliations	Federations Associations Coalitions	Consortia Networks	Joint Ventures or Projects
Current Relationships				
Outcomes				
Your Desired Relationships				

difficulty in this assessment is that often the costs of a relationship are quite apparent at the outset and in the short term, whereas benefits accrue over the long term. Thinking through desired outcomes is a form of cost–benefit analysis. Desired outcomes describe the hoped-for state of affairs. The success of a strategic alliance is judged by its outcomes. Outcomes are any measurable attainments in the furtherance of the alliance's goals and may include things like services or products as well as intangible outcomes such as change in the perception of the organization by the community.

In further considering a new alliance or deepening existing alliances, it is helpful to examine the potential of these relationships on an array of dimensions, such as common interests and domains, historic communication patterns, formal relationships, and mutual perceived value of collaboration. Common domains and interests may form natural opportunities for working together or may set up a competitive context. Existing communication patterns that have been regular and constructive can form the basis for effective joint problem solving, whereas relationships previously fraught with conflict and misunderstanding will require creative conflict-management approaches.

The requirement for a formal relationship may set some boundaries on working with a potential partner, but the quality of that relationship may be driven by other factors; informal opportunities can be as powerful as formalized ones. Examining a broad set of potential allies around a specific leadership challenge provides a template for considering what is needed in enhancing the desired strategic alliances. Worksheet 5.1 (Strategic Alliance Relationship Profile) at the end of this chapter, provides a tool to develop a picture of the alliances you as a leader identify in relation to a specific challenge.

Networks

A leader's networks are the relationships through which a leader gauges the possibility of new forms of strategic alliances. The plethora of networking literature available often tends to distinguish organizational and individual networking and, in the context of the individual, personal and professional networks. More recent literature on social networking provides a helpful context through which leaders can understand the power of *all* of these types of relationships. Social networks are formed around similar interests and provide a leader with the ability to go beyond his or her own personal knowledge and capability to involve others in adaptive challenges (Liebowitz, 2007). Social networks provide a forum through which leaders can get to know potential partners, exchange information, understand others' priorities and operating styles, and form strategic alliances.

Brafman and Beckstrom (2006) described the power of social networks through the comparison between the starfish and the spider. Their analogy goes that cutting off the leg of a spider yields a seven-legged spider, and cutting off its head yields a dead spider. However, cutting off the arm of a starfish results in its growing a new one, and, in fact, the severed arm can grow an entirely new body because starfish, unlike spiders, are decentralized: Every major organ is replicated across each arm.

Spider organizations, the analogy continues, are centralized and have a clear organizational structure. "Leadership" in a spider organization means that someone is "in charge." Starfish organizations, however, mirror the power of social networks and are changing the rules of leadership. Starfish organizations are based on principles such as shared ideology and communication. They may arise rapidly around the simplest ideas or platforms. They exist in social networking web-based tools such as LinkedIn, Blackboard, and Facebook, which allow people to share information, make connections, and learn from one another.

Continuing our earlier example, when looking for support, the state director for children's mental health connected with his old friend, the state director for juvenile justice. In the process of responding to this leadership challenge, it became clear that a systemwide effort required as many resources as possible to be brought to the table, including community awareness raising—both in the children's advocacy community, as well as in communities across the state. Using a web-based social networking site, the state director for children's mental health created a "cause" around the need for a system of care, which was joined by thousands of state citizens. This network enabled the development of even stronger programs as it catalyzed new resources and support. As a leader faces complex adaptive challenges, it is often starfish organizations that provide the response to these challenges.

A leader's social networks are the relationships through which a leader can increase support for adaptive challenges. Frances Hesselbein (2002), former CEO of the Girl Scouts of the USA and chairman and founding president of the Drucker Foundation, emphasized that in making transformational change, leadership is a matter of how to be, not how to do it. The next chapter provides a discussion of how to develop strategic relationships and collaborations. The material emphasizes a set of skills that support a way of being with others that is necessary for the development of strategic partners in adaptive work.

REFERENCES

Bailey, D., & Koney, K.M. (2000). *Strategic alliances among health and human services organizations*. Newbury Park, CA: Sage.

Brafman, O., & Beckstrom, R. (2006). *The starfish and the spider: The unstoppable power of leaderless organizations*. New York: Portfolio.

Heifetz, R.A., & Linsky, M. (2002). *Leadership on the line: Staying alive through the dangers of leading*. Cambridge, MA: Harvard Business School Press.

Hesselbein, F. (2002). *Hesselbein on leadership*. San Francisco: Jossey-Bass.

Kagen, E.B., & Hepburn, K.S. (Eds.). (2006). *Leadership in systems of care: An unpublished training curriculum*. Washington, DC: Georgetown University Center for Child and

Human Development, National Technical Assistance Center for Children's Mental Health. Washington, DC.

Liebowitz, J. (2007). *Social networking: The essence of innovation.* Lanham, MD: Scarecrow Press.

Lipman-Blumen, J. (1996). *The connective edge: Leading in an interdependent world.* San Francisco: Jossey-Bass.

Mattessich, P.W., & Monsey, B.R. (1992). *Collaboration: What makes it work: A review of research and literature on factors influencing successful collaboration.* St. Paul, MN: Amherst H. Wilder Foundation.

Plsek, P.E., & Wilson, T. (2001). Complexity, leadership, and management in healthcare organizations. *British Medical Journal, 323*(7315), 746–749.

Strimling, A. (2006). Stepping out of the tracks: Cooperation between official diplomats and private facilitators. *International Negotiation, 11,* 91–127.

Wheatley, M.J. (1992). *Leadership and the new science: Learning about organization from an orderly universe.* San Francisco: Berrett-Koehler.

Winer, M., & Ray, K. (1994). *Collaboration handbook: Creating, sustaining and enjoying the journey.* St. Paul, MN: Amherst H. Wilder Foundation.

Worksheet 5.1

Strategic Alliance Relationship Profile

The questions below are designed to profile your relationship with each of your potential allies or collaborators.

	Ally 1	Ally 2	Ally 3	Ally 4	Ally 5	Ally 6

1. Domain similarity

   In relation to your potential ally, to what extent do you

   a. Do the same kind of work (provide the same services)? — 1a
   b. Serve the same client population? — 1b
   c. Serve the same geographic area? — 1c

To no extent	Little extent	Some extent	Considerable extent	Very great extent
1	2	3	4	5

2. Task specialization

   In relation to your potential ally, to what extent do you

   a. Have similar operating goals? — 2a
   b. Have personnel with similar training? — 2b
   c. Use the same information, equipment, or technology? — 2c

To no extent	Little extent	Some extent	Considerable extent	Very great extent
1	2	3	4	5

(continued)

From Kagen, E.B., & Hepburn, K.S. (Eds.). (2006). *Leadership in systems of care: An unpublished training curriculum.* Washington, DC: Georgetown University Center for Child and Human Development, National Technical Assistance Center for Children's Mental Health; adapted by permission.

In *The Leadership Equation: Strategies for Individuals Who Are Champions for Children, Youth, and Families* edited by Gary M. Blau & Phyllis R. Magrab (2010; Paul H. Brookes Publishing Co., Inc.)

Worksheet 5.1 *(continued)*

		Ally 1	Ally 2	Ally 3	Ally 4	Ally 5	Ally 6
3.	**Interdependence**						
3a	a. For your ally to accomplish his/her goals and responsibilities, how much does your ally need services, resources or support from you?	——	——	——	——	——	——
	Not at all 1 Very little 2 Some 3 Quite a bit 4 Very much 5						
3b	b. For you to accomplish your goals and responsibilities, how much do you need services, resources, or support from your potential ally? (use scale above)	——	——	——	——	——	——
4.	**Leadership and central control**						
4a	a. To what extent do you look to your ally for leadership on definition of objectives, plans, or methods for your work?	——	——	——	——	——	——
4b	b. Is there an agency, committee, council, or consortium that governs relations between you?	——	——	——	——	——	——
	No committee or agency 0 Coordinating agency 1 Two-organization committee 2 Multi-organization committee 3						

(continued)

From Kagen, E.B., & Hepburn, K.S. (Eds.). (2006). *Leadership in systems of care: An unpublished training curriculum.* Washington, DC: Georgetown University Center for Child and Human Development, National Technical Assistance Center for Children's Mental Health; adapted by permission.

In *The Leadership Equation: Strategies for Individuals Who Are Champions for Children, Youth, and Families* edited by Gary M. Blau & Phyllis R. Magrab (2010; Paul H. Brookes Publishing Co., Inc.)

Worksheet 5.1 *(continued)*

5. Formalization and standardization of relations
   a. To what extent have the terms of your relationship between you and your potential ally

	Ally 1	Ally 2	Ally 3	Ally 4	Ally 5	Ally 6
1. Been explicitly discussed and detailed? — 5a1	___	___	___	___	___	___
2. Been written in contracts or affiliation agreements? — 5a2	___	___	___	___	___	___
3. Been mandated by law or regulation? — 5a3	___	___	___	___	___	___

To no extent	Little extent	Some extent	Considerable extent	Very great extent
1	2	3	4	5

   b. To what extent are interactions between you and your potential ally governed by standard operating procedures (e.g. rules, policies, guidelines, forms, formal communication channels)? (use scale above) — 5b

	Ally 1	Ally 2	Ally 3	Ally 4	Ally 5	Ally 6
5b	___	___	___	___	___	___

(continued)

From Kagen, E.B., & Hepburn, K.S. (Eds.). (2006). *Leadership in systems of care: An unpublished training curriculum.* Washington, DC: Georgetown University Center for Child and Human Development, National Technical Assistance Center for Children's Mental Health; adapted by permission.

In *The Leadership Equation: Strategies for Individuals Who Are Champions for Children, Youth, and Families* edited by Gary M. Blau & Phyllis R. Magrab (2010; Paul H. Brookes Publishing Co., Inc.)

Worksheet 5.1 *(continued)*

	Ally 1	Ally 2	Ally 3	Ally 4	Ally 5	Ally 6

6. Communication

a. During the past four months how frequently have you been in contact with your potential ally

		Ally 1	Ally 2	Ally 3	Ally 4	Ally 5	Ally 6
1. Through written letters, memos, or reports?	6a1	—	—	—	—	—	—
2. Through personal conversations?	6a2	—	—	—	—	—	—
3. Through committee meetings?	6a3	—	—	—	—	—	—

Not once	1–2 times	Monthly	Twice monthly	Weekly	Several times a week
0	1	2	3	4	5

b. In general, what percent of contacts were initiated

		Ally 1	Ally 2	Ally 3	Ally 4	Ally 5	Ally 6
1. By you?	6b1	—	—	—	—	—	—
2. By your ally?	6b2	—	—	—	—	—	—
3. By others?	6b3	—	—	—	—	—	—

(continued)

From Kagen, E.B., & Hepburn, K.S. (Eds.). (2006). *Leadership in systems of care: An unpublished training curriculum.* Washington, DC: Georgetown University Center for Child and Human Development, National Technical Assistance Center for Children's Mental Health; adapted by permission.

In *The Leadership Equation: Strategies for Individuals Who Are Champions for Children, Youth, and Families* edited by Gary M. Blau & Phyllis R. Magrab (2010; Paul H. Brookes Publishing Co., Inc.)

Worksheet 5.1 *(continued)*

	Ally 1	Ally 2	Ally 3	Ally 4	Ally 5	Ally 6
7. Competition To what extent do you compete with your ally for						
a. Clients?	7a ___	___	___	___	___	___
b. Funding?	7b ___	___	___	___	___	___
c. Staff?	7c ___	___	___	___	___	___
d. Leadership on policy direction or standard setting?	7d ___	___	___	___	___	___

To no extent	Little extent	Some extent	Considerable extent	Very great extent
1	2	3	4	5

	Ally 1	Ally 2	Ally 3	Ally 4	Ally 5	Ally 6
8. Awareness						
a. How many years have you been involved in some fashion with your potential ally?	8a ___	___	___	___	___	___
b. How well informed are you about the specific goals and services of your ally?	8b ___	___	___	___	___	___

Not at all	Little informed	Somewhat informed	Quite informed	Very well informed
1	2	3	4	5

(continued)

From Kagen, E.B., & Hepburn, K.S. (Eds.). (2006). *Leadership in systems of care: An unpublished training curriculum.* Washington, DC: Georgetown University Center for Child and Human Development, National Technical Assistance Center for Children's Mental Health; adapted by permission.

In *The Leadership Equation: Strategies for Individuals Who Are Champions for Children, Youth, and Families* edited by Gary M. Blau & Phyllis R. Magrab (2010; Paul H. Brookes Publishing Co., Inc.)

Worksheet 5.1 *(continued)*

	Ally 1	Ally 2	Ally 3	Ally 4	Ally 5	Ally 6
9. Consensus How do you agree or disagree with your potential ally on a. The way work is organized and performed in the service system? Disagree very much 1 Agree a little 2 Agree somewhat 3 Agree quite a bit 4 Agree very much 5	9a ___ 9b ___	___ ___	___ ___	___ ___	___ ___	___ ___
10. Quality interaction a. Overall, how much difficulty do you experience in getting ideas across clearly in communications to your potential ally? No contact 0 None 1 Little 2 Some 3 Quite a bit 4 Very much 5	10a ___	___	___	___	___	___
b. When you want to communicate with your potential ally how much difficulty do you have in getting in touch with him or her? (use scale above)	10b ___	___	___	___	___	___
c. To what extent has your potential ally hindered your performing during the past several months? To no extent 1 Little extent 2 Some extent 3 Considerable extent 4 Great extent 5	10c ___	___	___	___	___	___

(continued)

From Kagen, E.B., & Hepburn, K.S. (Eds.). (2006). *Leadership in systems of care: An unpublished training curriculum*. Washington, DC: Georgetown University Center for Child and Human Development, National Technical Assistance Center for Children's Mental Health; adapted by permission.

In *The Leadership Equation: Strategies for Individuals Who Are Champions for Children, Youth, and Families* edited by Gary M. Blau & Phyllis R. Magrab (2010; Paul H. Brookes Publishing Co., Inc.)

Worksheet 5.1 (continued)

	Ally 1	Ally 2	Ally 3	Ally 4	Ally 5	Ally 6

11. Mutual influence and accommodation

a. How much influence or say over the internal policies and operations of your work does your ally have?   11a   ___ ___ ___ ___ ___ ___

None	Little	Some	Quite a bit	Very much
1	2	3	4	5

b. How much influence or say over the internal policies and operations of your unit does your potential ally have? (use scale above)   11b   ___ ___ ___ ___ ___ ___

c. During the past few months how often were there disagreements or disputes between your unit and your potential ally?   11c   ___ ___ ___ ___ ___ ___

Not once	1 or 2 times	About monthly	Twice monthly	About weekly	Several times each week
0	1	2	3	4	5

d. How well are any differences worked out?   11d   ___ ___ ___ ___ ___ ___

Very poorly	Poorly	Adequately	Well	Very well
1	2	3	4	5

(continued)

From Kagen, E.B., & Hepburn, K.S. (Eds.). (2006). *Leadership in systems of care: An unpublished training curriculum.* Washington, DC: Georgetown University Center for Child and Human Development, National Technical Assistance Center for Children's Mental Health; adapted by permission.

In *The Leadership Equation: Strategies for Individuals Who Are Champions for Children, Youth, and Families* edited by Gary M. Blau & Phyllis R. Magrab (2010; Paul H. Brookes Publishing Co., Inc.)

Worksheet 5.1 *(continued)*

	Ally 1	Ally 2	Ally 3	Ally 4	Ally 5	Ally 6
12. Perceived value of relationships						
a. To what extent has your potential ally carried out his/her responsibilities and commitments in relation to you during the past several months? 12a	——	——	——	——	——	——
b. To what extent is the time and effort spent in developing and maintaining the relationship with your potential ally worthwhile? 12b	——	——	——	——	——	——
c. Overall, to what extent are you satisfied with the relationship between you? 12c	——	——	——	——	——	——

To no extent	Little extent	Some extent	Considerable extent	Very great extent
1	2	3	4	5

(continued)

From Kagen, E.B., & Hepburn, K.S. (Eds.). (2006). *Leadership in systems of care: An unpublished training curriculum.* Washington, DC: Georgetown University Center for Child and Human Development, National Technical Assistance Center for Children's Mental Health; adapted by permission.

In *The Leadership Equation: Strategies for Individuals Who Are Champions for Children, Youth, and Families* edited by Gary M. Blau & Phyllis R. Magrab (2010; Paul H. Brookes Publishing Co., Inc.)

6

Building Common Ground

Suganya Sockalingam and Elizabeth Z. Waetzig

uch work in children's mental health takes place in dynamic, functional systems. These systems are made up of ever-changing entities that are interrelated and interdependent. In other words, the people and pieces of the system are connected and function in an ongoing relationship to each other. For that reason, establishing common ground is critical to synchronizing work and moving the system forward within an ever-changing environment.

"Getting on the same page," "playing on the same team," collaboration, and many other descriptors of working together are discussed as the ideal way to work in a system. Collaboration, in fact, is one of the core principles of a system of care. And yet, leaders and groups struggle to build and sustain a collaborative culture within and among organizations. It does not seem innate or natural to do what it takes to work truly together. It is a value shift for most people to listen to, consider, and value the varied perspectives and ideas of all members of a group. It is also a shift to allow one's ideas, and even one's identity, to become a part of the whole. Sometimes contributions become unrecognizable and thus cannot be attributed to any single individual.

Building common ground requires a rethinking of values, process, and the environment around how work is done by a group. The role of the leader is critical in this rethinking. The leader has to be prepared to model the behavior required and to maintain focus on building and sustaining common ground, especially when it becomes difficult to do so. Moreover, because building and maintaining common ground is a journey that, although it can become easier, does not end, the leader must be steadfast in his or her attention to where the group is standing and where they need to be.

This chapter explores what it takes for a leader to build common ground. First, it offers several reasons why building common ground is challenging, and then it explores the justification for common ground—why it is worth the effort. A definition and strategies for building common ground are outlined, and the leader's role in motivating, managing, and measuring the development of common ground and the effort required to sustain it are offered.

SETTING THE STAGE FOR BUILDING COMMON GROUND

Prior to understanding the strategies and tools leaders use for building common ground, it is important to know what common ground is and some of the challenges leaders have faced in building it as well as why it is important. An understanding of the definition, challenges, and benefits will enable leaders to apply the strategies detailed in the subsequent section for their purpose and in the specific group within which they work.

DEFINING COMMON GROUND

Before a leader can build common ground, that leader must know how to define it. What is common ground? What does it feel like to be standing on common ground with a group of people? How did you get there? How do you stay there while the environment changes? There are some things all of you see. Some of them you see differently because you have different vantage points. Some things only a fraction of the group sees.

Interview #1. On Building Common Ground

The following interview is with Scott G. Reynolds, Nevada Children's Behavioral Health Consortium member and assistant superintendent of student support services for the Washoe County School District.

What does it feel like to be standing on common ground with a group of people?

It is comforting to know that you are not addressing any issue alone, that several people and agencies come together to develop a system of care. You are able to stand on high ground and from that perch to be able to see and move in a different way, having seen more. It becomes clear to those coming together that there are many more resources when we come together than when we work alone. We know when we are duplicating services and making it harder and more complicated for our clients to receive our services.

Did you get there? How did you get there?

We got parts of it by coming together as mutual stakeholders with the end in mind. When we came together and discussed the vision, then it was easy to see the strategies, easier than when we were alone. With the end-in-mind vision, we were able to work backwards.

How do we get there? It is a process of recommitting to that outcome. Of attending all the meetings and being committed to the path we've taken. We looked at the negotiables and the nonnegotiables. In common ground, we had to commit to the nonnegotiables. We identified nonnegotiables in terms of outcomes, and how we got there was open-handed. We looked at it from various points of views and allowed flexibility for each agency to come to that place to account for its differences. At the end of the day we found we had more similarities—that we shared common strategies as well. It is by paring down of both (the negotiables and nonnegotiables) that we could get action planning established.

How do you continue to stay there while the environment changes?

Systems change is person dependent. When we engage in working with different stakeholders, we have to cultivate a culture that is not person centered—matching, pacing, and leading the systems into new practice. Matching by first listening to each other on what is reality. Pacing, then, is the beginning of the conversation of what are some potential lists of strategies to explore. We brainstorm all the possibilities; we "get out of the box" with all possible options. Finally, we lead—that is, we decide what we are going to do and stay the course. The lead process is not person dependent—here there is co-leadership capacity that sustains change and can bring the work to scale.

There are some things that all of you see. Some of them you see differently because you have different vantage points. Then there are some things that only a fraction of the group sees. How do you handle a situation such as that?

If everyone understands that each system is on a journey of evolution—no right no wrong, that each agency has unique challenges, and each has respect for the change process—then we can all move forward together. Even if you're in front of boat, you are not getting there sooner than those at the back. This work requires patience and mutual respect, and comfort comes from that. It is having natural forces—harnessing those forces in a way that can maximize the change process sooner rather than later.

Building common ground is often thought of as a tool or strategy that groups use to get a decision made or problem solved. Although it can provide a context for doing this, common ground is much more: It is a way of being. The values tha t are required for building and sustaining common ground are deeply rooted in the norms of leaders and translated into their work with others. Common ground is a complex combination of mind-set, environment, and strategies that are based on a set of organizational values from which the culture of a group or organization is created and maintained. The framework also includes institutional processes that lead to norms of working that promote building and sustaining common ground. A definition proposed by Clark and Brennan (1991) is that common ground is a concept that refers to the "mutual knowledge, mutual beliefs, and mutual assumptions" that are essential for communication.

Reaching a mutuality of the knowledge, beliefs, and assumptions is the work of building common ground.

There is no single definition that truly captures the complex nature of "common ground." The term transcends disciplines and is found in music and art as well as the sciences—social, environmental, and engineering sciences, to state a few. Common ground allows for an exchange of ideas to determine differences and similarities in perspectives. It supports the building of consensus on a foundation of shared values and guiding principles. What serves to define and support common ground depends on the arena in which it is being articulated and addressed. Redman and colleagues described a group of libraries that see the Internet as their common ground because it serves as a "collaborative means of organizing and enhancing access to Internet resources" (Redman et al., 1997, p. 325) for their community—the world.

The "common ground movement" has even come to an arena (reproductive health) where once it would have been unimaginable to assume an acceptance of differences and a desire to understand and integrate these differences. Yet, this is precisely what has happened. How did this happen? First, many "pro-choicers" and "pro-lifers" (individuals on both sides of the debate) alike can validly claim as "foremothers" (as in forefathers), pioneering feminists who had an awareness of both women's and already-born children's "body" rights. Second, much of the movement toward a centrist attitude in this debate is the shared desire to improve women's lives. Today, the two proponents have found common points of view through dialogue, within the common ground movement. This has led to potential legislation such as preventing unintended pregnancies, reducing the need for abortion, and supporting parents—all signifying common ground goals (Paris, 2009).

Today's complex economic, social, and environmental issues require more than a "business as usual" approach. We need to create a new vision and new processes and access new capacities to handle these challenges successfully. Senge, Smith, Krushwitz, Laur, and Schley (2008) mapped a vision for how a group can cross boundaries and go from problem solving to creating new possibilities. It is about creating opportunities to understand and integrate different perspectives—weaving whole cloth out of individual threads of different hues. It is the foundation of common ground on which all else can be built.

For the purpose of this discussion, common ground will be defined as *that space in which the collective worldviews and experiences of members within the group serve as a foundation for shared learning and understanding in pursuit of a shared view of the world.*

Challenges to Building Common Ground

Why is it hard to build and to sustain common ground? According to Marvin Weisbord (1992), human beings have created a world of relentless change. It is hard to find ways to manage how work is done that match the complexity of the work itself. As people struggle with that mismatch, we insist upon absolute quality, growth, meaning, and dignity.

Many reasons for the difficulty with collaboration come from biology and culture. For human beings, a primary motivation underlying all behavior is to survive. In the very early years, humans were rewarded for collecting and hoarding resources with no reward for sharing or working together. As human beings organized into communities and then nations, there was much to gain by making enemies out of the "other." Leaders used a sense of fear with regard to other groups to gain power and control resources leading to survival of their group. Even as human culture has evolved, we continue to organize social systems in ways that promote noncollaborative behaviors.

To be sure, there are many societies around the world that have integrated collaborative values and behaviors into their culture, as is the case in many parts of rural United States where people are dependent on each other rather than institutions and governments. Yet, the prevailing trends in the United States are economic and social structures based on the ideal of individual effort leading to individual recognition. Taking the lead, being the "top dog," are values that work well with the incentives and rewards provided by business and institutions, particularly in Western cultures. These incentives and rewards reinforce aggressive and individually based values and behaviors.

It is tempting to think that human services systems are different. One might assume they are working to benefit others and therefore hold values and behave in ways that benefit teamwork and collaboration. But behaviors, skills, and processes to support collaboration are often not taught in tandem with the academic aspects of social work and psychology. In addition, government agencies that create policies and human services systems are not funded or mandated to collaborate. So without a foundation of awareness, knowledge, and the requisite skill and experience in collaboration and building common ground, it is very difficult for human service professionals to overcome biological and cultural tendencies in the context of disjointed government infrastructure. Within this fragmented context, collaborative relationships are difficult due to varying perspectives and philosophies about the nature of the work and the sought-after outcomes. Collaborative groups end up mistrusting each other and blocking each other's progress. A report to Congress on substance abuse and child protection (U.S. Department of Health and Human Services, 1999) concluded that the following were some of the factors that create mistrust: language differences (e.g., defining the term *client*), expected outcomes, expectations of timelines on deliverables, and response to setbacks.

Building a system of care for children's mental health is very complex. Children's mental health care has made considerable progress since the early days of orphanages and institutions. However, the system is still a collection of government systems such as mental health, education, child welfare, juvenile justice, and primary care as well as community and advocacy organizations, families, and youth. These entities maintain separate mandates, protocols, and funding streams that create service gaps, duplication, inefficiencies, and, of course, competition for resources.

The challenges of finding common ground for those entities that try to collaborate as systems of care often start at the very beginning. These agencies can come together to write a grant proposal, but when the grant comes through, roles may have changed, responsibilities may have shifted, and even the vision may have evolved. In addition, the degrees of accountability and ownership among partners may have shifted. Some groups immediately become stuck in a conflict from which they cannot emerge. Even agencies that come together on smaller initiatives because of similar visions and a common mission may not necessarily share the same philosophy of practice, language, values, and guiding principles. It may be necessary to take stock of what is currently happening within the collaborative that would support common ground and determine what potential challenges need to be addressed. See Worksheet 6.1 (Take Stock: An Assessment of the Current Status of Common Ground) at the end of this chapter.

Benefits to Building Common Ground

Common ground can facilitate the exchange of ideas and best practices of people working on a daily basis in the areas of mental health promotion, disease prevention, and case management. Through the process of creating common ground, we share our experiences, best practices, and effective approaches to address problems, which lead to the development of protocols and processes common to our collective needs. Finding common ground will help agencies share information and scarce resources. Weisbord (1992) wrote of a world moving from experts solving problems for people, toward everybody, including the experts, improving whole systems. He believes this is critical for long-term dignity, meaning, and community.

A problem-resolution process in which individuals with different perspectives gainfully explore their differences and search for solutions can occur when these individuals are brought together in constructive ways and with the appropriate information (Gray, 1989). Together they can not only create authentic visions and strategies for addressing their joint problems but also in many cases overcome their limited perspectives of what is possible. David Mathews (1994) wrote about a growing number of community organizations across the country that are focused more on building a public agenda and relationships than in advancing a specific cause. Finding mutuality and interdependency (as with any collaborative) will enable them to establish a give-and-take and will allow them to get to the solutions collectively. They depend on each other to produce mutually beneficial solutions.

What Building Common Ground Does for Systems of Care

If the agencies and organizations that make up a system of care commit to building common ground, the result is aligned perspectives. They all know 1) what they are doing, 2) why they are doing it, 3) for whom they are doing it, and 4) how they will accomplish their goals. And when they build that common ground together, they will incorporate competing and diverse perspectives, work through seemingly irreconcilable differences, and find areas of unity. They can create a shared vision for moving forward. Most important, if they work to build common ground from the beginning of their collaborative effort, they will instill organizational norms that allow their differences to lead to a richer outcome. In this environment, all are engaged and the processes instituted allow for, and promote, the building and sustaining of common ground.

Common ground is built when every diverse voice has value and is embraced, and through the process of building common ground, the purpose, processes, functions, and messages become owned and promoted by all. For all to feel a sense of ownership in the common ground, all must shift from focusing on their own part to focusing on the whole. There is shift away from individual agency ownership to ownership by the collaborative. It requires reflection on our own values, calls for us to change the norms of our systems, and yet acknowledges that moving forward should carry no guilt or shame for the way we have handled it in the past.

A Foundation

Between understanding the setting or context and applying the strategies, groups must identify and define the values that must guide their work together. Values help to keep leaders and their groups on track as they discuss difficult issues such as change and conflict and sensitive substantive issues that can arise.

A Process Grounded in Values

The process for building common ground must be built upon a foundation of values. (See also Chapter 2.) Leaders are most effective when their attitudes, behaviors, and values are evident in their leadership. Otherwise, expediency can get in the way of creating a culture of collaboration. If it is a credible process (it has both integrity and a fair chance of producing results) and an open process (the dialogue is both honest and receptive to different points of view), then people are more likely to invest the energy required to build common ground.

Four values that serve as the foundation for the *process* of building common ground are diversity, inclusiveness, equality, and community.

Diversity Each individual brings to the group unique knowledge, talents, ideas, and experiences. Common ground is promoted when we express our value of diversity by actively seeking diverse voices. Doing so sometimes creates discord in the short term but leads to an outcome that is richer for reflecting a wide range of individual experiences.

Inclusiveness   To achieve common ground, it is not only important to listen to diverse voices but to invite them to participate. All voices are invited and protected.

Equality   Everyone participating is considered an equal in that setting. Although individuals may come to the table with varied authority and stature, in the process of building common ground, their voices all have equal weight.

Community[1]   The community of collaborators is the source of the effort and is acknowledged for the outcomes achieved. Rather than individual effort and its acknowledgment as an incentive to participate, the success of the initiative is based on the engagement of the community and is experienced by all.

There are other related values that enhance the process of building common ground. One such value is love—love for your fellow human. President Obama stressed this in a speech to the joint session of Congress:

I know that we have not agreed on every issue thus far, and there are surely times in the future when we will part ways. But I also know that every American who is sitting here tonight loves this country and wants it to succeed. That must be the starting point for every debate we have in the coming months, and where we return after those debates are done. That is the foundation on which the American people expect us to build common ground [*emphasis added*].
—President Barack Obama
Address to joint session of Congress
Tuesday, February 24, 2009

Shared values guide peoples' decisions, priorities, behaviors, and organizational processes. In a sense, these processes institute the ways in which we as individuals and organizations operationalize our values. As a group goes through the process of defining its values of common ground, it begins to build a culture that supports collaboration, which in turns leads to building common ground. Upon the foundation of values, a leader can employ the strategies to motivate a group to build common ground, manage the building process, and measure progress.

STRATEGIES FOR BUILDING COMMON GROUND

The process of building common ground in collaborative work is a deliberate choice. It does not happen by default. If a group chooses to build common ground, it must commit to it as an ongoing process. For a group to commit (and recommit) to the continuous process of building common ground, the leader must be ready to frame, implement, and work to sustain the process. There are

---

[1]*Community* has a specific meaning among the disciplines in which we work—and it is also used in the broader context. In addressing the values of the process for building common ground, the value of community refers to the community of the collaborative group.

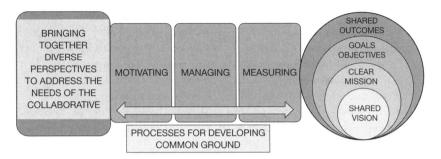

Figure 6.1. A framework for building common ground.

three primary components of the overall process, each with its own set of actions and required skills. First, a leader must motivate a group to build common ground. Second, the leader manages the process of both building and sustaining common ground. Third, leaders must measure aspects of common ground to determine if the group is making progress and moving effectively in a predetermined direction. Measuring should provide feedback for the processes of motivating and managing (see Figure 6.1). Leaders guiding these continuous processes need to juggle multiple skills and wear multiple hats within the collaborative.

Setting the Stage for Common Ground: Motivating the Group

At various points along the process, leaders must convey the importance of building common ground. Leaders must support the importance of taking time to participate and fully engage with a group of diverse stakeholders, and they must do so themselves. Leaders must model listening and learning as individuals within the collaborative. They must articulate personal values and visions and develop shared values and a shared vision. As the collaborative begins to build a mission and strategic direction from this shared vision, leaders need to be able to help the group negotiate and find common interests on which to base their mission and strategic directions.

Leaders can motivate a group to invest in building common ground by creating an environment of safety and trust and by ensuring that effective communication occurs. In addition, leaders ensure a collaborative process for decision making through consensus and by helping the group define a shared vision as well as utilizing collaborative process skills to help shape the vision.

Creating an Environment of Safety

An initial, critical piece in the process of building common ground is creating an environment that is inclusive, participatory, and safe. The leader must nurture an environment that supports building and rebuilding and sustains common ground. If the environment is inclusive and engaging, people from different backgrounds can integrate diverse perspectives, values, and beliefs through authentic communication. Also, there is a widespread expectation that there is an allocation of time, people, and process to reach an outcome that feels beneficial to the community as a whole. Lencioni (2002) emphasized the need to spend considerable time in face-to-face meetings and working sessions, as well as to identify individual strengths and weaknesses in developing the collaborative, to overcome the discomfort of being vulnerable as people learn about each other.

A safe environment is one in which people feel their voices are desired and valued. It is in this type of environment that members of a group will take risks and participate boldly. Each individual is protected against judgment and therefore will feel comfortable while honestly expressing diverse views. Although this does not mean there will be no disagreements, it does mean that disagreement will lead to a richer and more honest dialogue, thereby yielding better outcomes.

It is the responsibility of the leader to create an environment in which collaboration can occur. The environment must allow for being vulnerable and for risk-taking behavior. Leaders must not only endure being at risk but they must model risk-taking behavior. This requires leaders to be self-aware and understand their own strengths and weaknesses and to use them to build trust that leads to building common ground.

Ciancutti and Steding (2001) explored multiple factors that allow trust to develop: closure, commitment, communication, speedy resolution, respect, and responsibility.

- In *closure,* it is critical to convey the importance of relationship (connection and engagement) as well as outcomes when bringing processes of building common ground to completion. People need to acknowledge the approach and the achievement of a mutually determined destination. Through appropriate protocols and processes, the experience of closure can be created.

- In *commitment,* it is important to treat all commitments as promises with obligations and to model commitment through sharing personal values and vision while encouraging others to do the same.

- *Communication* involves receiving all information before responding and a separation of receiving from judging. It also requires developing the art of listening by including content, mood, and emotional subtext.

- In *speedy resolution,* leaders need to act on values and principles rather than reacting to issues in order to create an environment in which people feel free to dissent. It is important to model unity and agreement from the top down and bottom up using closure, commitment, and vision.

- The importance of *respect*—holding diverse opinions and values in high regard, while allowing people to feel heard by acting on the new understanding—is paramount. It is equally important to encourage and reward people for disagreeing and for innovative thinking, while tolerating failure and mistakes.

- In *responsibility,* there is a need for leaders to accept the requirement to create agreements to share responsibility, rewards, burdens, passion, and challenge, as well as to convey empathy, consistency, and integrity intentionally (see Table 6.1).

Communication

Communication is a fundamental human activity, yet one of the hardest to achieve continuously and productively. Information that is sent is coded by the different values, beliefs, and cultural worldviews of a sender and simultaneously decoded through different experiences of a receiver. From the moment contact is established, mutual and simultaneous perceptions occur.

It is not just who we are but also what we are (e.g., co-worker, friend, relative, supervisor) that informs how information gets communicated. Our role influences our perceptions and the perceptions of ourselves. These cultural identities, with their infinite variables and implicit rules, influence our behavior and

Table 6.1. Habits for building trust

Habits that strengthen trust	Habits that weaken trust
• Being responsible by being trustworthy, committed, and self-determined	• Nonclosure and false commitments
• Treating commitment as a promise with obligations	• Not shaping commitment through shared values and vision and compelling the larger environment to do the same
• Creating agreement to share responsibility, rewards, burdens, passion, and challenges	• Not modeling commitment by not taking the first risk, not sharing the risk, and by being an army of one
• Holding diverse opinions and values in high regard	• Failing to build authentic teams that model unity and agreement from the top down and bottom up using closure, commitment, and vision
• Receiving all information before responding	
• Separating receiving information from judging information	• Reacting to issues instead of acting on values and principles
• Developing the art of listening by including content, mood, and emotional subtext	• Believing that the outcome of an issue is more important than the connection between two parties
• Providing all participants with written agreements: who, what, when, how	• Allowing people to feel unheard by failing to act on new understanding

From Kagen, E.B., & Hepburn, K.S. (2006). Framing the work. In *Framing the leadership in systems of care: A training curriculum.* Washington DC: Georgetown University Center for Child and Human Development, National Technical Assistance Center for Children's Mental Health; reprinted by permission.

responses, ensuring that language and communication are bound by context. Identities add to the complexity of accurately decoding communication.

Language   An often overlooked and critical part of communication is a consideration of the language of the work. Particularly in a group made up of members from diverse cultural origins, common terms and definitions cannot be assumed. The term *mental health* is an example of this. The mental health field has struggled for some time with the use of the term and is still trying to define it. What does it mean? Should it be used? If so, how? As a group struggles with this issue, they not only reach consensus about the term to use and its definition, but along the way they also learn about each individual's perspective, experience, and values. This new understanding of each other creates compassion and a belief in good intent. The dialogue, if authentic and grounded in the values above, is instrumental in building a culture that supports common ground (see Worksheet 6.2 [Common Ground on Language] at the end of this chapter).

Meaningful Communication   For communication to truly serve as an instrument for building common ground, it has to be meaningful. Members within the collaborative need to feel that they can be heard and, more important, they need to hear. Factors that support and create opportunities for meaningful communication (Myers & Lambert, 1994) include the following:

- A comfortable and "safe enough" environment for communication[2]—Trust and safety are key, and the work of the leader is to ensure an environment that holds these as nonnegotiable.

- A sense of equal power within members of the collaborative—unequal power impedes true communication

- Acknowledgement of both cultural differences and similarities and how these influence individual worldviews and perceptions of reality

- Attention paid to the different patterns in nonverbal communication, such as eye contact, spatial difference, touching, tone of voice, and facial expressions

- Time allowed for the narratives—time to "tell our stories" in our own way

- A focus on "understanding" as the goal of communication—to listen intently and completely, to ask questions for clarification, to seek beyond the words and understand the perspectives that drive communication

Listening to Understand   A very effective way to model authentic communication and to break down existing communication barriers is to listen first

---

[2]There is recognition in leadership work that no matter how much a leader works to establish a safe environment, the concept of safety remains the personal experience of each individual. The sense of safety is relative, and every individual will need to determine what is safe and unsafe and how much he or she is willing to risk to support change.

with the intent to gain a thorough understanding of the speaker's message, both implicit and explicit. Listening with the goal of understanding means looking at an issue from the others' perspective and attempting to understand their expressed ideas and attitudes. The idea is for the listener to put him- or herself in the speaker's place and to recreate the experience as the speaker is speaking. To make sure that he or she is recreating the experience accurately, the listener must check his or her understanding, help the speaker elaborate and clarify, and seek feedback from the speaker along the way.

Effective listening also indicates to the speaker that you are listening. If the speaker feels that he or she is being heard, the speaker is less likely to remain emotionally charged and may even be able to explore and describe more fully his or her side of the situation. In addition, by truly trying to understand another person's perspective and message, an example is set, an example others are likely to follow.

Waetzig and Magrab (1997) outlined multiple steps critical to listening to understand: restating, reframing, asking open-ended questions, reflecting, summarizing (see Table 6.2). Worksheet 6.3 (Listening to Understand) at the end of this chapter provides opportunities to explore how to work through the steps on listening to understand.

Decision-Making Through Consensus When individuals come together as a group to make decisions, they come to their decisions in all sorts of ways. In some groups, majority wins. Some groups require a super majority or even unanimity. There is no right way. It depends on the values, culture, and norms of a particular group. However, as in most other aspects of building a collaborative process, ironically, there is no consensus on the term *consensus*. For purposes of this discussion, the definition that will be used is "agreement that is supported by all, or most all, of the affected and/or involved members who seek common understanding about a given situation and/or mutually beneficial responses to that situation" (Hanson, 2005, p. 4).

In collaboration, group members must believe the processes and protocols are fair and that they will likely lead to a win/win solution. When consensus is achieved, the collaborating group is assured that the common ground for which it is striving is strengthened and sustained. According to Hanson (2005), the presupposition at the heart of collaborative discourse is that all points of view are valid. This requires participants to respect everyone's truth as equally valid. By doing so, the group is assured that people are achieving common ground and therefore will be predisposed to move forward with the work of the collaborative.

Clear definitions and processes are fundamental ingredients in building consensus. All process must be designed to be clearly visible to the group. At times, the collaborative may choose to make decisions on the basis of majority vote or to allow even a smaller group of members who serve as a core or executive team to make decisions for the group. The decision-making protocols must be defined and normalized before the consensus and decision making occur (see Worksheet 6.4 [Consensus Protocols] at the end of this chapter).

Table 6.2. Strategies for listening to understand

Restating

You restate when you repeat the factual content of the speaker's message. You want to ensure that you understand the facts accurately and invite him or her to clarify his or her message. You do not judge or agree or disagree with the facts; you merely acknowledge that they are the facts of the speaker's message.

Some phrases that indicate you are restating:

Let me see if I understand what you are saying.

So, you are saying that . . .

Is that what you are saying?

Reflecting

You reflect when you state the emotional content of the speaker's message back to the speaker. In addition to understanding the facts, you must understand and acknowledge that you are aware of the speaker's emotions. Again, reflecting does not mean that you agree or disagree with the emotions the speaker feels. You are acknowledging that they exist and that they play a part in the conflict.

Questions on reflecting:

When you think about it, how do you feel?

What else do you feel?

What memories arise for you?

Open-Ended Questions

These questions do not contain or suggest the answer in the question. Open-ended questions are a tool that you can use to help the speaker to broaden and clarify his or her message. Using open-ended questions enables the speaker to come up with his or her own answer so the speaker can broaden and clarify the intended message and the listener can better understand it.

Ask questions that start with:

What

Why

How

Reframing

Reframing allows you to diffuse an emotional situation and point the discussion in the right direction. You are able to acknowledge and differentiate between the content of the message and the speaker taking that content to a level where it can be addressed productively. Reframing offers an alternative interpretation, eases tension, and makes communication more productive. Not only can you reframe the other speaker's statements into more focused and clear messages, but you can reframe your own message into one that speaks positively about the future and addresses your interests.

Here are some alternatives:

When the speaker states his or her view in the negative, turn it into the positive.

When the speaker states his or her view in terms of the past, turn it into the future.

When the speaker states his or her view as a position, turn it into an interest.

Summarizing

When you summarize, you give the factual and emotional content back to the speaker to acknowledge as accurate or to correct. You get a complete understanding, the speaker feels completely heard and understood, and the communication process can proceed.

Some phrases that indicate that you are summarizing:

So, this is where we are so far . . .

Let me see if I understand what has been expressed.

To summarize . . .

From Waetzig, E., & Magrab, P. (1997). *Negotiating together—conflict management manual.* Washington, DC: Georgetown University Child Development Center; reprinted by permission.

Clarity of role for the leader is critical—the leader must determine whether to serve as a neutral facilitator or to disclose his or her point of view while agreeing not to influence the outcome unduly. In addition, the leader needs to reiterate that the consensus developed is specific to that situation and is not a magic bullet for all issues to be addressed by the collaborative.

Shared Vision Creating a shared vision is important, as it defines the substantive picture of what a group is doing and why it is doing it. It is also an early experience that helps a group assess its values, process, and environment, all of which support building common ground. Shared vision is a group's collective picture of what they want to create as a culmination of their common aspirations. This "picture" is carried by all and represents their connections and commitment to each other. The process for creating a shared vision requires trust born out of a personal search, equal voice for each individual, and the emotional safety of trust and respect for the culture-bound values and beliefs of each individual (Georgetown University Center for Child and Human Development, 2006). The personal search must include examination of mental models and assumptions in the context of an individual's culturally informed worldview and its influence on thought and action. The process begins with careful listening to one's internal voice and personal truth—or mental models—as well as becoming quiet and open to the truths of others in the community. Only by listening, understanding the impact of mental models and assumptions, and by shifting to a co-created new and larger vision can leaders support the process of developing a shared vision.

A shared vision (Georgetown University Center for Child and Human Development, 2006) has these attributes:

- Keeps focus on the ultimate goal
- Engages everyone through personal ownership to achieve the ultimate goal
- Provides a rudder to keep process and progress on course
- Directs focus back to deeply held views and commitment
- Encourages risk taking in the interest of reaching the ultimate goal
- Supports persistence in the interest of reaching the ultimate goal
- Identifies and defines a long-term investment

Peter Senge, in his book *The Fifth Discipline* (1990), outlined multiple ways in which leaders can engage groups in developing a shared vision. He outlines the following strategies: co-creating, consulting, testing, telling, and selling. Each of these strategies can be effective under different circumstances and can be used to achieve specific outcomes (see Table 6.3). He went on to address possible negative attitudes people have toward a shared vision and ways to overcome them.

Table 6.3. Strategies for creating shared vision

Co-creating	Consulting	Testing	Selling	Telling
"Let's create the future we individually and collectively want."	*"What vision do members recommend that we adopt?"*	*"What excites you about this vision? What doesn't?"*	*"We have the best answer. Let's see if we can get you to buy in . . ."*	*"We've got to do this . . . be excited about it."*
The leader and the organization participate in a collaborative process.	The leader is puts together a vision and seeks creative input from the organization before moving forward.	The leader has an idea about the vision but wants to know organization reaction before moving forward.	The leader knows the vision and motivates others.	The leader knows what the vision is.
Leader's tasks:	Leader's tasks:	Leader's tasks:	Leader's tasks:	Leader's tasks:
• Create vision shared and owned together.	• Build in protection against distortion of the message.	• Provide as much information as possible.	• Keep the channels open for responses.	• Inform people directly, clearly, and consistently.
• Build on personal vision.	• Gather and disseminate results.	• Make a clean test.	• Support enrollment, not manipulation.	• Tell the truth about current reality.
• Treat everyone equally.				
• Have people speak only for themselves.				
• Encourage interdependence.				
Cautionary tips:	Cautionary tips:	Cautionary tips:	Cautionary tips:	Cautionary tips:
• Use facilitated processes.	• Don't tell and consult simultaneously.	• Protect people's privacy.	• Focus on benefits.	• Be clear about what is or is not negotiable.

Source: Senge (1990).

BUILDING COMMON GROUND: MANAGING THE PROCESS

The cohesion of any collaborative will ebb and flow with changing political, economic, social, and environmental climates. Leaders must manage dynamics to encourage members to remain engaged in the collaborative process when the group reaches an impasse in times of conflict. This requires leaders to ensure that the group continues to engage in effective and authentic communication. Leaders also need to manage, participate in, and even facilitate difficult conversations that may arise within a diverse collaborative when agreed-upon commonalities are challenged. To manage the process of building and sustaining common ground, leaders need to "hold the environment." Leaders must simultaneously maintain a level of tension to ensure shifts in thinking can be generated and at the same time not trigger destructive conflict. Leaders need to be able to recognize when to step into the fray and when to step out. Managing the environment is recognizing the difference between enabling a supportive versus a threatening environment and knowing how to intervene when necessary. In managing common ground, leaders must focus on protocols that sustain collaboration, engage in interest-based negotiation, and manage conflict when value and process conflicts arise within the group.

Collaboration

Collaboration requires an infrastructure with the norms, time, and supports to connect and build common ground. The infrastructure supports that enable effective collaboration are facilitators, topic experts, and resources—including fiscal resources (see Worksheet 6.5 [Creating a Collaborative Environment for Managing Common Ground] at the end of this chapter). The norms and ground rules that are developed to guide the collaboration should be based on the personal values, belief systems, and expected behaviors of the individuals within the collaborative. Finally, without the sharing of appropriate information, members of the collaborative will be unable to have meaningful dialogue, which leads to the building of common ground.

Time The lack of time is one of the greatest barriers to authentic communication. In our time-compressed organizations, where technology has fostered expectations of instantaneous responses, it is tempting to proceed without authentic communication. Groups must set aside time to communicate and engage in a collaborative process. Most people do not like (and, in fact, dread) meetings. Not everyone is patient with process. For that reason, deliberately setting aside time and expressing the expectation that process is important is more likely to lead the group to participate authentically.

Norms Individual behavior, personal values, and beliefs all affect the collaborative process. The group often develops its own norms in these areas and then monitors itself (see Worksheet 6.6 [Development of Norms—Points to Ponder] at the end of this chapter).

Supports   When a group or organization builds a culture that includes intentional collaborative processes, it must then take steps to sustain that part of their culture. To do so, resources and supports must be allocated. Supports can come in the form of an outside facilitator who can help move a group forward or help them through very substantial change or difficult conflict. A group might also need the help of an expert to move forward. The process of building common ground can be divisive, and sometimes the only way to find consensus is through the recommendations of an agreed-upon expert.

Building a team that can move to common ground requires attention to the team dynamics. Teams do not form and function well without planned opportunities to build the trust and mutual understanding that can lead to common ground. Resources, human and financial, as well as time must be dedicated to building healthy teams.

Interview #2: When and How Did You Get to Common Ground?

The following interview is with Pam Becker, vice chair of the Nevada Children's Behavioral Health Consortium, chair of the Washoe County Children's Mental Health Consortium, and director of community collaborations for the Children's Cabinet in Reno, Nevada.

We have had moments when we have stood on common ground, but the space is not so big. We have a common purpose, but the goals get difficult in terms of moving forward because they are not necessarily the same for everyone. That is when people feel limited by their own systems.

We got to common ground in our state consortium when we developed Nevada's definition, attributes, and principles for our system of care. We all agreed and everyone signed the commitment sheet—this made it concrete, and we were able to move forward. That was something; a major step forward. Now we are working on modifying the existing memorandum of agreement between two agencies (Division of Child and Family Services [DCFS] and Mental Health and Developmental Services [MHDS]), incorporating system of care principles so everyone in the two agencies will have and use a document that expounds what we have all agreed to. And the beauty of it is that a person will get system of care principles and attributes without having to sit through a separate training. It becomes how people do business.

Sometimes being in the same room and meeting on a constant basis helps to build trust. People open up a little more each time and share what is common and what is different. This takes time, and you have to make time for people to trust and work on something as large as a system of care. When we started at the local consortium, some members had previous bad experiences with some agencies in the room. They did not want to trust the person representing the agency because they had been burned before—but as agency people continue to come back, people open up a little each time they attend a meeting and begin to discuss their agency's protocol, and this helps others understand the difficulties people within the agency have when delivering services to children and families. As a leader I must keep a vision of the overall process—viewing the dynamics from 10,000 feet. I need to see it as a new experience and a new way of doing things with that agency with that individual. As progress is made in relationship building within the group, I need to start the celebration for any progress that we make. It is very important to celebrate all of our successes, because people like to associate themselves with success (even when it is small). As humans we feel things personally, and as the leader I need to point out the that the frustrations people in the group are feeling are with the systems, not the people. We have to remind ourselves of the higher purpose of serving children and families, which can help overcome the fear, distrust, and discomfort of being in the room sometimes and working together. We can see how we can be together and make shifts—moving forward and not continuing to see backward.

Interest-Based Negotiation

In collaboration, members of the group will have diverse and competing positions, making it difficult to reach common ground. Interest-based negotiation, according to Fisher, Ury, and Patton (1991), is a way to work together by reframing competing positions to positive, future-oriented, common, and shared interests. For example, one person taking a strong position against individual ownership of guns and another standing against gun control can mutually reframe their positions to a common interest in safe communities.

What Are Interests?   Interests move individuals from the "what" (positions; what you want) to the "why" (interests; why it is important to you). For example, one might express the desire for a clean house. However, the interest is that a mother-in-law is coming over and the homeowner wants to feel confident during the visit. Interests allow a broader, more honest and substantive discussion as well as a greater potential for finding common ground. There are three types of interests that affect the dialogue: substantive, psychological, and procedural. Although members of a group have many opinions about the substance of the work or the situation, they also have both procedural and psychological interests. In other words, they have an interest in feeling valued in the situation, and they want to feel as if the process is fair.

Why Focus on Interests?   In discussing interests, which include needs, hopes, fears and desires, the conversation moves to the heart of what is important—children and families or, alternately, profession, agency, and systems of services. When dialogue occurs at an interest level, more often than not mutual interests are readily identifiable. When proponents discuss their interests, they begin to understand individual interests and explore mutual interests so that they shift their relationship and begin to build common ground and move to a shared vision for their work together.

However, when people express positions, they are often doing so from a place of power or of rights. For example, one who has the power of the purse might use it to force a decision in line with his or her position. In a rights-based scenario, a person might advocate for his or her position and justify it using a perceived right (e.g., I have a right to a free and appropriate education) or because he or she simply believes that he or she is right. Justifying an outcome based on power or a right might not get the proponents very far unless all begin to discuss *why* the stated positions were formed and why they continue to be important.

How Do We Focus on Interests?   The leader who is intent on managing common ground by ensuring interest-based negotiation must facilitate the dialogue by exploring the group's interests, framing their interests in a way that everyone in the group can understand, and identifying the mutuality of the interests. One of the most basic ways to focus on interests is to continuously ask "why?" rather than "what?" when exploring for common ground within a group. Leaders need to direct focused attention to the topic at hand and consistently move members within the collaborative to work to understand in depth the perspective of all. Leaders need to make sure that the process allows for as many perspectives as needed to be brought to the table to consider all points of view. Once all the interests have been articulated, leaders can direct the group to work on a statement that frames the current issue in ways that are inclusive of everyone's needs. The group will then deliberate and determine the multiple creative options available that represent common ground. Worksheets 6.7 (Shifting Positions to Interests) and 6.8 (Shifting Positions to Interests: Alpha and Beta) at the end of this chapter provide opportunities to explore interests and to move from positions to interests.

Managing Conflict

When a group is unable to move forward because members are unable to see sufficient commonality to reach consensus, it is critical to assist them in aligning their perspectives. However, when the impasse continues and conflict arises, leaders need to be able to manage the conflict.

Alignment of Perspectives   Perspectives are an individual's view of, or outlook on, the world, shaped through experiences, personality, roles, and positions. It is the lens through which one looks at and understands situations and people. When we are confronted with a situation, perspective guides the response to that situation. Clarifying perspectives will enable the group to determine where there is an alignment of perspectives and where there is a dissonance in perspectives. An alignment of perspectives and interests allows for the creation of common ground, which is needed in a collaborative. Where there are irreconcilable differences, members within the collaborative need to agree to disagree and move on. This is where the leader must be vigilant to ensure that people do not continue to regurgitate differences and thus stymie forward movement.

An essential element in managing and sustaining common ground is bringing together disparate points of view to create something larger and more comprehensive, thereby ensuring true collaboration. Effective leaders understand their own perspectives and how they affect their interactions with people and situations. Perhaps more important, they have developed a way to gain an understanding of the others' perspectives. This enables leaders to come to the table to really listen, free of assumptions that often stall successful collaboration. They are able to untangle the snags of assumptions, mental models, and misperceptions to get to the underlying deeply held values and beliefs that can support and guide the collaborative. Leaders take on a role similar to a mediator in this case. At other times, an outside neutral mediator can be helpful to aid in the alignment of perspectives.

Utilizing Conflict Toward New Ways of Thinking and Framing Issues

Conflict is often feared and avoided because people's experiences inform them that this is a negative experience. Unfortunately, they are not taught as children how to handle conflict, and this deficit haunts them into their adulthood. People either avoid it or aggressively pursue it—neither of which necessarily provides the results they seek.

Conflict that arises from genuine differences in the way a specific situation is viewed can launch diverse ideas and lead to the development of mutually beneficial solutions. A group can engage in collaborative decision making when all perspectives in the room are heard, clarifying questions are asked to inform our mental models and assumptions, and options that will serve the group's needs are collectively determined.

When different perspectives are used judiciously to engage, learn from, and teach others, there is movement toward a closer understanding of our dreams, our hopes, and our vision for all. Common ground is built and collaboration is strengthened.

SUSTAINING COMMON GROUND: MEASURING SUCCESS

Building and maintaining common ground is a continuous and circular process, and at many points along the way, leaders need to determine if the process is working and if common ground is being built. Leaders will have to keep track of the environment that supports the process, elements that make up the collaborative process, and the group's progress in building common ground. This requires that the leader and the collaborative develop criteria for success.

In other words, what does it look and feel like if the group is successfully building and sustaining common ground? These outcomes and indicators can include the health of relationships as well as the cohesiveness of the group and the ability to achieve consensus. In addition, the level of safety and trust experienced by the group for the partners to discuss issues that test assumptions and diverse perspectives and opportunities to anticipate, prevent, and manage conflict.

Measuring the process of building common ground along the way allows for midcourse corrections and innovations in this continuous journey. In addition, leaders are able to articulate the benefits and outcomes of building common ground. This can motivate a group to continue the process and maintain the commitment as the process becomes part of the culture of the group.

Last, measuring processes that are put in place by a leader to get to and maintain common ground are distinct from measuring the work itself. In other words, if common ground is sought in developing a new initiative, it is critical to build an evaluation component for the new initiative. Evaluating the environment and the processes used to come to common ground involves separate tools.

Measuring Outcomes

The first step in evaluating a process is to have the group define the outcomes and indicators. What are the desired outcomes of a process that leads to common ground? Each group will define shared outcomes based on the unique work of each individual within the group. In general, however, outcomes will likely focus on the above pieces of the process. Examples of shared outcomes might include the following:

- Each member of the group participates in a way that is individually comfortable.

- Divergent views are not only heard, but sought.

- The group has deliberately defined the way in which decisions are made.

- Collaborative communication skills are used by each member of the group.

- A shared vision is defined and the group works in concert to achieve that vision.

Process Evaluation

After defining outcomes, the group must look at the norms and processes that must be in place to achieve the outcomes. For instance, if safe participation for each member is the stated outcome, the leader must engage the group to define the indicators of success and the tools that will be used to measure their progress. Some of those tools will include anonymous individual evaluation. Some tools will assess team-building efforts to gauge the level of safety among the group. Measures may also include individual satisfaction with the process, adherence with collaborative norms, and output from the process that indicates common ground has been attained. Evaluation should be routine so that processes and behaviors will continue to evolve. Worksheet 6.9 (Questions to Consider When Developing an Evaluation) at the end of this chapter addresses a list of questions to consider as evaluation is developed.

Measuring Shared Vision

Shared vision is both an output of common ground and an indicator that common ground has been achieved. It is defined through a process that includes the elements detailed in this chapter, such as an inclusive and participatory environment, collaborative communication, interest-based dialogue, conflict management, and methods employed to measure the progress in achieving the shared vision. A shared vision also provides the leader with tools to continue to motivate the group and to manage the ongoing work of building common ground.

SUMMARY

Most people who work in children's mental health have spent considerable time and effort in the work they are doing. They are passionate and committed to making the lives of children, youth, and families better. Unfortunately, the process of how to do the work has not historically been given much attention. The result has too often been that good people have a hard time moving things forward and are left feeling defeated, isolated, and stressed.

Leaders from all levels are beginning to realize that it takes thought, time, and effort to create expectations, processes, and environments that bring diverse people together to create the comprehensive, coordinated, and efficient systems that communities need. It starts with a commitment to building common ground.

REFERENCES

Clark, H.H., & Brennan, S.E. (1991). Grounding in communication. In L.B. Resnick, J. Levine, & S.D. Teasley (Eds.), *Perspectives on socially shared cognition.* (pp. 127–149). Washington, DC: American Psychological Association.

Ciancutti, A.R., & Steding, T.L. (2001). *Built on trust: Gaining competitive advantage in any organization.* New York: McGraw-Hill.

Espiritu, R. (2009) *Developing an evaluation for building common ground.* Houston, TX: Change Matrix.

Fisher, R., Ury, W., & Patton, B. (1991). *Getting to yes: Negotiating agreement without giving in* (2nd ed.). New York: Penguin.

Gray, B. (1989). *Collaborating: Finding common ground for multiparty problems.* San Francisco: Jossey-Bass.

Hanson, M.P. (2005). *Clues to achieving consensus: A leader's guide to navigating collaborative problem solving.* Lanham, MD: Rowman and Littlefield Education.

Kagen, E.B., & Hepburn, K.S. (2006) Framing the work. In *Framing the leadership in systems of care: A training curriculum.* Washington DC: Georgetown University Center for Child and Human Development, National Technical Assistance Center for Children's Mental Health.

Lencioni, P. (2002). *The five dysfunctions of a team: A leadership fable.* San Francisco: Jossey-Bass.

Mathews, D. (1994). *Politics for people: Finding a responsible public voice.* Urbana: University of Illinois Press.

Myers, S., & Lambert, J. (1994). *Diversity icebreakers: A guide to diversity training.* Amherst, MA: Diversity Resources.

Obama, B. (2009). Remarks of President Barack Obama—as prepared for delivery address to joint session of Congress—Tuesday, February 24th, 2009. Retrieved from http://www.whitehouse.gov/the_press_office/remarks-of-president-barack-obama-address-to-joint-session-of-congress/

Paris, K. (2009, July 23). A landmark for common ground. *RH Reality Check: Information and Analysis for Reproductive Health.* Retrieved August 5, 2009, from http://www.rhrealitycheck.org/commonground/2009/07/23/a-landmark-common-ground

Redman, P.M., Kelly, J.A., Albright, E.D., Anderson, P.F., Mulder, C., & Schnell, E.H. (1997). Common ground: The HealthWeb project as a model for Internet collaboration. *Bulletin of the Medical Library Association, 85*(4), 325–330.

Senge, P.M. (1990). *The fifth discipline: The art & practice of the learning organization.* New York: Doubleday.

Senge, P., Smith, B., Krushwitz, N., Laur, J., & Schley, S. (2008). *The necessary revolution: How individuals and organizations are working together to create a sustainable world.* New York: Doubleday.

U.S. Department of Health and Human Services. (1999). *Blending perspectives and building common ground. A report to congress on substance abuse and child protection.* Washington, DC: U.S. Government Printing Office.

Waetzig, E., & Magrab, P. (1997). *Negotiating together—Conflict management manual.* Washington, DC: Georgetown University Child Development Center.

Weisbord, M. (1992). *Discovering common ground.* San Francisco: Berrett-Koehler.

Worksheet 6.1

Take Stock: An Assessment of the Current Status of Common Ground

1. What are the points of diversity among the people in the group?

2. What current processes are in place that lead to common ground?

3. How are individuals included in those processes?

4. What is the level of participation in those processes?

5. How are diverse voices protected?

6. What happens when there is a disagreement?

7. How consistent are the messages coming from various individuals within the group?

 **Worksheet 6.2**

Common Ground on Language

Term(s) Currently in Use	Existing (Common) Definitions	Issues of Concern and Tension	Agreed-Upon Terms and Definitions

Worksheet 6.3

Listening to Understand

RESTATE the content of the following statements:

1. It really frustrates me to have to justify every method of care that I propose for my patients.

   _____

2. My child's teacher is really trying my patience. She insists on keeping him with the other students all day long when it is clear to me that he is falling further and further behind, which is frustrating to him.

   _____

3. This meeting is a waste of my time. We are not getting anywhere, and I think I am going to end it here.

   _____

Change the following questions to OPEN-ENDED QUESTIONS:

1. Are you as frustrated as I am about the way Crisis Insurance has limited the treatment options we can provide to our patients?

   _____

2. So, it is your intention to keep this child in the special education class for at least half of the day?

   _____

REFRAME these sentences as a response to the speaker:

1. The managed care companies are gaining all of the power to dictate how we will practice medicine.

   _____

2. Every time I have contacted you to discuss this child, you are unable to grasp what I believe to be the issue.

   _____

3. I do not want my child to be placed in foster care.

   _____

From Waetzig, E., & Magrab, P. (1997). *Negotiating together—Conflict management manual.* Washington, DC: Georgetown University Child Development Center; adapted by permission.

In *The Leadership Equation: Strategies for Individuals Who Are Champions for Children, Youth, and Families* edited by Gary M. Blau & Phyllis R. Magrab (2010; Paul H. Brookes Publishing Co., Inc.)

Worksheet 6.4

Consensus Protocols

1. Is there mutual understanding among group members of how decisions are made?

   _____

2. Has there been an intentional conversation among group members about how decisions are made?

   _____

3. Does that process apply to all decisions? If not, how do you choose the decision-making norm?

   _____

4. How should decisions be made to achieve common ground?

   _____

5. Is there a contingency plan if a decision is not possible using the preferred process?

   _____

Other questions to consider:

1. What decisions are governed by the consensus process?

   _____

2. What decisions are outside of this process?

   _____

3. How are decisions to be made?

   _____

4. What is the *quorum* for a decision to be made?

   _____

5. What constitutes a *majority* for a decision to be made?

   _____

6. How do you attend to those in disagreement with the decision?

   _____

7. When might you revisit issues already decided upon?

   _____

Worksheet 6.5

Creating a Collaborative Environment for Managing Common Ground

Describe the ideal environment in which common ground will be built.	
Time: *How much time is allocated to build and sustain common ground?*	
Norm: *What would be appropriate norms for this process?*	
Supports: *What supports do you need (e.g., facilitator, subject matter expert, transport, child care, food)?*	

 **Worksheet 6.6**

Development of Norms—Points to Ponder

1. How do people talk about issues of significance?

   _____

2. Is it customary within the organization to send an e-mail or discuss in person?

   _____

3. Do people discuss issues in groups versus one-to-one?

   _____

4. Do small groups take on issues, or is it the norm within the organization to wait until a person with authority brings an issue to the table?

   _____

5. What is the norm around information disclosure?

   _____

6. How is information viewed within the organization?

   _____

7. Who has access to information?

   _____

8. How is information shared?

   _____

9. How are individuals able to contribute to information?

   _____

Worksheet 6.7

Shifting Positions to Interests

Change the following positions into interests:

Position: If clients miss appointments, they will have to reschedule. No exceptions!

Interests:

_____

_____

Position: I do not want my child to be placed in a residential treatment facility. A day treatment program will be fine for him.

Interests:

_____

_____

Position: We professionals are perfectly capable of representing the child's interests at these meetings.

Interests:

_____

_____

Position: I want to schedule the surgery for my back now. I do not want to wait for 6 months to see if the physical therapy makes a difference.

Interests:

_____

_____

Position: These parents need to understand.

Interests:

_____

_____

From Waetzig, E., & Magrab, P. (1997). *Negotiating together—Conflict management manual.* Washington, DC: Georgetown University Child Development Center; adapted by permission.

 **Worksheet 6.8**

Shifting Positions to Interests: Alpha and Beta

The Alpha Organization is a community advocacy organization that serves children, youth, and their families with severe emotional disorders at both the local and state level. They serve families throughout the state through two main offices—one in the south and the other in the north—and through a network of paid staff and volunteers.

Beta Organization is a provider agency that also has statewide presence. They have one main center at the business capital of the state and three other centers geographically located to correspond with the main population centers within the state.

Beta Organization has just successfully applied for a state award to increase capacity and enhance services throughout the state. The primary goal of the grant is to provide mobile crisis and intervention services for children and youth with serious emotional disturbance throughout the state.

Alpha Organization is strongly opposing this decision. They feel that the state should have awarded the funds to an organization that has previously clearly demonstrated its commitment to rural communities and has shown utilization patterns for services beyond the four centers. They are threatening to take the issue to other advocacy and family organizations and stage protest demonstrations.

The state leadership has invited both organizations to a meeting to discuss this issue.

What are the organizations' positions?

How can they reframe these positions as interests?

What common interest(s) do they both share?

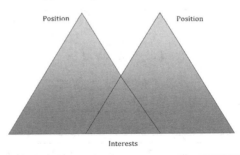

Triangles image reproduced with the kind permission
of the Justice Institute of British Columbia (www.jibc.ca).

Worksheet 6.9

Questions to Consider When Developing an Evaluation

General

Who should conduct our evaluation?

Does the team represent the diversity of our group?

How do we ensure meaningful stakeholder participation?

Who will participate in the evaluation? What strategies will be used?

How will evaluation results be shared with the group and used to improve the process?

Process Evaluation

What are the common ground strategies that have been implemented? What have been the challenges and successes in implementing these strategies?

Do the common ground strategies do what they were intended to do?

How are diverse voices included in the group?

Are group members satisfied with common ground strategies?

(continued)

From Espiritu, R. (2009). *Developing an evaluation for building common ground.* Houston, TX: Change Matrix; reprinted by permission.

Shared Vision

What is the shared vision of the group?

_____

What were the challenges and successes in developing the shared vision?

_____

How is the shared vision being used?

_____

Outcomes

What will successful common ground look like for the group?

_____

How will people feel, behave, and communicate with one another?

_____

How will the leader operate?

_____

How will the group operate, communicate, and make decisions?

_____

What will the environment be like? How will it feel to group members?

_____

From Espiritu, R. (2009). *Developing an evaluation for building common ground.* Houston, TX: Change Matrix; reprinted by permission.

7

Adaptation and Innovation

GARY M. BLAU, SHANNON CROSSBEAR, AND CORETTA MALLERY

Quite simply, effective leadership requires adaptation and innovation (Anthony & Huckshorn, 2008; Quinn, 1996). Many authors write that a leader must be flexible and creative in dealing with individuals, organizations, and systems (Anthony & Huckshorn, 2008; Quinn, 1996; Sternberg, 2007) because of the ever-changing environment in which human services are delivered. Constant flexibility and creativity are not easy to achieve.

Try this exercise: Be honest with yourself. If you were asked to rate yourself on a scale from 1 (*not at all*) to 10 (*all the time*), how "adaptable" or "innovative" would you be? How would others rate you? How hard is it to answer the questions?

What do *adaptation* and *innovation* really mean? The dictionary definition[1] of *adaptation* is "something, such as a device or mechanism that is changed or changes so as to become suitable to a new or special application or situation." The dictionary definition[2] of *innovation* is "a new way of doing something; the successful implementation of creative ideas." Taken together and applied to leadership in the context of this book, adaptation and innovation mean that the effective leader is sufficiently flexible and malleable so as to apply new and creative strategies to challenges faced in the field of children's mental health.

In many ways just saying that leaders should be adaptable and innovative is unfair. For one, a person's level of adaptability or creativity differs across different circumstances and settings. Take, for example, the clinician who relates well to teenagers and has excellent strategies for engagement and intervention. Should this person also be expected to have the same ability with older adults or when addressing "system" challenges rather than "individual" challenges? Also, the environment in which a person operates plays an important role. How can one be adaptive and innovative when the fiscal and economic climate is uncertain or in

---

[1,2]By permission. From *Merriam-Webster's Collegiate Dictionary* © 2009 by Merriam-Webster, Incorporated (www.Merriam-Webster.com).

chaos, when the needs of families and communities are overwhelming, and when there are drastic changes in service delivery models and practices?

On the surface it seems like it should be easy to define and recognize the qualities and characteristics of adaptability and innovation, and yet exploration shows them to be very complex. Consider all of the changes currently demanded within behavioral health care for children, youth, and their families. The challenging economic climate provides threats and uncertainty. These economic changes are happening simultaneous to dramatic changes in family structures and cultural backgrounds of community members. Systems must be prepared to adapt to these significant changes through the modification of service approaches.

In addition, the relationships between care recipients and care providers are undergoing dramatic changes, creating the need to forge new partnerships. There is a continuing devolution of service responsibility to local units of government, broadly outstripping the available resources while contributing to wide disparities across communities. There are also wide disparities between what is known to work and implementation of those strategies, a result of continuous growth in knowledge about how to care for the special needs of children and their families. These disparities make it very difficult for communities to keep up, possibly adding to conflicts between "old" and "new" practices.

To add another layer of complexity, these factors and circumstances are also affected by individual characteristics, such as temperament, the ability to tolerate stress, and cultural background. It is important to note that the terms *adaptability* and *innovation* are subject to interpretation and subjectivity in their meaning, and there is not always agreement on how to define these qualities in leadership (Anthony & Huckshorn, 2008).

Many authors have written about the important qualities of adaptable and innovative leaders (Hackman & Wageman, 2007; Kaiser, Hogan, & Craig, 2008; Quinn, 1996; Sternberg, 2003, 2007; Zander & Zander, 2000). These qualities include the ability to respond quickly to changing circumstances, developing new solutions to old or emerging problems, the capacity to communicate and demonstrate empathy, and the ability to see the big picture to create a specific course of action. The literature seems clear that these characteristics and behaviors are desirable qualities, yet there is no manual for how to develop these skills. One could argue that real, effective leaders are born with this ability, but the authors of this chapter argue that adaptive and innovative leadership in fact comprises a set of skills that can be learned and behaviors that can be enhanced and improved. The key is not to say, "Today I will demonstrate an ability to be adaptive," or "By the end of the week I will develop two new innovative ideas." Rather, the key is to create the necessary conditions that allow adaptability and innovation to occur.

Such conditions are about more than the leader's own abilities; they must also nurture other people's abilities. A good example of this is the leader who recognizes and acknowledges his own limitations. Perhaps it is limited knowledge of organizational skills or interpreting legislation or understanding the nuances of financing and budget. In all of these situations the leader can augment his own strengths by engaging others who can complement his talents and abilities. Putting the right people in the right places, giving them the tools and supports they need, and rewarding their efforts serve to increase adaptability and innovation within the group or organization. One of the authors of this chapter has often commented that the best decisions he ever made, that ultimately enhanced the work and improved the lives of children, youth, and families, were not about policy—they were about people, the people chosen to do the job. Thus, a leader's ability to be adaptable and innovative goes beyond himself and extends to those around him.

This chapter will shift the emphasis beyond individual qualities of good leadership to a broader context of an operating style and set of skills and ideas that can be cultivated and developed. Such an approach is consistent with the system of care philosophy (Stroul & Blau, 2008) and the values of collaboration, engagement, and shared decision making. With this as a backdrop, the remainder of this chapter is dedicated to identifying a set of challenges that leaders face because of traditionally established modes of thinking. Such thinking may limit a leader's ability to adapt and respond effectively.

DEVELOPING LEADERSHIP INSTINCTS

The book *Unnatural Leadership* (Dotlich & Cairo, 2002) offers "Ten New Leadership Instincts" regarding how effective leaders succeed. These authors developed their ideas and concepts by interviewing leaders in the business world and found that successful leaders move beyond old stereotypes of leaders being viewed as infallible to leaders working collaboratively and being perceived as vulnerable. In this chapter, many of the basic tenets of Dotlich and Cairo are borrowed, explored, and applied to systems of care and the delivery of services to children, youth, and families. Although the examples come from the authors of this chapter, the application of unnatural leadership to children's mental health is built on the innovation of Dotlich and Cairo. In addition to being grateful for their work, the current authors highly recommend the original source material.

Move Past Prior Experience

The first way that effective leaders succeed is to "refuse to be a prisoner of experience" (Dotlich & Cairo, 2002, p. 71). This means letting go of preconceived ideas of how things are done and being willing to change. Most can recall a time when someone has suggested something at a meeting, often a newer employee, and a more seasoned employee has quickly closed down the idea because it does not fit with old patterns of "how we do things." Norms are formed within organizations about how things are typically done. Effective leaders within systems of care are not trapped by these norms and are open to new ideas.

Think briefly about your own experience of the system chaos inflicted by the economic crisis. A successful system leader recognizes chaos as a changing of the old and an opportunity for the new. As the old proves less durable than imagined, what opportunities arise? It is important to learn from past experiences without remaining bound by them. Innovative leaders are willing to let go of almost anything previously believed about what works if a new and better approach arises, as solutions often emerge and from unlikely sources. Past solutions that worked gloriously will stop working, and leaders must be willing to move forward. Innovative leadership must focus on changes that lead to improvement, avoiding dogma and rigidity. It can be difficult to completely "wipe the slate clean," but one can suspend previous beliefs for a time to enter into new approaches. This suspension of previous beliefs allows new models to emerge, but it is important to note that, while being open to change, effective leaders stay focused on fundamental values and vision.

In children's mental health, a good example of being locked into past experiences is the way clinicians are trained. The majority of clinical staff have been trained in the "deficit model," in which problems are identified and diagnosed. Some are even trained in the medical model, in which the goal is to identify the disease state so a cure can be developed. In systems of care, however, the focus is to emphasize strengths and partner with youth and families. If one is a prisoner of experience to the medical model, he or she might not be open to a strength-based approach. As another example, in the early days of the family movement in children's mental health there was a great deal of adversarial conversation between child serving "systems" and families. It took the suspension of mistrust to create opportunities for conversations to begin to move toward collaboration. Leading in a time of change requires suspending our past messages around what will and will not work.

Be Authentic and Expose Vulnerabilities

Innovative leaders learn to be authentic and expose their vulnerabilities, meaning that they acknowledge their weaknesses and imperfections. It is not possible for any one person to have all the answers and solely make correct decisions. Likewise, it is unrealistic that someone is skilled in every facet of the organization he or she leads. Contrary to more traditional thinking, it is important for leaders to admit to these flaws. Systems of care leaders invite and explore a variety of perspectives, regularly learning and gathering information from a variety of sources. This collaborative philosophy is promoted across organizations.

It is a myth that all good leaders are consistently self-confident, decisive, and error free. Great leaders do not purport to be invincible, as this only succeeds in setting them apart from the community with which they are trying to engage. Successful leaders must show humanness to become a part of the system. This is particularly important in a cultural context. In some cultures, for example, being too self-assured or unilateral in decision making would be seen as arrogant and disrespectful.

There are consequences to feigning invincibility or hanging on to past successes. The first is that those being led think the leaders expect them to always be strong and confidant. This may lead to dishonesty out of fear of challenging this illusion of strength and confidence. This false behavior may also make it hard to gain the trust of certain populations. It is hard to build a rapport if leaders are seen as dishonest and incapable of thoughtful consideration of others and the collective human condition of imperfection. The final consequence of this behavior may be that the leader is set up on a pedestal that may eventually result in a long fall and harm to the larger goal. Leaders are not expected to have all the answers but frame the necessary questions for the group to answer. They express uncertainty, acknowledge complexity, and accept input. Working with a team means the leader is "one of" not "one over." This does not mean that the leader relinquishes authority or ultimate decision making. Rather, it means that the leader must create the conditions for collaboration and problem solving.

Perhaps the best example of this comes from the highly successful *Star Trek* series. Captain Kirk demonstrated many leadership qualities and in fact acknowledged that he did not always have the answer (e.g., vulnerability). He called upon his team (e.g., Spock, Bones, Scotty) to provide input and feedback so that a course of action could be determined. A reader less familiar with *Star Trek* might think of other examples from popular television series. A leader who takes the time to listen and ask questions, in addition to being comfortable with ambiguity, is a leader better prepared to deal with the rapidly transforming mental health care system. These behaviors promote finding shared solutions and gaining stakeholder buy-in, which in turn result in shared responsibility for outcomes.

Another example where exposing vulnerabilities led to positive outcomes is the coming together of families and mental health professionals in systems of care communities. Family members often bring fear of being blamed or vilified into the relationship, while professionals may have fear of turning over some of the power, while remaining responsible for the results. When a person is forthcoming about his or her fears, it aids in building empathy and strengthening relationships. Once fears are shared openly, the family members may be able to use their passion to become leaders. One might think that exposing those fears would weaken leadership, but it is through sharing vulnerabilities that other strengths can be identified.

Acknowledge Your Shadow Side

Leaders must work to uncover and acknowledge their shadow side, meaning their flaws and faults. Whereas exposing one's vulnerability relates to an identified area of weakness, acknowledging one's shadow side relates to recognizing one's character flaws. Such openness is respected by others and often invites openness in return. For example, vulnerability could be poor organizational skills or low self-esteem, whereas a person's shadow side could reflect an overemphasis on power, control, or competitiveness. When leaders model imperfections and are seen working on their flaws, other are freed to acknowledge and work on their own flaws.

Many people revert to what was known and safe in the past. Known and safe could mean hanging on to a particular title that once had power and authority attached or staying quietly tucked away in a back office. Leaders promote the belief that no one is perfect. Knowing that, leaders who present themselves as not having some form of shadow side may appear arrogant. Maybe the shadow side is the need for recognition, a fierce desire to compete, or be known as the "best." Leaders who acknowledge their faults invite expertise from others.

One of the authors of this chapter learned a painful lesson about arrogance that is remembered to this day. The story begins with a promotion, a new title, and an increase in authority. This was an exciting and challenging time, and several meetings were held with "subordinates" to discuss vision and plan strategy. Following one of these sessions, the leader was asked by one of the staff if he could have a one-on-one discussion. The leader thought that his expertise was being tapped and was all too happy to arrange the private meeting. However, the conversation did not begin as the leader expected. The staff member started by saying that he was nervous about the discussion but was sufficiently upset and concerned that he was willing to take the risk and potential consequences of sharing his thoughts. The leader was unsure how to react, especially since he had known and trusted the person for many years and considered him a friend. He could not understand what had made his friend and colleague so upset, so he decided to wait and hear what the staff person could have to say. The staff member proceeded to share that since receiving his promotion the leader had become arrogant, dismissive, and self-absorbed. In fact, the leader's behavior and his seemingly new obsession with power and control (and perhaps a desire to show off and be recognized) was so offensive that the staff member was prepared to look for a new job.

Consider the dynamics and intensity of this conversation and the complexity of this interaction. This discussion had many levels and involved roles, conflict styles, and relationships, along with a direct confrontation to the leader's shadow side. At first, not surprisingly, the leader was taken aback, but within moments he realized that he had just been given the gift of a life lesson that has never been forgotten. This spurred the leader to take a moment to reflect and consider what type of leader he wished to be and how he would like to be perceived by others. In many ways, the retelling of this story is the public acknowledgment of a private moment that has forever improved the way this author and leader behaves and interacts with others.

Develop a Right-versus-Right Decision-Making Mentality

Clear-cut answers to complex, challenging questions are difficult to find and agree on. There are often multiple right answers, and leaders should be flexible to hearing them all. Unfortunately, in American culture many are socialized at a very young age that there is a right way and a wrong way. In fact, competition and a culture of winning are taught from the very early stage of life. To illustrate the importance of this, one just has to follow sporting events. What is the second place person called? The first loser. What about the Olympic athlete who feels the need to apologize for a silver medal? Leaders help groups move away from "winning and losing" and discussions of "right and wrong" toward discussions that lead to "improvements." System improvements depend on diversity of ideas and freedom in input for decision making. This is a change in mind-set from a "we–they" position toward "us," as solutions are often best when implemented through partnerships.

Innovative leaders view multiple options generated through partnerships as multiple opportunities for growth and improvement. It is also critical to recognize that the "right" answer yesterday is not necessarily the "right" answer for today. A leader who learns to change within a "right versus right" mind-set helps a group continue to seek improvement. Take the following lesson learned by one of the authors. After a meeting, the leader (the author) was approached by a colleague who said that he was setting up a competition by using language that could be interpreted as devaluing other people's ideas. During a brainstorming session, a member of the team had offered an idea, and the response was, "That was an interesting idea, but . . ." In this instance, the word *but* served to completely negate the idea and stifled the discussion. In fact, the word *but* often creates an adversarial stance and tends to squelch any attempt at innovation. The colleague suggested that the word *but* be replaced with the word *and. And,* it turns out, is a word that validates and connects. It is a word that allows for a value-added conversation. This is a simple change that makes a significant impact on decision making.

Consider how often you use the word *but* in conversation. You will probably be surprised by how helpful the word *and* can be when collaborating and trying to gain consensus. Using the example from above, one would say, "That was an interesting idea, and . . ."

Create Teams that Create Discomfort

Innovative leaders avoid surrounding themselves with yes-people. Teams are deliberately built to avoid sameness and to encourage diversity and contradictory perspectives. This approach allows some discomfort and healthy tension. The system of care philosophy depends on collaboration among multiple stakeholders, therefore leaders must create the best opportunities for effective collaboration. This requires each stakeholder to hear other points of view, which may be uncomfortable for some people. To the contrary, homogenous groups simply share similar beliefs and affirm each other's opinions. This affirmation is helpful for quickly pushing agendas through, but dissonance is sometimes necessary for innovative thinking. Alternatives must be aired, even though such airing may be contentious and uncomfortable.

Innovative leaders help to create teams that seek and embrace a diversity of perceptions. These teams manage discomfort so that solutions are found. Solutions often depend on avoiding "group think" while promoting independent thinking and loyalty to the group process. Thus, leaders are always prepared to let go of their solution when better solutions emerge from the group. An example of this in children's mental health can be found in the National Building Bridges Initiative (Blau et al., in press).

For over 20 years, since the advent of the system of care movement, there has been tension between community and residential service providers. Community-based providers have voiced concern that their residential colleagues have kept children too long and have failed to demonstrate the effectiveness of their services. Residential providers have asserted that their community-based colleagues have not collaboratively supported their efforts, assisted with discharge planning, or provided intensive service options as necessary follow-up. Families and youth have often expressed mixed reactions and opinions about both sets of providers, asking that all providers become more family-driven and youth-guided and encouraging them to create a more integrated array of services.

In this climate, made more complex as systems vied for limited resources, a group of community-based and residentially based treatment and service providers, policy makers, advocates, families, and youth, spearheaded by the Substance Abuse and Mental Health Administration's Center for Mental Health Services, began a dialogue in the fall of 2005 to discuss ways to improve relationships and practice. The result was the initiative now known as the Building Bridges Initiative (BBI).

National Building Bridges Summits occurred in 2006 and 2007, bringing together recognized experts in the field of children's mental health, including family members, youth, advocates, community and residential providers, and policy makers. The 2006 summit, inspired by compelling youth and family voices, resulted in a drafted and signed joint resolution (JR) of common principles and a shared commitment to a coordinated, integrated, comprehensive, flexible, individualized, strength-based, family-driven, and youth-guided array of culturally and linguistically competent services and supports that are evidence based and practice informed and consistent with research on sustained positive outcomes. The JR has since been endorsed by 24 national organizations and 20 agencies, and hundreds of staff in residential and community programs across the country are operationalizing the BBI principles and/or implementing BBI tools to achieve the mission articulated by the JR. All of this was the result of creating a team of people who were historically in conflict and uncomfortable with each other and encouraging them to work collaboratively toward a common goal.

Trust Others Before They Earn It

Leaders accelerate team chemistry by trusting others even before they earn it. They actively work to turn competitors into colleagues and allies. Freely given trust is a catalyst for forming more trust. Society has internalized an idea that trust must be earned over time and experience, but does this have to be the case?

First impressions strongly guide how we interact with others, and people sometimes feel they need to see someone's list of accomplishments or a resume before trust can be gained. Systems of care leaders often ask families to trust them, so trust freely offered to the families first could change the dynamics of a relationship. Recent system history shows multiple levels at which systems and agencies are distrustful, often having to compete for limited resources. Perhaps there is a history of conflict and harsh words. Leaders can help system components move beyond past hurts and differences by attempting to engage in a trusting relationship, even before it has necessarily been earned. Of course, this doesn't mean being reckless. What it does mean is that in many circumstances there may be an opportunity to collaborate on an activity that is positive and mutually beneficial. An example of this can be found in the tremendously successful collaboration between the Founding Partners of National Children's Mental Health Awareness Day. Despite historical tensions between the Federation of Families for Children's Mental Health, the National Alliance for Mental Illness, and Mental Health America, these organizations teamed up to provide a unified voice to promote and advance the cause of children's mental health.

Coach and Teach as Well as Lead and Inspire

Leaders must do more than just lead and inspire, and the importance of their roles as coaches and teachers cannot be underestimated. Innovative leaders commit time to engage team members individually, giving support and guidance in personal ways.

Administrators and managers carry a significant burden to demonstrate compliance with funding and operational requirements. Meeting compliance requirements is not the same as providing leadership, but often the same person is expected to provide both. Thus, leaders are required to wear many hats. Leaders look to each interaction as an opportunity to teach and coach others, while also looking at each opportunity as a chance to learn and be coached.

Systems success is contingent upon personal contact by leaders. These leaders must seek creative ways to stimulate thinking among others. This may involve looking for the potential contribution from each group member and behaving in ways that reflect this potential. Consider an example from Joe Paterno, arguably the most successful college football coach in history. In his acceptance speech for the Distinguished American award, given by the Football Hall of Fame, he said, "What are coaches? Number one, we are teachers and we are educators." In essence, being a leader both on and off the football field means being a teacher.

Even though most leaders understand that coaching and teaching are important, the temptation to focus on being an inspirational figure is often too compelling to pass up. Successful leaders know that they must make time for those they work with and be available to coach and teach. This approach requires a closer connection and increased expectations both for the leader and the person being coached.

The importance of this leadership quality was brought to the attention of one of the authors in a very personal way. Early in his career he had the opportunity to become the clinical director at a private, nonprofit agency. This meant moving from a full-time staff psychologist to a position where program oversight and supervision of other clinical staff would be expected. As part of his departure from the first agency, the executive director asked for an "exit interview." Amidst the typical chit-chat and questions, the executive director offered two pieces of advice that continue to have merit. The first was that a good leader offers people consistency. As he put it, "One should not get too high in the good times and too low in the bad times." Leadership is helping people maintain balance. The second piece of advice was that when it comes to your staff, no matter what level they are at (at the beginning of their careers or more experienced than you), it is your responsibility to help them grow and develop. The point of this story, beyond the obvious good information, is that this executive director took the time to mentor, coach, and teach in a way that was specific and meaningful, and this brief interaction provided guidance that has lasted for nearly 20 years.

Connect Instead of Create

People tend to want to "leave their mark" by creating something. Perhaps it is a program, or a policy, or a building. While this is admirable, successful leaders also talk about building connections and creating alliances. With this perspective, leadership is about cultivating relationships. It is also about reflecting the multiple contributions that are necessary to effect change. Although sometimes considered a discrete program, systems of care done properly serve to connect mental health and other child-serving systems. The idea is less about creating a program and more about developing relationships. One of the authors of this chapter is often heard talking about the importance of "giving mental health away." This means that mental health must connect with juvenile justice, child welfare, substance abuse, education, and primary care in ways meaningful to those systems. It is ultimately through such connections that creation can occur. In essence, building functional relationships and creating effective care and success within each system depends on connections with other systems. Connections and alignment become more important than ownership, and this provides the benefit to children, youth, and families.

Give up Some Control

Loosen the grip. Strive for balance between compliance and autonomy. Many leaders today grew up in a system that rewarded those who asserted control, which is in direct opposition to the values of certain cultures. Mental health is moving from an era of take-control management to participatory decision making.

One of the authors facilitated a weekend retreat and decided to let the group determine the agenda and activities. One of the participants arrived and panicked when there was no set agenda: "What are we going to do? When will we eat? Who will do the cooking?" On a whiteboard, everyone wrote what they wanted to do within the 4 days. The leader decided to give up control of exactly when and how something would happen to "allow" it to happen. The participants ended up taking leadership and real ownership of the weekend, and what was created was far beyond what one could have planned alone.

Another example is the development of the national youth organization called Youth MOVE (Youth Motivating Others through Voices of Experience). This organization has grown and evolved over the past several years and is becoming an authentic voice for youth who have had a history and experience with mental health and other child-serving systems. In the initial stages of organizational development, one of the authors of this chapter exerted considerable influence and control. He had the goal and the funding and provided more than his fair share of direction. Over time, however, he had to learn to relinquish some control as the young people demonstrated their own creativity and innovation. Today they continue to forge an effective partnership, and the youth of Youth MOVE continue to take on more responsibility and exert more control (with, of course, support from the adult mentor!).

Challenge Conventional Wisdom

There was a time when a popular bumper sticker said "Question Authority." Effective leaders have to challenge conventional thinking while preserving culture and vision. Leaders must be open to challenging their own individual wisdom and accepted group wisdom such as myths and ideas a group accepts without thought.

It is often said that a healthy organization is a learning organization. Is it possible that this is not true? How would we know? We can only prove that it is true by studying it, which proves the underlying premise.

When one challenges conventional wisdom there are risks, and people have to act in ways that reflect their comfort level with risk. The authors do not advocate for readers to act out; rather, it is hoped that readers will think differently. Leaders should encourage group members to think, speak, and continue to learn, as new circumstances will always demand new solutions. Instead of putting color on a white piece of paper and calling it culturally diverse, representative, and inclusive, change the color of the paper! Emerging leaders are invited to take a look at their acquired wisdom and question the sources and its current validity, invite others to challenge their wisdom, and help the groups they are affiliated with challenge their accepted wisdom.

These 10 innovative leadership strategies are not really strategies at all. They are simply challenges to established modes of thinking that limit a leader's ability to adapt and respond effectively. Leadership means hearing the diverse views of stakeholders and recognizing that answers can come from unexpected sources. This ability to think and listen should also be fostered in others. In the final analysis, this chapter is NOT advising readers to think outside the box. This chapter challenges the reader to realize that the boxes are not real!

REFERENCES

Adaptation. (2009). In *Merriam-Webster OnLine*. Retrieved October 27, 2009, from http://www.merriam-webster.com/dictionary/innovation.

Anthony, W.A., & Huckshorn, K.A. (2008). *Principled leadership in mental health systems and programs*. Boston: Center for Psychiatric Rehabilitation.

Blau, G., Caldwell, B., Fisher, S., Kuppinger, A., Levison-Johnson, J., & Lieberman R. (in press). The Building Bridges Initiative: Residential and community-based providers, families and youth coming together to improve outcomes. *Child Welfare*.

Dotlich, D.L., & Cairo, P.C. (2004). *Unnatural leadership: Going against intuition and experience to develop ten new leadership instincts*. San Francisco: Jossey-Bass.

Hackman, J.R., & Wageman, R. (2007). Asking the right questions about leadership. *American Psychologist, 63*(2), 43–47.

Innovation. (2009). In *Merriam-Webster OnLine*. Retrieved October 27, 2009, from http://www.merriam-webster.com/dictionary/innovation.

Kaiser, R.B., Hogan, R., & Craig, S.B. (2008). Leadership and the fate of organizations. *American Psychologist, 63*(2), 96–110.

Quinn, R.E. (1996). *Deep change: Discovering the leader within*. San Francisco: Jossey-Bass.

Sternberg, R.J. (2003). *Wisdom, intelligence, and creativity synthesized*. New York: Cambridge University Press.

Sternberg, R.J. (2007). A system model of leadership. *American Psychologist 63*(2), 34–42.

Stroul, B.A., & G.M. Blau (Vol. Eds.). (2008). *Systems of care for children's mental health. The system of care handbook: Transforming mental health services for children, youth, and families*. Baltimore: Paul H. Brookes Publishing Co.

Zander, B., & Zander, R.S. (2000). *The art of possibility: Transforming professional and personal life*. New York: Penguin.

IV

Aspiration, Inspiration, and Survival

8

Understanding and Overcoming Pitfalls

JAMES R. WOTRING AND SANDRA A. SPENCER

Leaders will encounter many different pitfalls when developing and implementing systems of care. How a leader predicts or deals with obstacles determines whether he or she can strategically maneuver through or around them. Some common pitfalls a leader may experience while developing systems of care are discussed in this chapter. A leader may commonly encounter three primary types of pitfalls: personal, organizational, and environmental.

Leaders may encounter personal pitfalls as they react to personal challenges faced while leading change, as they interact with others and express their leadership style. Organizational pitfalls may emerge from the nature or culture of organizations, especially when working in partnership with multiple organizations/systems, and they affect how a leader handles changes. Lastly, environmental pitfalls are challenges generally beyond the control of the leader or organization. Environmental pitfalls can come in the form of statewide budget cuts, the death of a client, or a lawsuit.

The authors suggest strategies for overcoming some common pitfalls and provide examples to add clarity, while recognizing that other chapters in this book offer leadership strategies that can overcome pitfalls. Many pitfalls can be anticipated and overcome in part by laying groundwork before they appear. Unfortunately, some pitfalls develop into problems to be worked through or circumnavigated.

Successful leaders know that pitfalls will appear and can use the system of care infrastructure to address them. The eight pitfalls described in this chapter are as follows. *Personal pitfalls:* 1) being a beacon of loss, 2) becoming a martyr, 3) using dictatorship instead of collaborative leadership, 4) and confusing passion with leadership; *organizational pitfalls:* 5) not understanding organizational culture, 6) confusing technical challenges with adaptive challenges, 7) and experiencing changes in leadership; and an *environmental pitfall:* 8) enduring economic changes.

Leadership is like navigating, rather than steering, a boat. Almost anyone can steer a boat in a given direction if he or she has some basic understanding of driving. Navigation is much different. While navigating a boat, the destination point has to be determined in advance and a course charted to ensure that the boat arrives at its destination. This involves mapping out the coordinates of the boat's starting point, planned stops along the way, and the boat's final destination. It requires determining the direction the boat will be heading, the speed the boat will be running, guiding the boat around obstacles, monitoring the depth of the water to make sure the boat does not run aground, monitoring the weather and wind, and taking the current into consideration, all while watching out for other boats. Even with a precise course charted, the captain will have to make midcourse adjustments, sometimes charting a whole new direction because of unforeseen circumstances.

Leadership requires similar actions. Certain pitfalls will show themselves and can be circumnavigated. Others will be less obvious and require different, more drastic actions to reach a final destination. The eight strategies for overcoming pitfalls described in this chapter are examples drawn from the authors' experience in developing systems of care: 1) separating self from role, 2) creating distance to gain perspective, 3) using collaborative leadership, 4) applying technical solutions to technical challenges and adaptive solutions to adaptive challenges, 5) being willing to compromise, 6) employing continuous self-reflection, 7) pacing the work through communication, and 8) building partnerships.

EXAMPLES OF COMMON PITFALLS IN LEADERSHIP

The examples that follow are some common pitfalls a leader may experience when developing systems of care. However, these are only a few of the many pitfalls a leader will experience as he or she leads a change initiative.

Personal Pitfalls

1. *Being a beacon of loss:* A leader stands out like a beacon of loss (Heifetz, 1994). As a leader moves an organization or multiple organizations in new directions, other initiatives may be left behind or become less of a priority for one or more of those organizations. Individuals who are committed to the prior efforts will experience a loss, sometimes resulting in individuals blocking or attempting to block the new direction. Some individuals may take this loss personally and attempt to make it a personal matter for the leader. Leaders need to be prepared for these challenges, to listen and talk with the

individuals who are experiencing this loss, and not take it personally. When a leader experiences criticism from within her own organization or from partner systems, she needs to remember the difference between one's self and one's role. (Heifetz, 1994). Leaders must remember that people will respond to the role they play and the perspectives they represent. Leaders must interpret the responses from these individuals in relation to the leadership role to gain a deeper understanding of different perspectives.

2. *Becoming a martyr:* Leaders will experience setbacks as they work to move an initiative forward. Forces much stronger than an individual, or even a team of individuals, can stop an initiative in its tracks (Heifetz, 1994). When this occurs, a leader may be tempted to become a martyr or "fall on his sword" in sacrifice for the mission, thinking if he makes a dramatic show he will be able to counter the forces attempting to end the effort. This usually does not result in moving the issue or initiative forward; it is likely to bring a quicker end. Jumping off the boat or shutting down the engine will not help it reach its destination.

3. *Using dictatorship instead of collaborative leadership:* One of the easiest personal pitfalls to avoid is taking a top-down approach rather than a collaborative approach. Building systems of care requires collaboration across systems and within systems, both vertically and horizontally, as well as with non-system partners, such as families and community leaders. Taking a top-down approach will meet with certain failure. It is hard to determine why so many leaders still take a top-down approach to leadership. This traditional form of leadership is often perceived to be the easiest to implement, but it yields the least favorable results. Top-down leadership resembles a dictatorship, where the person with the power makes all of the decisions and others simply follow the rules. Sometimes leaders have to use this approach, such as on a battlefield, but for most human service organizations a more participatory approach is recommended (Finzel, 1994). If a leader is using a top-down approach, she may be confusing leadership with management. A manager has subordinates and a leader has followers. Although both are positions of authority, a manager gets people to act because it is her job to do so, whereas people follow a leader because they want to follow her.

4. *Confusing passion with leadership:* Another common personal pitfall is confusing passion with leadership. This pitfall is common in systems of care, as family and youth leaders work to improve services in their community. Family members and youth are often very passionate about improving services and supports for children, youth, and their families. This commitment is visible when families and youth advocate for themselves and their families, share their stories, and offer suggestions to improve services and supports. The advocate, and his voice, may be well known on these issues, and he may

often be called upon to serve on collaborative committees and boards. The assumption made is that if he is passionate enough to make people listen to him, he must be a good leader. These family and youth are then put in positions of leading family and youth organizations, where they are expected to be managers, entrepreneurs, and great business leaders.

Passion coming from life experience can resemble leadership because people listen and sometimes follow. Passion reflects strong feelings and sometimes serves as a driving force for a leader. However, leadership is much more complicated than simply being passionate about something. Leadership involves building relationships, modeling the way and enlisting, enabling, and strengthening others to act (Kouzes & Posner, 2007). Passion and leadership are much different; passion alone cannot sustain a leadership position.

Passion drives people to become advocates for their causes. Advocates speak up and become the "voice" for what they believe. Families and youth generally do not want to give up their role in being the "voice" of change, but the community often expects them to lead the efforts and raise up others to carry the "voice." Leaders need an overarching view and must have the ability to create distance to gain perspective (Heifetz, 1994). Gaining distance, or getting on the balcony, does not mean one has to lose passion; he or she just has to get a clear perspective. One can have passion without being a leader, but it is more difficult to be a leader in this work without passion. The best family, youth, and community leaders have both.

Organizational Pitfalls

5. *Not understanding organizational culture:* A leader may fall into a common pitfall by not taking the time to understand the culture of the organization or of its partnering organizations, by not understanding the way things are done and why they are done that way in an organization. Sometimes organizational culture is described as the unspoken rules of the organization (Finzel, 1994). These rules are the principles and values that drive the organization, and the leader must know them, know why they are important, and understand the ramification of not following them or changing them. *Merriam-Webster's Collegiate Dictionary* (1996) defines *culture* as "the integrated pattern of knowledge, belief, and behavior . . . the customary beliefs, social norms, and material traits of a racial, religious, or social group."[1] Every organization has its own unique culture. A leader who misses or misreads the cultural clues will have limited success in helping lead that organization in new directions.

6. *Confusing technical challenges with adaptive challenges:* Leading finance work in systems of care requires a leader to have or acquire technical skills and use adaptive skills to align everyone's values before the technical work of

---

[1]By permission. From *Merriam-Webster's Collegiate Dictionary* © 1996 by Merriam-Webster, Incorporated (www.Merriam-Webster.com).

blending or braiding funding begins (see also Chapter 5). For example, a leader must have some understanding of multiple federal funding (e.g., Medicaid, Title IV) rules and laws to successfully lead an effort to blend or braid funding across systems. A leader must also be aware of the underlying adaptive work that has to be done when working in the area of finance. As defined by Heifetz (1994), the adaptive challenge consists of a gap between the shared values people hold and the reality of their lives, or a conflict among people over values or strategy.

When working in the area of finance, one may experience an adaptive challenge described as a technical problem. For example, someone may say something can or cannot be done with Medicaid and everyone accepts that as a technical problem that cannot be overcome, or they fail to look into what may be the underlying adaptive issues. One or more of the individuals charged with blending or braiding funding may not want to blend or braid funding, allowing the situation to be defined as a technical problem, when in fact it is an underlying adaptive challenge.

Understanding major funding rules and laws is technical knowledge a leader will need if working in the area of finance to find ways around or through technical barriers. The leader must also listen for the adaptive challenge that may or may not be underlying the described technical problem. Such adaptive challenges may come up when one system or organization loses resources, such as when funding is redirected from residential care to community-based services, or when funding is reallocated and combined into one system. These are real losses to an organization or system and require creativity and adaptation.

7. *Experiencing changes in leadership:* Some pitfalls can be expected and prepared for. When a new leader comes into an existing organization, there are pitfalls that can be expected. It is especially challenging when an organization transitions from a founding leader of an organization to the next leader, even more so if the former leader left on good terms and was viewed as a successful leader. A new leader must know that many of the staff will be committed to the former leader and the way that leader operated. One pitfall to expect is that some staff may leave the organization because they cannot accept the change in leadership. The new leader needs to see this as a developmentally important process and not take it as a personal attack. Another pitfall to expect is that the staff may view any changes and new directions from the new leader as criticism of the former leader, even though this may not be the case. As a new leader in an existing organization, it is important to learn its history and cultural values and to build relationships within the organization before making too many major changes.

Another area of leadership change that one must prepare for is being promoted to leader from within the organization and going from co-worker and peer to boss. Such a new leader must deliberately change relationships with co-workers in a thoughtful way, managing those relationships and making changes before problems arise. For example, as a co-worker, one may share work challenges and process conflicts with a friend at work. Once promoted to leader, these conversations must end, and it is up to the leader to facilitate the change in these relationships. These pitfalls can be expected during leadership changes, and a leader can be prepared to handle them and help others within the organization deal with the changes as well.

Environmental Pitfall

8. *Enduring economic changes:* Systems and organizations are constantly changing, perhaps from social changes, legislative changes, changes in political leadership, the death of a client, or economic changes in a state or community. Environmental influences often come from outside the organization and result in one or more organizations having to develop a response to these external influences. New services may have to be developed and implemented in response to legislation. Often the recommendations of a commission provide a strong enough external influence to require changes in a system or organization. Budget cuts or merging of departments or divisions within departments are common responses to economic changes in the environment. How a leader responds to these environmental pitfalls will vary depending on the external influence.

STRATEGIES FOR OVERCOMING PITFALLS

1. *Separating self from role:* Leaders need to be prepared to hear criticism and not take it personally. A good mental exercise for a leader to use when receiving criticism is to separate himself from the role and tasks at hand. This is not easy to do, because most leaders are very passionate about what they are trying to accomplish. However, it can provide some space and allow a leader not to take the action of others personally. It can provide the leader with just enough distance to look objectively at what he is trying to accomplish and get a fresh look at where he is going. Distinguishing self from role does not mean giving up emotions or passion for a goal and simply acting as if playing a role. Distinguishing self from role enables leaders not to take things personally and be misled by emotions. This provides leaders with the distance needed to objectively understand the issues that are being presented or discussed. Distinguishing self from role allows one to focus attention on the issues and not on the individuals involved (Heifetz, 1994).

2. *Creating distance to gain perspective:* Keeping perspective or gaining a new perspective about a change process requires a leader to occasionally stand back from her day-to-day activities and get a fresh look at what she is trying

to accomplish. It allows a leader time to back away from the day-to-day challenges or conflicts in the environment and reflect. It allows a leader to look for new directions or try new strategies, even if it is going to result in having to take a whole new direction that will require more time. A new perspective may require finding more or new partners from outside an organization, such as advocates to help increase the sense of urgency and need for change. It may require additional support from a boss or colleagues to combat a force that is threatening to end or stall an initiative. Heifetz (1994) referred to this as "getting on the balcony." Others refer to it as getting out of the bushes or climbing a ladder (Covey, 1990). Regardless, it calls for creating distance to gain perspective.

3. *Using collaborative leadership:* A leader in systems of care must practice collaborative leadership. A collaborative leader offers the team the opportunity to give input before moving to a new course of action. A collaborative leader sees himself as a "facilitator" of the collaborative process. A collaborative leader can lead the charge but must also empower the team to lead the process. This means that a collaborative leader is willing to share information, power, and decision-making authority and involve partners in creating the plan. Building strong interpersonal relationships is a critical skill that a leader must master and use to bring other individuals along in a new direction. A leader is only as powerful as the group being led. If no one is following, then a leader is not leading. Individuals must want to follow a leader. There is a great leadership proverb: "If you think you're leading and no one is following you, then you're only taking a walk" (Maxwell, 1999, p. 5). Leaders must look ahead, back, and beside themselves as they are moving systems of care forward. A collaborative leadership approach is more likely to draw followers. People tend to follow a plan when they were involved in creating the plan, and they will be more invested in making sure the plan succeeds.

4. *Applying technical solutions to technical challenges and adaptive solutions to adaptive challenges:* Agreeing on a shared vision is critical to the success of any interagency initiative. When all of the partners can agree to a common vision, mission, goals, and outcomes, they can move forward together. Building a common vision helps align the values that different systems, organizations, and individuals bring to an interagency initiative. Aligning the values of these systems, organizations, and individuals is the adaptive challenge collaborative leaders face (Heifetz, 1994). The technical work of a collaborative initiative may include completing a study of the different laws or rules that influence certain policies or the various funding sources a group wants to use to serve the population of focus. A technical challenge may be gaining a deeper understanding of how certain funding sources are aligned

to affect a particular population and identifying how those funds can be moved from out-of-home care to support community-based care. Another technical challenge may be completing a finance matrix to study the various funding sources.

In the previous examples, the adaptive leadership work is aligning the values of the group and gaining consensus to support intensive community-based services instead of more restrictive care, such as residential care or hospitalization. The technical work requires individuals with special skills or practical knowledge in identifying the various rules or laws influencing the funding sources to determine if the funds can be shifted from restrictive care to community-based care and to determine the amount of funding available from each funding source. Strategies can be used to help minimize loss, such as helping a residential provider learn to provide intensive community-based services rather than residential care and entering into agreements that these organizations will be given the opportunity to bid on community-based contracts. Because of the concern of losing resources or control of certain funding streams, a leader must know when to use adaptive skills to make sure the values are aligned and when to use technical skills to accomplish a certain task. Even when stakeholders know they should work together to better serve a population of focus, technical pitfalls will arise and agreement on the common vision, mission, and values is critical to address the adaptive challenge. Understanding the difference between the adaptive and technical differences is critical (see also Chapter 5).

5. *Being willing to compromise:* In collaborative leadership, an individual leader will never achieve everything she sets out to achieve because a leader must be willing to compromise. This does not mean compromising personal values or principles, but it may require letting a few things go or delaying completion of some tasks to get an initiative started.

    To illustrate, a leader (one of the authors) in a particular collaborative effort had three primary system partners—mental health, child welfare, and juvenile justice—and the leaders of those system were all committed to a common set of goals and outcomes. The goals were to maximize federal revenue, blend/braid funding to expand community-based services, and reduce the need for hospitalization and residential care with Medicaid as a key funding source. Two systems were initially able to blend and braid funding— juvenile justice and mental health. Having two of the three systems ready to blend/braid funding allowed for the development of a 1915(c) waiver. The child welfare system was not able to initially participate because of funding cuts. Leaders will not always get perfect alignment of all of the system partners and will sometimes have to compromise to move forward. In this illustration, the leader had a chance to move forward and build momentum with two of the three systems or wait until all of the systems were aligned. The leader chose to move forward with two systems, which allowed the initiative to continue to build momentum and bring along the third system, child welfare, when its alignment was better.

6. *Employing continuous self-reflection:* A leader must be aware of self and continually evaluate what he is trying to accomplish. A leader must use self-reflection as a critical tool to both monitor what he is doing and feeling and monitor others to determine if they are moving forward with the initiative. The pressures of leadership are significant. A leader signifies loss as well as progress, change as well as stability. A leader must always look within and make any personal changes needed to continue to lead the team. This may require seeking feedback from individuals on the team or others outside of the team who are being influenced by the team. Since leadership involves trial and error, a leader has to listen to input after something has been tried, reflect upon it, and make adjustments to minimize errors the second time.

   Listening to self and others is a critical skill leaders must exercise when leading an initiative. Reflecting upon self does not mean a leader has to do it alone. Leaders need coaches to help them reflect upon their behavior. A good friend or boss can help one see blind spots as well as strengths. It is similar to how a good therapist works with a client. Coaches, consultants, and good supervision can provide space for an individual to debrief and talk openly about what has occurred, reflect upon his behavior, learn, and move forward.

7. *Pacing the work and communication:* Pacing the work of change requires a leader to check in with the team and individuals in the organizations who are being affected by the change. Organizations and individuals can experience significant stress during efforts to change. Stress can come from the uncertainty of a new effort. There is a lot of trial and error in new initiatives, and individuals need to feel safe to make mistakes that are inherent in trying anything new. Stress can come from leaving the old and familiar behind or from the addition of new work while still doing much of the old work. Pacing the work gives individuals time to adapt to the new and make needed midcourse corrections. Pacing the work also allows individuals time to let go of the old and adapt to the new.

   A leader may be seen as a threat to others as she moves an organization or multiple organizations in new directions. Communication is key to any change initiative regardless of whether the change is planned within an organization or in response to influences outside of an organization. A leader has to be willing to communicate as much information as possible and be willing to dig in and help out in any way necessary to support those being affected by the change. Predicting and communicating about the change helps individuals adapt to the new situation. Budget cuts can often be anticipated, and communicating details on such developments well in advance helps soften the shock individuals may experience from the actions related to the budget cuts, such as layoffs or cutting of programs. Involving individuals in the decision making also helps them feel some control over a situation in which they may have little control. Teams can also help as an organization strategizes new actions it can take to adapt to new realities.

8. *Building partnerships:* Building systems of care requires a leader to work across multiple systems and with numerous partners to achieve a common goal or mission. In doing the collaborative work of system building, one has to engage in broad participatory planning and work with diverse groups of individuals and ensure that everyone is committed to the common vision. Sometimes this may include individuals and organizations very different than the "typical" collaborative partner. The following story is an example of building a partnership between two very different organizations. The story also highlights several of the other pitfalls and strategies covered in this chapter.

   The National Federation of Families for Children's Mental Health (NFFCMH), a family-run organization that focuses on offering support, education, and training to families raising children with mental health challenges, and the International Association of Chiefs of Police (IACP) needed to work together to improve the outcomes of police interaction with youth in a mental health crisis. The IACP organization appeared to be rigid, whereas the NFFCMH viewed itself as a very family friendly and flexible organization that allows family members to feel comfortable and supported in the process of working with police officers. The leadership structure of the NFFCMH was very different from that of the IACP. The IACP was a very top-down, hierarchical organization. Policies and procedures were strictly followed and obeying orders was critical. Everyone addressed each other with formal titles (e.g., Sergeant Walker, Chief Smith, Officer Dan). As a very family-oriented organization, the NFFCMH used a more collaborative type of leadership, with everyone on a first-name basis. Team building and collaboration are important values to the family organization.

   A meeting was convened between the NFFCMH and the IACP to address the very serious issue of negative outcomes for young people in mental health crisis when police get involved. Some families became very angry and did not trust police officers. Other families reported they have watched their children be hurt, traumatized, or even killed by police officers whom they called on to help. Families have viewed police officers as lacking sympathy or understanding for the needs of their children. Police officers, on the other hand, thought that these were bad parents who did not teach and discipline their children when they were young, because if they had there would be no need for police involvement.

In the process of their work, the leaders of both organizations began to realize how much they had in common. Both the NFFCMH and the IACP honored at their national conferences those whom they lost each year. The police organization honored fallen police officers, and the family organization honored those lost by suicide or died as a result of their mental health disorder. The two ceremonies were very much alike. A joint summit of the two organizations, along with other supportive national organizations, held a shared ceremony honoring the lost of both organizations.

The NFFCMH and the IACP found common ground in the area of stigma and negative press. The police revealed that because the media only reported when a police interaction goes wrong, or on the wrongdoing of a few bad police officers, the public does not trust the police, and this puts officers at greater risk of losing their own lives or having to use deadly force more often. The families talked about the negative way the media portray people with mental health issues and how stigma keeps people with mental health issues from seeking help. In the process of building their partnership, the two groups began to find common ground. They wanted the same results or outcomes for their constituencies' safety. A mom said, "I just want my family to be safe and for my son to make it home after he has had an intervention with police." The police officer said, "My wife and kids want me to come home safe each night." This opened the door for the two groups to create a set of values, principles, and outcomes they could agree on, and thus work began to improve the outcomes of police responding to youth in mental health crisis. Finding common ground around values and outcomes proved to be the best way to build the partnership between two contrasting organizations.

SUMMARY

Leadership is about taking chances and being innovative. A leader tries new and different things and, as a result, is constantly running into pitfalls, most of which can be navigated around or through. A leader may experience personal, organizational, and environmental pitfalls. Regardless of the specific pitfall, a leader is constantly solving problems and helping align the values and vision of others. This chapter has described a few of the many pitfalls a leader may experience when developing systems of care. The strategies and stories are simply illustrations to help the reader gain a deeper understanding of some of the pitfalls he or she will experience. There are probably a thousand times as many pitfalls as have been described here and thousands of different strategies a leader could use to overcome or avoid them. The one mistake a leader cannot make is to stop trying new and innovative strategies and stop learning as he or she implements those new strategies. When a leader stops learning and taking chances, he or she is no longer leading; navigating through and around pitfalls is part of leading.

REFERENCES

Covey, S.R. (1990). *The 7 habits of highly effective people.* New York: Simon & Schuster.

Culture. (1996). *Merriam-Webster's Collegiate Dictionary.* (10th ed.). Mish, F.C. (Ed.). Springfield, MA: Merriam-Webster.

Finzel, H. (1994). *The top ten mistakes leaders make.* Colorado Springs, CO: Cook Communications.

Heifetz, R.A. (1994). *Leadership without easy answers.* Cambridge: The Belknap Press of Harvard University Press.

Kouzes, J.M., & Posner, V.Z. (2007). *The leadership challenge* (4th ed.). San Francisco: Jossey-Bass.

Maxwell, J.C. (1999). *The 21 indispensable qualities of a leader: Becoming the person others want to follow.* Nashville, TN: Thomas Nelson.

9

Resilience for Leaders in Times of Change

VIVIAN HOPKINS JACKSON AND W. HENRY GREGORY, JR.

L eading in times of change and challenge requires vigilance, insight, and, often, extraordinary actions and measures. Success is never assured, and the leader may come face-to-face with his or her fears of incompetence and defeat. Managing the associated stress of such challenges is necessary to every leader's continued effectiveness and personal survival. Those who lead systems change and transformation efforts, as is the task in building systems of care, are particularly susceptible to the assaults on self-esteem. This work requires both change in the structures and processes of service provision and change in the philosophical and attitudinal approach to service delivery. Although the stimulus for change may come from within the mental health system in which the leader may have some formal authority, the changes must also come within other child-serving systems, within which he or she has no formal authority. Surely this is a daunting task that tests the resilience of the leader at every turn.

In Chapter 8, readers were introduced to a variety of personal, organizational, and environmental pitfalls, as well as a variety of strategies to address those pitfalls. Clearly, not all leaders will recognize these pitfalls or employ these strategies all of the time. Even when employed, these strategies will not always yield the desired outcomes. Successful implementation may even trigger new sets of unforeseen challenges. It is in those moments of stress, when the leader feels like failure is imminent, that the very personal dimensions of resilience are most critical. The health and well-being of the leader and successful movement of the transformation agenda require resilience.

Resilience—the process of self-righting, or the capacity to withstand hardship, bounce back, and move forward—provides a viable framework to address this stress. This chapter 1) describes key concepts related to resilience, 2) presents protective factors that ameliorate stress, and 3) suggests strategies that promote leadership resilience and foster protective factors.

RESILIENCE

A True Person is more calm and deliberate. He or she doesn't worry about interruptions.
—Rumi (Barks, 1995)

Resilience is the ability to rebound from adversity, strengthened by the experience. It refers to manifest competence in the context of significant challenges to adaptation or development (Masten & Coatworth, 1998). Resilience entails more than merely surviving, getting through, or escaping a harrowing ordeal (Walsh, 1998). Survivors are not necessarily resilient; some become trapped in a position as victims, nursing their wounds and blocked from growth by anger and blame (Wolin & Wolin, 1993). Resilient people learn from their experiences and heal from painful wounds. They take charge of their lives, living fully and loving well. Resilient people build on their experience of adversity and become stronger, more effective people. Leaders who are resilient people are better able to thrive in the chaotic environment of systems change and promote resilience in those with whom they work.

ADVERSITY

Life is a moving target and as such it challenges a leader to handle a variety of stressors through varying levels of consciousness (his or hers and others), including feeling out of control, feeling directionless, feeling inadequate, facing more commitments than time available, experiencing uncertainty, and maintaining high expectations of self and responding to change, especially changes that are not self-initiated. Adversity can be experienced as a sense of loss of the familiar, the comfortable, the desirable, or the necessary. These kinds of adversity create negative stress (or distress) for the leader. When any type of stress escalates to the point that it compromises the ability to manage emotions and make good decisions, it can set off chain reactions that further exacerbate one's ability to feel competent and successful in the leadership role.

Leadership is a risky business that requires courage and tenacity to face the personal threats to one's self-image and public persona in formal and informal positions of leadership. Distress is created by conscious and unconscious fears of loss, including loss of confidence, credibility, relationships, political capital, self-worth and self-esteem, and status. Although all stress is not bad, a leader's functioning is diminished when overwhelmed. For example, changes in partnerships, funding, staff, or the political landscape all bring stress, whether the changes are perceived to be positive or not. Even pleasant changes, such as succeeding in getting a grant, discovering budget surpluses, or finally getting the 501(c)(3) status, challenge the ability to cope.

Stress occurs when the demands of a situation or event are perceived to outweigh a person's ability to cope with or handle the situation. In essence, it seems that a leader's perception of the events occurring in his or her life determines whether and to what degree the events are perceived as adversity. The meaning attributed to the situation affects the intensity and potency of the experience and consequently the response to it.

Adversity—threats to homeostasis and stability in structure, relationships, performance, and process—may be categorized as fundamental, developmental, or hazardous (Wolin & Wolin, 1993). *Fundamental adversity* in business or organization includes those routine activities that demand cognitive and emotional resources. These would include such tasks as ensuring sufficient budget, space, transportation, and technology to perform the work. *Developmental adversity* may include the changes in management, staff, contracts, or even seasons that are generally expected to occur over time yet require an accommodating shift. *Hazardous adversity* is represented by the unexpected, unanticipated events that disrupt the normal and expected functioning of people's lives, programs, or organizations. Hazardous adversity may include events with life-threatening implications, such as incarcerations, the death of a client, or termination of contracts or employment. At the organizational level, hazardous adversity arises when governments shut down or agencies are closed due to state budget problems. To some extent, adversity is a personal matter, determined by the perceptions and preferences of the leader. Adversity is not a product of the situation itself—it is a byproduct, determined by thoughts and feelings in response to a challenge. Ultimately it is the mental model (see Chapter 4), or mind-set, that determines whether an event is threatening to us.

Adversity is a way that life gets one's attention. Adversity challenges the person to reevaluate efforts and reprioritize, for effectiveness's sake. When there is comfort and things are going well, there is less inclination toward in-depth analysis and assessment. Efforts to be comfortable compete with efforts to grow. Much behavior supports efforts to control and predict life's events and circumstance. Adversity threatens these efforts by pushing circumstance into the realm of the uncontrollable. Control itself is an illusion, but one that is held dear. Adversity confronts leaders with the reality that they have no real control. It forces leaders to play unfamiliar games with new rules, thereby allowing for opportunities to experiment with new definitions and ways of being.

Adversity may facilitate positive psychological changes. It also provides the opportunity to learn new skills, discover new capacity, and experiment with new attitudes and perspectives. Adversities force people to come out of their comfort zones to address issues that they may not otherwise address.

Resilience Theory: Review of the Literature

Resilience theory and inquiry have proceeded through three stages, or waves (Richardson, 2002). Each of these stages—personal qualities, relationships and context, and metaphysical and spiritual—offers perspectives on ways to promote resilience. Leaders should consider these perspectives as they apply to their understanding of self, of colleagues and workforce, and of the community and families of service. The stages reflect the shifts in the study and conceptualization of resilience that initially employed a reductionist, problem-oriented approach, then moved to a nurturing, strengths-based approach, more recently moving to a postmodern, "spiritual" approach to the understanding of responses to personal dilemmas.

Resilience Theory: Personal Qualities

Much of the early work on resilience arose as investigators who were studying risk realized that there were children flourishing in the midst of adversity (Anthony, 1974; Garmezy, 1974; Murphy & Moriarty, 1976; Rutter, 1979; Werner & Smith, 1982). These investigators recognized that such children could teach better ways to reduce risk, promote competence, and shift the course of development in more positive directions. Such studies countered the predominant view that familial and environmental risk factors and negative life events inevitably produce childhood and later adult disorders. For instance, most survivors of childhood abuse do not go on to become abusers (Kaufman & Zigler, 1987). Similarly, according to Rutter (1985), no combination of risk factors, regardless of severity, gave rise to significant disorder in more than half of the children exposed to such factors.

The next focus of study emerged in the 1980s, as a number of child development and mental health experts directed attention toward understanding protective factors (in contrast to risk factors) that fortify the resources of children and encourage their resilience (Dugan & Coles, 1989; Luthar & Zigler, 1991; Masten, Best, & Garmezy, 1990; Rutter, 1985, 1987). Most of these inquiries sought to understand how children of parents with mental illness or from dysfunctional families are able to overcome early experiences of abuse or neglect to lead productive lives (Cohler, 1987; Garmezy, 1987). The key resilience factors included personality disposition, a supportive family environment, and an external support system. Similarly, a concept of *hardiness* grew out of another line of research on stress and coping (Murphy & Moriarty, 1976). Kobasa and her colleagues (Kobasa, Maddi, & Kahn, 1982) proposed that people who experience high degrees of stress without becoming ill have a personality structure characterized by hardiness.

Resilience has been studied in a wide variety of situations throughout the world, including war, living with parents who have severe mental illness, family violence, poverty, natural disasters, and in situations with many other risk factors and stressors (Garmezy, 1985; Haggerty, Sherrod, Garmezy, & Rutter, 1994; Luthar & Zigler, 1991; Masten, Best, & Garmezy, 1990; Rutter, 1990; Wright & Masten, 1997). Results of these studies are remarkably consistent in pointing to qualities of child and environment associated with competence and better psychosocial functioning, during and following adverse experiences. The features include attributes such as happiness, optimism, faith, self-determination, wisdom, excellence, creativity, morality, self-control, gratitude, forgiveness, dreams, and humility.

Reflecting Western culture's heroic myth of the rugged individual, most interest in resilience during that period focused on strengths found in individuals who have mastered adversity. These qualities have usually been viewed in terms of personality traits, temperament, disposition, and coping styles (Kobasa & Pucetti, 1983; Walsh, 1998) that enable a child or adult to overcome harrowing life experiences. Resilience from this perspective is seen as inborn, as if resilient people grew themselves up. They either had the "right stuff" all along (a biological hardiness) or acquired it by pulling themselves up by their bootstraps (survival of the fittest). This fosters the expectation that they must become self-reliant and survive through fierce independence. The unfortunate corollary to this ethos is a contemptible view of those who do not succeed as deficient, weak, and blameworthy when they cannot surmount their problems on their own (Walsh, 1998). It is the old "If I can do it, you can (and if you can't, then there must be something wrong with you)."

Many leaders believe that they should possess these characteristics, and some question themselves if they do not have the "right stuff." Indeed, it is helpful if a leader does have many of the qualities described in this section, but these qualities are not established just by a function of biology. As the next sections describes, these qualities can be fostered and developed through relational and spiritual processes.

Resilience Theory: Relational and Contextual Perspectives

The second wave of resilience inquiry was an attempt to answer the question, "How are resilient qualities acquired?" (Richardson, 2002). According to Cross (1998), there are two major worldviews: linear and relational. The linear view encourages the idea that a problem resides in the person, and the relational view sees a problem as a product of human interaction and the meaning assigned to it. A relational, rather than an individualistic or linear, mode of adaptation may be key to understanding resilience (Jordan, 1992; Miller, 1988; Surrey, 1985), particularly for many ethnic minorities whose worldviews are relationship oriented (Nichols, 1976). A relational perspective assumes the centrality of relationships in human development. Psychological growth is viewed as a process of differentiation and elaboration in relationships, rather than disengagement and separation from relationships (Surrey, 1985). It is the focus on the "we" in contrast to the "I." Relationships involve dimensions of reciprocity (Antonucci & Jackson, 1989; Rook, 1987), interdependence (Kelley et al., 1983), shared meaning (Duck, 1994), relationship awareness (Acitelli, 1992), and mutuality (Miller, 1988).

Mutuality suggests that resilience is a function of bidirectional movement of feelings, thoughts, and activity between people (Genero, 1998). It involves openness to influence, emotional availability, and a constantly changing pattern of responding to and affecting the other's state. Miller (1988) found that both members of a dyad experience an increased sense of vitality, by virtue of feeling connected to one another, and acquire an increased sense of self-worth and validation and desire more connection with others, beyond immediate interaction. These findings suggest that resilience may be the product of an adaptation process that is both interactive and reciprocal. If true, leadership actions that promote team processes not only lend themselves to the development of high-quality decisions but foster resilience within team members.

Resilience must be accompanied by an understanding of the environmental context in which adversity is experienced. Research on families notes that the combination of culture and community relationships shapes the process and determines the level of resilience of families (McCubbin, Futrell, Thompson, & Thompson, 1998). Gregory (2001) delineated several resilience processes that were applicable to African American families and expanded the understanding of relational resilience to include subtle aspects of relationships such as 1) expression of empathy, compassion, and forgiveness, 2) use of rituals, 3) the practice of remembering, 4) expression of gratitude and humility, and 5) dreams and clairvoyance.

Another thread of this contextual phase of resilience study is conveyed in positive psychology. Proponents of positive psychology (Seligman & Csikszentmihalyi, 2000; Vaillant, 2000; Taylor, 1989) promote the idea that adaptive and resilient behavior is indicative of positive mental health. Vaillant (2000) classified coping mechanisms or adaptive defenses that mitigate adversity into three categories: 1) social support, 2) conscious strategies that people intentionally use to make the best of a bad situation, and 3) involuntary mental mechanisms that distort our perception of internal and external reality to reduce subjective distress. Another perspective was offered by Flach (1988, 1997) and Richardson, Neiger, Jensen, and Kumpfer (1990), who suggested that resilience is the process of experiencing a disruption of equilibrium and reintegrating the experience to foster growth, knowledge, self-understanding, and increased resilient qualities.

This phase reinforces that resilience is not solely a function of individual, inborn characteristics. This phase promotes the role of relationships, social support, and perspectives on the disruptions of life to thrive and grow. The leader is encouraged to use relationships to reinforce the development of a life perspective that views all experiences as opportunities for growth and development. The next phase seeks to understand even better how it is that people make the choices to interpret life's challenges in a manner that supports that growth.

Resilience Theory: Metaphysical and Spiritual

After paying enough attention (always the key word) you begin to see that events form patterns; you see that they also hold lessons or messages or signs—the out world somehow is trying to communicate—and then you see that these outer events are actually symbols for inner events.
—Deepak Chopra (2000, p. 64)

A third wave of resilience theory says resilience requires energy to grow, and the source of the energy is a spiritual or innate resilience. (*Spirituality* is used to reference the human spirit or a person's relationship to a higher reality and not necessarily a religious orientation.) Further, it says that there is a force within everyone that drives them to seek higher manifestation of truth and reality, as well as altruism, wisdom, and harmony with a spiritual source of strength. "The energy or force that drives a person from survival to self-actualization may be called quanta, chi, spirit, prana, God, or resilience" (Richardson, 2002, p. 315). It is a capacity that everyone has, albeit sometimes dormant.

This perspective is derived from multiple disciplines, such as neuroimmunology, philosophy, physics, psychology, Eastern medicine, and neuroscience (Richardson, 2002). Using this perspective, the leader is encouraged to examine his or her experience of self in relationship to the Universe. This theory suggests that resilience is grounded in the nature of that relationship.

The motivational force/energy that some call resilience wills many toward growth, or the ability to actualize their potential. From this perspective, the purpose of adversity may be to get the leader's attention to attend to reality with a gradually elevating consciousness. Without adversity many would languish in the comfort of the status quo without approaching the essential life questions: Who am I? What is real? What is my purpose? Adversity provides the opportunity to reset a leader's priorities by continually bringing up these questions. The answers provide a compass to use as a guide in making decisions as to how to act in response to the adversity.

Reality is what we take to be true. What we take to be true is what we believe. What we believe is based upon our perceptions. What we perceive depends upon what we look for. What we look for depends upon what we think. What we think depends upon what we perceive. What we perceive determines what we believe. What we believe determines what we take to be true. What we take to be true is our reality.
—Gary Zukav (2001, p. 344)

The circular reasoning presented by Zukav (2001) highlights the role of perception as the basis for what people declare to be the "truth." What each person experiences is not external reality, as it is, but the meaning discerned from the person's interaction with that external reality (Walker, 2000). Therefore, the leader's label of an event or circumstance as a "problem" or an "opportunity" is a function of how that person has created meaning from the interaction with the events or circumstances.

Some physicists (e.g., Bohm, 1980; Herbert, 1985) in the past 20 years have said what mystics have said for millenniums—that the human experience is a part of and not separate from a larger ordered whole. It may follow that living in harmony with that larger whole would reduce stress and provide energy to adjust, accommodate, and adapt to change. Studies show that people who have positive (e.g., optimistic, hopeful, grateful) outlooks have high immune levels, and, conversely, those who perceive themselves as helpless, hopeless, and depressed have weaker immune systems, implying that our outlook influences health and the ability to bounce back physically, mentally, and emotionally (Richardson, 2002).

When making decisions, listen to what your head says; then listen to what your heart says. If they differ, follow your heart! Whenever you listen to your heart, you listen to that part of you that is most interested in your well-being.
—Anonymous

Resilient leadership requires an adherence to one's innate moral framework or a natural love of others, as well as openness to learning. It also requires intuitive abilities, as cognitive logic alone is frequently not enough to manage the challenges involved in leading people. To some extent, resilience is a choice to trust and tap into our innate nature, which is based in love (Richardson, 2002).

CONSTRUCTIVIST CHANGE: CHANGE YOUR MIND AND YOU CHANGE YOUR SITUATION

There are no victims. Everything is well ordered; things happen as they should. Random events are guided by a higher wisdom. Chaos is an illusion; there is total order to all events. Nothing happens without reason.
—Deepak Chopra (2000, p. 108)

Problems can be conceptualized as the result of the way one thinks about a situation, and solutions can be conceptualized as a product of changing one's perceptions of those situations. This section provides additional information in support of the idea that shifting perspective creates opportunities for new or unforeseen solutions. Leaders who can acknowledge their own perception of the situation are in a good position to experience resilience.

Constructivism refers to a family of theories about mind and mentation that 1) emphasizes the active and proactive nature of all perception, learning, and knowing; 2) acknowledges the structure and functional primacy of abstract (tacit) over concrete (explicit) processes in all experience; and 3) views learning, knowing, and memory as phenomena that reflect the ongoing attempts of systems to organize (and endlessly reorganize) their own patterns of action and experience. These patterns are related to changing and highly mediated engagements with their momentary worlds (Neimeyer, 1993). Each individual is, at least, co-constructor of the personal realities to which he or she responds. Leaders neither passively receive sensory experience nor mechanically process information. At the core of constructivist theory is a view of human beings as active agents who, individually and collectively, co-constitute the meaning of their experiential world (Neimeyer, 1993).

The constructivist understands that what is observed is always influenced by the observer. From this point of view there is no such thing as objectivity (Nobles, 1988). The knower always influences what is known, so consequently one is both subject and object of one's own personal knowing and aware of only a few of the processes that underlie one's efforts (Mahony, 1991). The knower always takes his or her investments and values into the process of knowing. Kuhn (1970) asserted that science (observation) is never value free but proceeds within (and promotes) a certain paradigm.

Resilience often requires shifting paradigms. Fighting, whether small debates, advocacy campaigns, or large wars, usually goes on without end until one party or the other gives up a belief in absolute "right and wrong" and shifts the paradigm to a more conciliatory and inclusive one—one that takes into account or accommodates the other's point of view.

Accordingly, constructivism implies that there are no victims. Leaders help to create circumstances by how they think about them and, consequently, behave. Nelson Mandela was in prison but he was never a prisoner because he continued to live by his own moral framework, even within his confinement. One becomes a prisoner, slave, or oppressed when one behaviorally accepts the other's definition of one's self.

Resilience literature suggests that as leaders experience the challenges of systems change, they will always have the opportunity to frame the challenges in a manner to promote finding solutions and personal, organizational, system, and community resilience. Resilience is a function of personal qualities, relationships with others, and relationship with the Universe. Further, labeling a set of circumstances as a source of distress is, in part, a function of how the person perceives and interprets those circumstances.

The following sections discuss protective factors that may ameliorate experiences of distress and offer strategies that promote leadership resilience in the midst of distress.

Protective Factors

In the face of the multiple challenges that a leader will face, maintenance of "self" is an essential aspect of effective leadership. The instruction one receives during any airline flight—to "first put your own oxygen mask on and then assist others"—applies in leadership as well. The leader cannot serve effectively if he or she is not physically, cognitively, and emotionally able to lead. This section introduces strategies to develop and strengthen the personal attributes discussed throughout this chapter.

The work to develop protective factors is intensely personal. Guidance is directed to the *person* behind the role of *leader,* behind the title of "lead family contact," "project director," or "program manager." Each individual comes to a leadership position with a personal story—family history, cultural context, personality characteristics, economic status, challenges and triumphs, faith experiences, work experiences, mental health experiences, childhood stories, and parenting stories. Each person has a family and social network that preceded the work and exists external to the work. This guidance not only affects the leadership role but all aspects of a person's life and relationships. Key themes from the literature suggest that the leader can benefit from positive external supports and relationships. Further, there are personal attributes, including one's relationship with the Universe, that are key factors to promote resilience (Gregory, 2001). Finally, there are specific actions that a person can engage in that will enrich one's experience with others, with self, and with the Universe to enhance one's ability to develop greater resilience. Each of these domains will be discussed in greater detail in the following sections.

External Supports and Structure: Who Is in My World?

Leaders need relationships to promote their own resilience. Leaders need people with whom they can process their experiences and discover ways to incorporate challenging experiences into a new, functional worldview. These relationships come from family members and friends, role models and mentors, allies, and confidants.

Trusted Family Members and Friends   As noted earlier, protection is garnered in part through the support and "cover" provided by those around us. In studies of resilience in children, it is noted that if a child has at least one caring adult in his or her environment, there is greater likelihood of surmounting the challenges of trauma than for those children without such support (Kagan, 2004). This relationship provides a buffer from the trauma. Support of trusted family members and friends provides a protective, nurturing cushion for the leader, offering affirmation of the person and a wall of protection from the assaults of the world. It is the person with whom the leader feels safe enough to be vulnerable and who can help the leader process messages, acknowledge critiques, discover new perspectives, and engage in planning new ways of acting. It is often from these people that the leader can hear the critiques of his or her performance and engage in discussions to promote corrective actions. It is from the trusted family members and authentic friends that the leader can find the most ardent fans and the most severe critics. In the midst of the good and bad, it is within this group that the leader feels safe to be him- or herself.

Good Role Models and Mentors   Positive role models are important, signaling to the leader that goals can be achieved, thereby offering a source of hope to the leader. Role models relating to specific tasks, such as facilitating collaboration of system partners, are useful, and role models demonstrating the achievement of work–life balance are beacons of resilience. These role models articulate beliefs and values that provide a foundation for the approach they take to the work and to their lives, living demonstrations that a dream can become reality.

Mentors are those people who provide guidance and coaching to assist leaders in increasing knowledge and understanding of the environment of their work. Mentors assist the leader in considering the implications of decisions made for the work and for professional growth and development. Oftentimes, the guidance includes coaching related to personal developmental matters and in specific domains related to the work. Mentors facilitate leaders to become proficient in the work, facilitating linkages with others who can support success in the work, and offering guidance for personal development.

Allies and Confidants   Leaders need allies and partners to accomplish shared goals. *Allies* are those people who share the vision on specific issues and concerns and will contribute to the thinking and the implementation of strategies to accomplish the goals related to those specific issues and concerns. Allies' contribution may be limited to their partnership on specific issues; their loyalty is to the issue and not to the person.

Although allies are important, another essential member of the leader's network is the *confidant*, whose loyalty is to the person. The confidant is a person with whom the leader can be honest and forthright without fear of retribution or risk. It is with this person that the leader can share worries and frustrations, doubts and questions, and triumphs and victories, knowing that the person understands the implications of these thoughts and feelings within the work environment. A confidant can provide meaningful feedback and honor the confidential nature of the communication.

All of these external factors assist a leader in not feeling alone. They support resilience, giving the protection, partnership, and authenticity that all need to thrive. However, leaders cannot depend on others alone to offer protection from distress. Leaders who have developed inner strengths and personal attributes will fare well in many dimensions of life, including leadership roles.

Inner Strengths and Attributes: Who Am I? What Do I Bring to the Universe?

Resilience requires a stance toward life and the Universe that allows the leader to survive and thrive from adversities. Elements include sense of purpose, sense of self-worth, optimism or positive outlook, flexibility, empathy, sense of humor, and emotional competence or intelligence. Each of the elements is discussed in the following text.

Sense of Purpose   A leader needs a personal vision for his or her life and must be able to place specific leadership efforts within that vision. That sense of purpose serves as a source of sustenance through the ups and downs of any endeavor. Covey wrote, "Correct principles are like compasses: they are always pointing the way. And if we know how to read them, we won't get lost, confused or fooled by conflicting voices and values" (1990, p. 19). He makes a differentiation between practices that represent the tasks to be performed and the principles that are the reasons for doing the tasks. Principle-centered leadership begins with the principles grounded in the personal domain—refining one's relationship with oneself, moving to the interpersonal, with a focus on one's relationship and interaction with others. It is followed by the managerial tasks of fulfilling one's responsibility to get the work done within the organization. These tasks focus on organizing people through recruitment, training, compensation, team building, problem solving, and aligning structures, strategies, and systems toward the goals of the organization.

A sense of purpose protects leaders from distress in the midst of what may seem like chaos. That sense of purpose facilitates a centering of the leader and allows the opportunity to gain useful perspective 1) when movement toward a goal seems to be stalled, 2) with an unending flow of crises and urgent needs, and 3) about distractions and expectations posed by others. This purpose fosters resilience grounded in one's connection with the Universe.

Sense of Self-Worth   Closely linked with the sense of purpose is the sense of self-worth. One must believe in the value of the "I" to be able to withstand multiple types of leadership challenges. This sense of self-worth is not egotism or narcissism but rather a reflection of a sense of security in oneself as a valued entity. This sense of security helps keep the challenges in perspective.

Optimism/Positive Outlook   Each person brings his or her own lens to any situation or circumstance. The implications of the frequently used question "Is the glass half empty or half full?" are documented in positive psychology. If one brings a perspective of positive expectation, there is greater likelihood that there will also be greater degree of energy, motivation, and alertness to the task. A sense of hopefulness generates an atmosphere in which others may also feel more positive and energetic. Thus, in a mutually reinforcing manner, that sense of optimism that one brings can be reinforcement for the leader. Seligman (1991), the father of positive psychology, discusses the following attributes of optimism. Optimism suggests an expectation of the desired outcome and the belief that there is the capability of achieving the desired outcome. Optimism is more likely to be observed in a person who sees bad events as temporary and good events from permanent causes; one who sees failure as specific to the incident rather than an indictment of the whole person. He or she believes that bad events have specific causes. He or she does not take blame for a negative result. Optimists see hope (Peterson, 2000; Seligman, 1991; Seligman & Csikszentmihalyi, 2000).

Optimism does not mean that the person is not realistic, nor does it mean that one believes the outcome will be the outcome that was sought. Nor does optimism absolve leaders from acknowledging their shortcomings. Optimism alone does not predict success; resources and social context influence outcomes, as well. However, optimism means that a leader uses every experience as an opportunity for growth, both individually and organizationally (Diener, 2000; Richardson, 2002).

Flexibility   The ability to be flexible is closely aligned with optimism or positive outlook. Flexibility allows the leader to be comfortable with the variety of pathways that can be taken to achieve the vision. It even allows for revisions of the vision with new information or priorities. Flexibility protects the leader from unnecessary battles and removes the weight that comes with absolute control. Leadership that trusts the contribution of the group and the group process more likely will yield quality results that will far surpass the outcomes of a pathway that may have been rigidly directed by the leader alone.

Empathy   Empathy, also sympathy, understanding, and compassion, allow the leader to "be in the shoes of the other." Empathy serves as a protective factor to support resilience and guard against stress in a number of ways. Empathy requires a shift in focus away from the leader. In so doing, the leader gets distance and becomes able to see context. The extension of empathy embodies connection with the spirit of another. Within that connection, a leader can both offer to and receive something from the other that allows the leader to grow.

In many ways, leadership is about empathy. It is about the ability to relate and connect to people for the purpose of inspiring and empowering their lives. Empathy builds self-awareness, and when leaders facilitate awareness, they have better tools for decision making. Empathetic leaders are attuned to the pulse and capacity of those that they lead. The messages cannot be received if the leader is not able to connect to people, no matter how sound or valuable the information may be. If the leader does not connect with people, they will not be open to the leader's influence.

Empathy allows one to see people's intentions, rather than being distracted by their behaviors that may or may not seem antagonistic to the leader's goals. On a personal level, resilience is supported by the connection of one human being to another. On a practical level, empathy supports resilience by reducing the potential for volatile conflict and, in contrast, promotes constructive interactions (Pink, 2005).

Sense of Humor   Leaders need to view themselves as "human," with strengths and challenges, and recognize the irony of imperfect leaders. Although goals of system reform are important, all are small within the Universe, and leaders must be able to laugh at and with self and others. There is a physiological component of play, the joke, and humor that provides physical and emotional release and relief. It allows a resizing of the issues and promotes release and reframing. It supports the positive outlook.

Humor, and even laughter, is sometimes incorporated into clinical services. Humor is one of the many ways of "untwisting" a client's cognitive distortions. Laughter stimulates a cathartic process that releases emotional pain, some anger, some fear, and boredom. Laughter does not change the facts but does change the way in which one relates to those facts (Junkins, n.d.). Humor and laughter allow one to put things into perspective, to reinterpret or reframe distressing events. Laughter distances an individual from the stressor, creating the space to gain perspective and experience a sense of safety.

Emotional Competence or Intelligence   Along with the perspectives noted above, the leader needs to bring a skill set that will assist him or her in navigating interactions with others. Emotional competence or intelligence, as described by Daniel Goleman (1995), focuses on those skills and competencies that drive leadership performance. Over the years, the framework has evolved to include two major types of competence: personal and social. Personal competence is described as 1) emotional awareness, which is the ability to recognize one's emotions and their effects; 2) accurate self-assessment, which is knowing one's strength and limits; and 3) self-confidence, a sureness about one's self-worth and capabilities. Leaders with such personal competence are self-aware, maintain self-control, and demonstrate self-motivation.

Social competence is described as the ability to successfully navigate relationships with others. A socially competent leader demonstrates social awareness, to include empathy, and the ability to sense the needs of others. In addition, he or she possesses social skills to be able to influence others, build relationships, manage conflict, and make good decisions regarding his or her own behavior (Cherniss, 2000; Consortium for Research on Emotional Intelligence in Organizations, n.d.; Goleman, 1995).

The leader who possesses protective factors will be prepared to withstand the tumult and adversity that naturally accompanies work toward system change. The following section introduces some specific steps a leader can employ to develop and demonstrate these factors.

SKILLS AND STRATEGIES

There are specific actions that a leader can take to stimulate the development and enrichment of protective factors that promote resilience. The specific skills and strategies discussed in this section are listening, reflecting, counteracting self-doubt, making meaning, prioritizing, developing a learning mind-set, creating alliances and forming positive connections, reaching out for help, staying on the task, generating new ideas, and accepting and adjusting to change.

Listening

A little-recognized value of listening relates to the realization that, in human relationships, it is frequently not what the facts are, but what people think the facts are, which is truly important. There is benefit in learning what someone else's concept of the reality of the situation is, no matter how wrong it might be.
—Bryan Bell (2008)

One of the most important, but least used, skills in the leadership repertoire is listening. This is the skill of listening to understand the message of the other—to be fully present with the other and attentive to the words and the meta-communication, via body language and paralanguage, to be able to grasp the meaning. The leader must be attentive to the words and the meanings behind the words within the cultural context of the messengers. In so doing, the leader has the opportunity to be informed and is able to focus the communication on what is real, rather than what is assumed.

Oftentimes, the leader is engaged in a type of listening in which the cues from the speaker prompt the listener to react. Rather than truly listening, the leader may be waiting for the opportunity to assert his or her point of view, to offer a rebuttal, or even to counterattack. Another possibility is that the leader may listen and assume that the message is understood but fail to verify the understanding. Active listening is a type of listening in which there is attention to what the person is thinking, feeling, and wanting and the true meaning of the message. The leader is active in checking the understanding to be sure. After the message has been heard and understood, the leader can offer a response in a manner that affirms that the message was understood.

An example of the differences in communication frameworks is visible in a distinction that is made between discussion and dialogue (Sockalingam, 2006) (Figure 9.1). Discussion promotes each individual speaking his or her point of view. Dialogue requires each person to listen fully to the message and meaning of each other's point of view and use that understanding creatively.

Reflecting

Reflection is the opportunity to take a comprehensive view of a situation and assess objective and subjective contributions. A leader is expected to take time to assess the nature of the issue. Does it require technical solutions or adaptive solutions, or some combination of both? Is the leader providing leadership tasks that match the circumstances? (See Chapter 6.) With a reflective analysis, the leader can create and implement a "leadership corrective action plan."

Discussion is the way that most people communicate.
- Ideas are presented and everyone analyzes and dissects them from their different points of view.
- The purpose of discussion, though, is to make sure you win, that your point of view is the one that is accepted.
- The purpose is to support your idea and give your points more strongly until, eventually, others agree with you.

Dialogue, on the other hand, is an exploration of ideas.
- During dialogue everyone works together contributing toward the idea.
- More is achieved from the dialogue as each person's ideas add to the last.
- In a dialogue, no one is trying to win. They are trying to learn and create.
- They suspend their individual assumptions and explore ideas and issues.

Figure 9.1. Discussion versus dialogue. (From Sockalingam, S. [2006]. *Dialogue as a tool for building consensus.* Unpublished manuscript; reprinted by permission.)

The second type of reflection is that in which the person takes a look at oneself—in relationship with self, one's purpose, individuals in one's Universe, the issues in one's life, and their relationship to each other. Research conducted by Kounios and Jung-Beeman (Hotz, 2009) documents that the ability to "quiet" one's mind may be a pathway to problem solving and creativity. They note that "a-ha" moments often materialize when the mind is wandering or when people are daydreaming. Clearly, taking the time to reflect provides an opportunity for a leader to assess how the dilemmas of the day interact with the leader's personal vision, principles, and mission. Taking time to reflect allows one the opportunity to experience renewal. It also provides the opportunity to gain perspective—not make mountains out of molehills, or, conversely, not to assume that a tsunami is just another wave.

Each person has his or her own preferred method of engaging in reflection—meditation, prayer, journaling, reading inspirational literature, or just being quiet. The challenge for the leader is devoting time to this activity.

Counteracting Self-Doubt

The leader can be his or her own worst enemy with self-doubt. Although doubt is inevitable, staying in a place of doubt is dangerous. Use of external structures (family and friends, role models and mentors, and confidants) and revisiting one's purpose (reflection) are approaches to counteract self-doubt. First, one must acknowledge the issues and then express the concerns to both self and others. One's image of leadership must allow for imperfection and expect movement to occur unpredictability as a consequence of the actions of other complex entities. Feelings of self-doubt are normal and expected, but leaders are confident enough to hear the self-doubt and not be paralyzed by it and instead work to understand it.

In some ways, the linear, "cause and effect" way of thinking, so prevalent in Western-oriented societies, exacerbates this challenge. If a leader believes that a linear process will facilitate achievement of the goal, and that process is implemented but the goal is not achieved, it is easier for the leader to feel doubt. Complexity theory offers another perspective on the cause-and-effect notions about goal achievement. This theory suggests that there are at least three types of tasks: simple (cake baking), complicated (rocket building), and complex (system building). It is when the leader treats the issue or task as simple when it is actually complex that the opportunities for self-doubt emerge. The limitations of the sphere of influence are made clearer as one recognizes that each of the actors required to be involved in a change process is attending to multiple issues himself. The outcome is a function of the interplay of each of these complex entities (McDaniel & Driebe, 2001; Westley et al., 2006).

Making Meaning

Leaders are constantly trying to make sense of the multiple issues with which they are confronted. When confronted with adversity, the leader engages in a process of making meaning by seeking to understand the adversity and attribute causal factors and influence. Coherence is important to one's attempt to make sense of disruptive events (Cohler, 1991). To make sense of life, the leader must continually construct, organize, and synthesize experiences. Ideally, the reorganization should incorporate the challenges in a way that produces growth. In some situations it is reasonable to see adversity as just a detour and the leader resumes previous conceptions of the world. The negative scenario would be one in which the reorganization leaves the leader feeling diminished or on a totally self-destructive path (Richardson, 2002). All concepts of the self and constructions of the world are fundamentally products of relationships, and it is through interdependence that meaning is derived in life. The optimal solution is resilience in which the person gains a sense of coherence, rendering any given crisis experience more comprehensible, manageable, and meaningful (Antonovsky, 1998).

Prioritizing

A leader must be clear that not all actions can be completed at the same time, not all actions have equivalent impact, and not all actions are equal in resources required nor time required to implement. The leader is constantly challenged with decisions regarding which goals to pursue, in what order, with what allocation of resources, and in what time frame. Those decisions must be guided by personal vision, the shared vision guiding the work, and the strategic thinking of the organizational collective regarding achievement of the vision. Some would suggest that one should use resources to achieve maximal benefit with the most efficient use of resources possible. Others would suggest going after the "low-hanging fruit" first to achieve demonstrable success and thereby inspire followers to continue their efforts toward the goal. The important message is that a leader must be focused, realistic, and thoughtful about the process of decision making. A well-designed process to articulate priorities offers the opportunity of comfort to the leader as he or she encounters competing demands from multiple sources. That process also helps the leader create opportunities to change priorities based on new information or changing contexts.

Developing a Learning Mind-Set

The leader who remains open to new information, develops new skills, and gains new knowledge is the leader who continues to adapt, grow, and thrive in an environment of constant change. Knowledge can come from any source or experience; thus, it is in every encounter with another, or in every experience with any phenomenon, that a leader has the opportunity to reflect and discern a lesson about him- or herself, the other, or the Universe. The leader can use experiences of "perceived" failure to frame the experience as a learning opportunity. Similarly, the leader can take experiences of conflict as opportunity to learn about self and to discover differing perspectives on shared data. Clearly, a sense of confidence and efficacy can grow as the leader continues to seek opportunities for knowledge and skill acquisition in his or her chosen field. That sense of efficacy can expand as the leader expands his or her domains for knowledge development. The continual curiosity about the world enables the leader to place his or her work within a context that both contributes to the vision and also places that vision within context.

Creating Alliances

A leader cannot achieve any vision alone. Every vision is achieved through the multiple talents of an aligned network. The leader who can establish positive relationships based on mutuality, respect, and shared vision will garner a network of alliances that will make the work easier to achieve and of higher quality.

Alliances or positive relationships within the work are special sets of relationships constructed to advance the furtherance of a goal. Alliances can be external to the organization, as with representatives of entities that have a stake in the outcomes of the work. In addition, alliances can be formed with other people who share similar goals with the leader. These could be family leaders, community leaders, or individuals in organizations and agencies who share the goals but do not have formal representational roles.

Similarly, alliances are necessary within the organization. The leader must create a network of people who share the vision. Through that network the leader may gain access to information, resources, and other decision makers through both the formal and informal mechanisms of the agency. This network can be available to assist with problem solving in the midst of adversity.

Chapter 5 provides various tools to help with the analysis of a network. It is important to identify alliances, assess the quality of relationships, and measure the strength of those relationships. From that analysis the leader can identify those with whom the leader has yet to develop positive relationships. The leader can also identify those in opposition to the vision to develop an approach to address that opposition. At times, there may be a desire to engage the opposition in a process to seek mutually beneficial outcomes. At other times, it may be most prudent to simply be aware of the opposition.

This type of analysis assists the leader by providing a concrete, visual picture of his or her alliances in this work. The follow-up tasks of establishing and reinforcing alliances moves the leader into a position in which the work can be achieved via a multitude of resources and opportunities for co-creating solutions to the problems that inevitably arise.

Reaching Out for Help

A network of alliances is of little value if the leader does not use those resources. The leader cannot achieve the vision alone. He or she must not perceive him- or herself as the sole source of solutions for challenges that arise. As is indicated by Dotlisch and Cairo (2002), the leadership instincts to "expose vulnerabilities" and "acknowledge your shadow side" actually enable the leader to be more effective. Leaders must be able to accept that they are not required to know everything, not required to be perfect. The freedom to be relieved of the pretense of the all-knowing, perfect person allows the leader to seek knowledge, assistance, guidance, and correction, as needed. The freedom to be a human being allows for a greater sense of resilience, as contrasted with those who expend great energy denying their weaknesses and faults to themselves and to others.

Staying on the Task

Heifetz (1994) described one role of the leader as to "direct disciplined attention" to the work. This is a task that the leader must impose on him- or herself. It is not unusual to be tempted to avoid that which may be perceived as uncomfortable. Further, the tasks may become more difficult, more time-consuming, or more complex than originally predicted. Even so, the maintenance of effort, even if the outcome is not as desired, can yield a sense of satisfaction and affirmation that in its own right becomes a source of resilience. The leader is challenged to revisit mental models to better understand the temptations to avoid the work and to use networks more creatively to assist in addressing the challenges of the work.

Generating New Ideas

The creative is the place where no one else has ever been. You have to leave the city of your comfort and go into the wilderness of your intuition. What you'll discover will be wonderful. What you'll discover is yourself.
—Alan Alda

It is through the use of networks that the leader can stimulate the generation of new ideas. This is another effort to move the leader from a status of rigidity to one that is flexible. As the leader is able to stimulate creative thinking, the options for action, the opportunities for success, and the identification of additional partners and resources all contribute to new ways of fulfilling the vision. Sometimes this creativity can stimulate a new vision. Wheatley (1999) warned that the things we fear most in organizations—fluctuations, disturbances, imbalances—are the primary sources of creativity. The leader is charged to establish an environment that is open to the new. Resilience is fortified by the opportunity to discover the new.

Accepting and Adjusting to Change

The key to resilience is the ability to accept and adjust to change. The resilient leader maintains the belief that change is inevitable and that within that inevitability resides an opportunity for growth and development, for self and the organization. Change has many dimensions. One can examine the location of change (e.g., external societal forces, management structure, allies becoming opponents, opponents becoming allies), depth of change (e.g., budget reductions that are mild or budget reductions that are catastrophic, requiring layoffs and even organizational closure), source of change (e.g., externally imposed rule changes or outcome of co-created strategic plan), duration of change (e.g., short-term illness or permanent loss of vision, hearing, or mobility), and so forth. As is discussed in the following section, resilience requires the ability to shift from "what was" to "what is" and to "what will be" in a manner that affirms our humanity.

Reframing

A major theme throughout these strategies to establish protective factors that promote resilience is the ability to gain perspective and create positive meaning. Reframing is a central skill to address distress that can accompany the experience of adversity.

Reframing is a deliberate and thoughtful reexamination and revising of the meaning one has assigned to an event or experience. Adversity and stress are expressions of the experience or threat of loss. Loss is made manageable when meaning can be attributed to the experience. The construction of meaning helps one to adapt to change, as it becomes the foundation of a reframe. Frequently, the reconstruction in the meaning-making process, although generally unconscious, serves to make adversities not only tolerable but also enlightening. If purpose is revealed and valuable lessons are gleaned from the adversity, then neither the life nor the loss is in vain.

To accept a change/loss, what was lost must be acknowledged and grieved in proportion to its significance. Then the task becomes to discern the benefit of the change. When the focus is changed from what was lost to what was gained, it is possible to move out of the past and into the present with a more optimistic attitude. Of course, a moral person who receives a gift or benefit is then obligated (by desire to maintain harmony with the source) to give something in return to show appreciation. What was a loss becomes a motivating force to serve the larger good. In the larger sense, resilience is an innate self-correcting force that enhances both individually and collectively.

SUMMARY

What doesn't kill you makes you stronger.
—Anonymous

Resilience is a process of living a positive moral framework in response to adversity and stress. The moral framework informs and directs the thoughts and behavior of a leader experiencing challenges. The moral framework is activated as one begins to look at situations, circumstance, and experience from another point. This changing of perspectives, or reframing, reduces stress and thereby creates energy. There are three primary points to consider as one reflects on the experience of adversity.

1. *Adversity is instructive.* It may be life's way of trying to get our attention. It focuses us by delineating priorities and helping us to determine what is real from what is not real. Pain is the teacher, and it subsides as we receive our messages and learn our lessons. Adversity seldom comes without warning. When we miss the signs of pending challenge and are confronted with it, it throws us into an assessment of priorities, actions, and inactions.

2. *Submission (adaptation) is key to resilience.* If one considers adversity as a message, the questions become, "What does life require of me? What am I supposed to do, as opposed to what do I want to do? What change is being required of me? What mission or task is calling me? What am I supposed to learn about myself through this process? What is the message that this experience has for me?" When these questions are adequately addressed, a new perspective dawns.

3. *Mutuality in all relationships is of optimal value.* Mutuality is the harmony or bidirectional feedback between beings, or between being and environment, that promotes connectedness in relationships. Connectedness in relationships validates existence for relationship-oriented people. Ultimately, adversity forces us to balance our experience of disruption with efforts to create or recreate harmony (homeostasis) in our lives by living within one's moral framework (being loving) to counterbalance the experience of loss. Resilience is an innate self-correcting force that can be enhanced.

As noted at the beginning of this chapter, the development of resilience is an intensely personal journey. Although one can describe characteristics of the resilient person and the power of relationships and context, even these components are reflections of who one is in his or her core being. Steps to take to guide this journey are outlined in the following section.

STEPS TO MOVE FORWARD ON A LEADERSHIP JOURNEY

As with most activities, it is difficult to develop a plan to advance an agenda without first knowing the situation. The leadership journey begins with self-assessment, followed by specific actions to seek feedback, use stress-management strategies, enrich one's spiritual foundation, and create a personalized action plan.

1. *Conduct an assessment of self.* The search for a starting place begins with a self-assessment process to clarify where one is in the journey. Worksheet 9.1 (Resiliency) at the end of this chapter is one assessment tool that focuses specifically on an assessment of resilience. It provides a useful guide to examine perspectives on self and habits of life. Worksheet 9.2 (Leading for the Long Haul: Tool Kit for Leaders Self-Assessment) at the end of this chapter is another tool that guides the user to examination of a range of strategies and habits that can contribute to resilience of a leader. Explore for additional tools that will help to articulate strengths and areas to consider for personal and professional growth and development.

2. *Seek feedback.* Although it is important to use one's own lens as a means of assessment, it is also important to seek input from close others. Insights from friends, family, colleagues, and associates provide opportunities to get input in domains to which one has no personal insight. There are a variety of tools for such a review. The Leadership Practices Inventory (LPI), developed by Kouzes and Posner (2003), is one example that offers opportunity to learn about the frequency of leadership behaviors.

3. *Use basic stress-management techniques.* A discussion about resilience overlaps many principles of stress management. Stress management encourages an orientation toward life and change that builds a network, maintains a flexible approach to life, establishes a positive frame on life, and enriches one's spiritual connection to the Universe. Stress management includes the establishment and maintenance of a physically fit lifestyle, including proper diet, physical activity, rest, and play. Finally, stress management includes the use of a variety of relaxation techniques, such as meditations, affirmations, breathing exercises, and visual imagery. Some practices, such as yoga, include both spiritual and physical components.

4. *Identify and strengthen one's spiritual foundation.* Some find the connection with a life force greater than oneself to be a critical component in the development of resilience. Within that frame of reference they find purpose, peace, and solace that brings order and coherence to their efforts. They experience the majesty of this Universe and place their work within perspective.

    Membership within a spiritual or faith community can be a resource for personal growth and development. Activities such as meditations, journaling, reading of inspirational literature, or reflective walks in nature are additional pathways to nurture the human spirit. Find the places, moments, or environments that facilitate communion with the Universe.

5. *Develop a personalized developmental action plan.* The work of becoming more resilient requires a strategic plan. A strategic plan acknowledges that, as humans, we have imperfections, and taking steps toward improvement can be deliberate and intentional. Due to our own frailties, that plan should be developed in concert with a guide, mentor, coach, or teacher who will be a second set of eyes and provide assistance in the life domains in which we need help. Our humanness also means that the work of creating and strengthening our resilience is ongoing. We need to practice, practice, and practice new attitudes, ways of thinking, and ways of behaving. Hopefully, this journey will expand joy in your life and have you on a path that has merit for society as a whole. For some, it may mean staying on your current path and becoming more effective on that path. For others, it may mean initiating a change of small or great magnitude. In either case, let us celebrate the journey!

REFERENCES

Acitelli, L. (1992). Gender differences in relationship awareness and marital satisfaction among young married couples. *Personality and Social Psychology Bulletin, 18*, 102–110.

Alda, A. (n.d.). Brainy quote. Retrieved December 20, 2009, from http://www.brainyquote.com/quotes/quotes/a/alanalda402848.html

Anthony, E.J. (1974). The syndrome of the psychologically invulnerable child. In E.J. Anthony & C. Koupernik (Eds.), *The child in his family: Children at psychiatric risk* (pp. 529–545). New York: Wiley.

Antonovky, A. (1998). The sense of coherence: An historical and future perspective. In H. McCubbin, E. Thompson, A. Thompson, & J. Fromer (Eds.), *Stress, coping, and health in families* (pp. 3–20). Newbury Park, CA: Sage.

Antonucci, T., & Jackson, J. (1989). Successful aging and life course reciprocity. In A. Warnes (Ed.), *Human aging and later life: Multidisciplinary perspectives* (pp. 83–95). London: Hodder & Stoughton.

Barks, C. (1995). *The essential Rumi*. New York: HarperCollins.

Bell, B. (2008). *Lessons in lifemanship: Listening*. Retrieved December 15, 2009, from http://www.bbll.com/index.html#Ackn

Bohm, D. (1980). *Wholeness and the implicate order*. London: Routledge and Kegan Paul.

Cherniss, C. (2000). *Emotional intelligence: What it is and why it matters*. Paper presented at the Annual Meeting of the Society for Industrial and Organizational Psychology, April 2000. Retrieved October 4, 2009, from at http://www.eiconsortium.org

Chopra, D. (2000). *How to know God*. New York: Harmony Books.

Cohler, B. (1987). Adversity, resilience and the study of lives. In E. Anthony & B. Cohler (Eds.), *The invulnerable child* (pp. 363–424). New York: Guilford.

Cohler, B. (1991). The life story and the study of resilience and response to adversity. *Journal of Narrative and Life History, 1*, 169–200.

Consortium for Research on Emotional Intelligence in Organizations. (n.d.). *The emotional competence framework*. Retrieved October 4, 2009, from http://www.eiconsortium.org

Covey, S.R. (1990). *Principle-centered leadership*. New York: Simon & Schuster.

Cross, T.L. (1998). Understanding family resiliency from a relational worldview. In H.E. McCubbin, E. Thompson, A. Thompson, & J. Fromer (Eds.), *Resiliency in Native American and immigrant families* (pp. 143–158). Newbury Park, CA: Sage.

Diener, E. (2000). Subjective well-being. *American Psychologist, 55*, 34–43.

Duck, S. (1994). *Meaningful relationships: Talking, sense and relating*. Newbury Park, CA: Sage.

Dugan, T., & Coles, R. (Eds.). (1989). *The child in our times: Studies in the development of resiliency*. New York: Brunner/Mazel.

Flach, F. (1988). *Resilience: Discovering a new strength at times of stress*. New York: Ballantine.

Flach, F. (1997). *Resilience: How to bounce back when the going gets tough*. New York: Harleigh Press.

Garmezy, N. (1974). The study of competence in children at risk for severe psychopathology. In E.J. Anthony & C. Kopernik (Eds.), *The child in his family: Vol. 3. Children at psychiatric risk* (pp. 77–97). New York: Wiley.

Garmezy, N. (1985). Stress-resistant children: The search for protective factors. In J.E. Stevenson (Ed.), *Recent research in developmental psychopathology: Journal of Child Psychology and Psychiatry Book Supplement 4* (pp. 213–233). Oxford, United Kingdom: Pergamon Press.

Garmezy, N. (1987). Stress, competence, and development: Continuities in the study of schizophrenic adults, children vulnerable to psychopathology, and the search for stress-resistant children. *American Journal of Orthopsychiatry, 57*, 159–174.

Genero, N. (1998). Culture, resiliency and mutual psychological development. In H. McCubbin, E. Thompson, A. Thompson, & J. Futrell (Eds.), *Resiliency in African-American families* (pp. 31–48). Newbury Park, CA: Sage.

Goleman, D. (1995). *Emotional intelligence: Why it can matter more than IQ.* New York: Bantam.

Gregory, W.H. (2001). *Resiliency in the black family.* Unpublished doctoral dissertation, Fielding Graduate Institute.

Haggerty, R., Sherrod, L., Garmezy, N., & Rutter, M. (1994). *Stress, risk, and resilience in children and adolescents.* New York: Cambridge University Press.

Heifetz, R. (1994). *Leadership without easy answers.* Cambridge, MA: Harvard University Press.

Herbert, N. (1985). *Quantum reality: Beyond the new physics: An excursion into metaphysics and the meaning of reality.* New York: Random House.

Hotz, R. (2009, June 19). A wandering mind heads straight toward insight. *Wall Street Journal.* Accessed on June 30, 2009, at http://online.wsj.com/article/SB124535297048828601.html

Jordan, J. (1992, April). *Relational resilience.* Paper presented at Stone Center Colloquium Series, Wellesley College, Wellesley, MA.

Junkins, E. (n.d.). *Laughter therapy.* Retrieved October 4, 2009, from http://www.laughtertherapy.com

Kagan, R. (2004). *Rebuilding attachment with traumatized children: Healing from losses, violence, abuse and neglect.* Binghamton, NY: Haworth Maltreatment and Trauma Press.

Kagen, E.B., & Penn, M. (2008). *Leadership development for systems change.* Washington, DC: Georgetown University.

Kaufman, J., & Zigler, E. (1987). Do abused children become abusive parents? *American Journal of Orthopsychiatry, 57,* 186–192.

Kelley, H., Bercheid, E., Christensen, A., Harvey, J., Huston, T., Levinger, G., et al. (1983). *Close relationships.* New York: Freeman.

Kobasa, S., Maddi, S., & Kahn R. (1982). Hardiness and health: A prospective study. *Journal of Personality and Social Psychology, 37,* 1–11.

Kobasa, S., & Pucetti, M. (1983). Personality and social resources in stress resistance. *Journal of Personality and Social Psychology, 45,* 839–850.

Kouzes, J., & Posner, B. (2003). *Leadership Practices Inventory (LPI)* (3rd ed.). Hoboken, NJ: John Wiley & Sons.

Kuhn, T. (1970). *The structure of scientific revolutions* (2nd ed.). Chicago: University of Chicago Press.

Luthar, S., & Zigler, E. (1991). Vulnerability and competence: A review of research on resilience in childhood. *Journal of American Orthopsychiatry, 61,* 6–22.

Mahony, M. (1991). *Human change processes: The scientific foundations of psychotherapy.* New York: Basic Books.

Masten, A., Best, K., & Garmezy, N. (1990). Resilience and development: Contributions from the study of children who overcome adversity. *Development and Psychopathology, 2,* 425–444.

Masten, A., & Coatsworth, J. (1998). The development of competence in favorable and unfavorable environments: Lessons from research on successful children. *American Psychologist, 53,* 205–220.

McCubbin, H., Futrell, J., Thompson, E., & Thompson, A. (1998). Resilient families in an ethnic and cultural context. In H. McCubbin, E. Thompson, A. Thompson, & J. Futrell (Eds.), *Resiliency in African-American families* (pp. 329–352). Newbury Park, CA: Sage.

McDaniel, R., & Diebe, D. (2001). Complexity science and health care management. *Advances in Health Care Management, 2,* 11–36.

Miller, J. (1988). *Connections, disconnections & violations.* Wellesley, MA: Stone Center, Wellesley College.

Murphy, L., & Moriarty, A. (1976). *Vulnerability, coping and growth: From infancy to adolescence.* New Haven, CT: Yale University Press.

Neimeyer, R. (1993). An appraisal of constructivist psychotherapies. *Journal of Consulting and Clinical Psychology, 6*(2), 221–234.

Nichols, E. (1976). *The philosophical aspects of cultural differences.* Ibadan, Nigeria: World Psychiatric Association.

Nobles, W. (1988). African-American family life: An instrument of culture. In H.P. McAdoo (Ed.), *Black families* (2nd ed., pp. 44–53). Newbury Park, CA: Sage.

Peterson, C. (2000). The future of optimism. *American Psychologist, 55*(1), 44–55.

Pink, D.H., (2005). *A whole new mind: Why right brainers will rule the future.* New York: Penguin.

Pulley, M., & Wakefield, M. (2001). *Building resiliency: How to thrive in times of change.* Greensboro, NC: Center for Creative Leadership.

Richardson, G.E. (2002). The metatheory of resilience and resiliency. *Journal of Clinical Psychology, 58*(3), 307–321.

Richardson, G.E., Neiger, B., Jensen, S., & Kumpfer, K. (1990). The resiliency model. *Health Education, 21,* 33–39.

Rook, K. (1987). Reciprocity of social exchange and social satisfaction among older women. *Journal of Personality and Social Psychology, 52,* 143–154.

Rutter, M. (1979). Protective factors in children's responses to stress and disadvantage. In M. Kent & J. Rolf (Eds.), *Primary prevention of psychopathology: Vol. 3. Social competence in children* (pp. 49–74). Hanover, NH: University Press of New England.

Rutter, M. (1985). Resilience in the face of adversity: Protective factors and resistance to psychiatric disorder. *British Journal of Psychiatry, 147,* 598–611.

Rutter, M. (1987). Psychosocial resilience and protective mechanisms. *American Journal of Orthopsychiatry, 57,* 316–331.

Rutter, M. (1990). Psychosocial resilience and protective mechanisms. In J. Rolf, A.S. Masten, D. Cicchetti, K.H. Nuechterlein, & S. Weinstraub (Eds.), *Risk and protective factors in the development of psychopathology* (pp. 181–214). New York: Cambridge University Press.

Seligman, M.E.P. (1991). *Learned optimism.* New York: Knopf.

Seligman, M.E.P., & Csikszentmihalyi, M. (2000). Positive psychology: An introduction. *American Psychologist, 55,* 5–14.

Sockalingam, S. (2006). *Dialogue as a tool for building consensus.* Unpublished manuscript.

Surrey, J. (1985). *The "self-in-relation": A theory of women's development.* Wellesley, MA: Stone Center, Wellesley College.

Taylor, S. (1989). *Positive illusions: Creative self-deception and the healthy mind.* New York: Basic Books.

Vaillant, G.E. (2000). Adaptive mental mechanisms: Their role in a positive psychology. *American Psychologist, 55,* 89–98.

Walker, E.H. (2000). *The physics of consciousness: The quantum mind and the meaning of life.* New York: Basic Books.

Walsh, F. (1998). *Strengthening family resilience.* New York: Guilford Press.

Werner, E., & Smith, R. (1982). *Vulnerable but invincible: A study of resilient children.* New York: McGraw-Hill.

Westley, F., Zimmerman, B., & Patton, M. (2006). *Getting to maybe: How the world is changed.* Toronto: Vintage Canada.

Wheatley, M. (1999). *Leadership and the new science: Discovering order in a chaotic world.* San Francisco: Berrett-Koehler.

Wolin, S., & Wolin, S. (1993). *The resilient self: How survivors of troubled families rise above adversity.* New York: Villard.

Wright, M.O., & Masten, A.S. (1997). Vulnerability and resilience in young children. In J.D. Noshpita (Series Ed.) & S. Greenspan, S. Weider, & J. Osofsky (Vol. Eds.), *Handbook of child and adolescent psychiatry: Vol. 1. Infants and preschoolers: Development and syndromes* (pp. 202–224). New York: Wiley.

Zukav, G. (2001). *The dancing Wu Li masters: An overview of the new physics.* New York: HarperCollins.

Worksheet 9.1

Resiliency

Look over the items in this checklist and darken the circle that most closely matches your assessment of yourself in each of the nine resiliency areas. What does your list tell you about your degree of resiliency? What resiliency strengths can you rely on during times of change? What areas should you develop to become more resilient?

Resiliency Strength *(indicates a skill you can rely on in times of change)*	Resiliency Development Need *(indicates a skill you should develop to increase your resiliency)*
Acceptance of Change	
I am comfortable with change. I see it as an opportunity to grow as a leader.	Change makes me uneasy. I do not like facing new challenges without having some kind of control over the situation.
O O O O O O O	
Continuous Learning	
Change provides a chance for me to learn new skills and test new ideas. I like to build on the lessons of the past—my successes and my disappointments.	I want to stick with what I know best and with the skills that got me to this point in my career. Other people expect that—it is part of who I am.
O O O O O O O	
Self-Empowerment	
I regularly assess my strengths. I keep my eye out for work assignments that will let me build new managerial skills and develop as a leader.	I have enough on my hands guiding the work of my direct reports. If this organization wants me to develop, it has to give me some kind of plan.
O O O O O O O	

(continued)

From Pulley, M., & Wakefield, M. (2001). *Building resiliency: How to thrive in times of change.* Greensboro, NC: Center for Creative Leadership. Used with permission.

In *The Leadership Equation: Strategies for Individuals Who Are Champions for Children, Youth, and Families* edited by Gary M. Blau & Phyllis R. Magrab (2010; Paul H. Brookes Publishing Co., Inc.)

Worksheet 9.1 *(continued)*

Sense of Purpose

I like to think that my work reflects my personal values. I try to make decisions based on what is important to me and balance that with the organization's mission.

If the organization demands a certain way of working, who am I to say if it is right? My work is not designed to follow a value system. It is my life the way it is—I cannot just change it around to make it into something else.

○   ○   ○   ○   ○   ○   ○

Personal Identity

I really like my job, but it does not define who I am. I have other pursuits outside of work that are just as important to me as my job.

I live for my work. Why not? What is the first question a person usually asks you? It is "What do you do?" not "How would you describe yourself?"

○   ○   ○   ○   ○   ○   ○

Personal and Professional Networks

I really appreciate my family, my friends, and my colleagues. There have been many times that those relationships have helped me out of a jam. I like to stay connected to those people who are close to me and take a personal interest in their lives.

Networking is really helpful in case there is a downturn and my company downsizes me. I wish I could stay more current with what my friends and colleagues are doing outside of work, but there never seems to be enough time.

○   ○   ○   ○   ○   ○   ○

(continued)

From Pulley, M., & Wakefield, M. (2001). *Building resiliency: How to thrive in times of change.* Greensboro, NC: Center for Creative Leadership. Used with permission.

Reflection

I make some room in each day to reflect on my decisions and actions. I like to look back to see if there was another choice I could have made.

There are always so many things to do. It is like running ahead of an avalanche. I do not have time to sit back and daydream about where I am going and how I am getting there.

O   O   O   O   O   O   O

Skill Shifting

My skills could prove useful to this organization in another role. I can translate my experiences outside of work into developmental opportunities.

Every position calls for a distinct set of skills. It takes a long time to develop those skills. It is inefficient to take somebody out of a familiar role and ask them to perform some other function.

O   O   O   O   O   O   O

Relationship to Money

I like things. Does not everybody? But I do not want to get caught in the trap of working long hours and taking on extra assignments in order to pay for things that do not really reflect my interests and values. I make my money work for me. I think about my purchases before I make them.

I have responsibilities. They cost money. There is no way around that. Besides, there is a certain expectation that when you reach my position you can afford a certain kind of lifestyle. You just have to work hard if you want the good things in life.

O   O   O   O   O   O   O

From Pulley, M., & Wakefield, M. (2001). *Building resiliency: How to thrive in times of change.* Greensboro, NC: Center for Creative Leadership. Used with permission.

In *The Leadership Equation: Strategies for Individuals Who Are Champions for Children, Youth, and Families* edited by Gary M. Blau & Phyllis R. Magrab (2010; Paul H. Brookes Publishing Co., Inc.)

# Worksheet 9.2

Leading for the Long Haul: Tool Kit for Leaders Self-Assessment

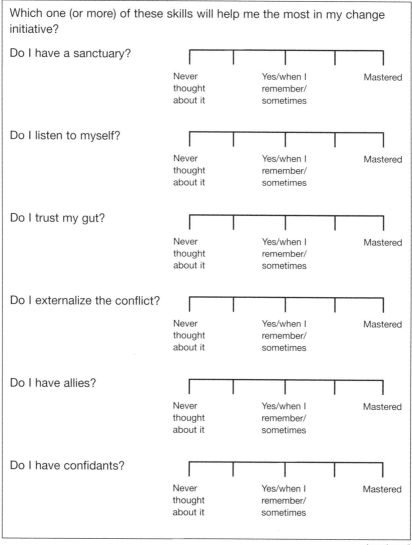

Which one (or more) of these skills will help me the most in my change initiative?

Do I have a sanctuary?

Never thought about it — Yes/when I remember/ sometimes — Mastered

Do I listen to myself?

Never thought about it — Yes/when I remember/ sometimes — Mastered

Do I trust my gut?

Never thought about it — Yes/when I remember/ sometimes — Mastered

Do I externalize the conflict?

Never thought about it — Yes/when I remember/ sometimes — Mastered

Do I have allies?

Never thought about it — Yes/when I remember/ sometimes — Mastered

Do I have confidants?

Never thought about it — Yes/when I remember/ sometimes — Mastered

(continued)

From Kagen, E.B., & Penn, M. (2008). *Leadership development for systems change*. Washington, DC: Georgetown University; reprinted by permission.

In *The Leadership Equation: Strategies for Individuals Who Are Champions for Children, Youth, and Families* edited by Gary M. Blau & Phyllis R. Magrab (2010; Paul H. Brookes Publishing Co., Inc.)

Worksheet 9.2 *(continued)*

Do I know the difference?   Yes ☐
                            No ☐

Do I have a mentor?   Yes ☐
                            No ☐

Do I have a way to preserve
my sense of purpose?

Never thought about it		Yes/when I remember/ sometimes		Mastered

Can I distinguish my self from
my role?

Never thought about it		Yes/when I remember/ sometimes		Mastered

Do I balance work and family?

Never thought about it		Yes/when I remember/ sometimes		Mastered

From Kagen, E.B., & Penn, M. (2008). *Leadership development for systems change.* Washington, DC: Georgetown University; reprinted by permission.

V

Leadership within a Cultural and Organizational Context

10

Culture and Leadership in Systems of Care

KING E. DAVIS AND DNIKA J. TRAVIS

I n this chapter, we seek to examine the challenges presented by cultural diversity and racial and ethnic disparities in leaders' efforts to answer the call to lead and build multiethnic, multiracial partnerships and alliances within a system of care model. As such, the key focus is on *how leadership can foster inclusion among collaborative organizations with different racial and ethnic histories and experiences.* To this end, the chapter 1) explores both the history of these narrowly conceptualized approaches to children as well as the influence of culture and leadership on the vision of change that was chosen, implemented, and reinforced; 2) examines dynamics and models of cultural diversity in human service organizations; 3) surfaces the challenges of bridging differences and fostering inclusion among collaborative organizations; and 4) offers practical, action-oriented recommendations for potential leaders to address these challenges.

IDENTITY AND THE CALL TO LEAD

When L. Douglas Wilder announced his intent to run for governor of Virginia in 1989, many political figures expressed grave doubts about his candidacy and his potential for leadership in a former confederate state (Edds & Duke, 1990). Although Wilder had served 4 years as lieutenant governor and close to 20 years in the senate, it was concluded that Wilder's race and cultural background disqualified him from the ultimate political prize of occupying the governor's office. Although his Republican opponent had far less experience than any former candidate for the office, senior leaders of the state's Democratic Party sought to find ways to secretly discourage Wilder from answering this historic call to lead. Some party members concluded that Wilder's name at the head of the ticket would torpedo their chances of election and control of the state congress. Others privately expressed the belief that Wilder would concentrate his efforts toward an African American agenda, unacceptable in Virginia. Other leaders in the party concluded that the larger white population of the state would potentially not accept Wilder's leadership as governor, producing long-term risks for the Democratic Party. Legislators in Wilder's party privately indicated that his past vocal efforts to change the racial wording of the state's song made it impossible for them to work comfortably with Wilder at the helm. Wilder's run for the number one leadership position in the state precipitated numerous questions and debates about the linkage between race and leadership in the 20th century (Edds & Duke, 1990). The key issues, however, centered on how Wilder would personally answer the call to lead if elected.

Wilder won the Virginia governor's race by a respectable margin and became the nation's first African American governor since reconstruction (Edds & Duke, 1990). Despite his significant victory, the range of questions about race and leadership in the state did not cease. Once elected, the questions focused on his ability to lead a predominately white legislature, his temperament, assertiveness, and interest in a subsequent run for president. However, when asked about his call to leadership, Wilder recalled that it was not so much a factor of his race that influenced leadership but rather the external perceptions and the low expectations. He used the critical commentary and doubts about his leadership potential to buttress his decision to answer the call to lead at such a high level. External doubts fueled and guided his internal sense of leadership and his external strategies. Wilder and his two campaign staff believed that he should eschew matters of his race, deemphasize open debates over racial disparities, and place their meager financial resources in public television advertising. In addition, Wilder believed that his ability to establish a clear vision for the state and specific goals would lessen the chatter about race and leadership. In his view, the most significant factor in determining his success as a leader was how he defined and managed himself amidst a chorus of doubt (Edds & Duke, 1990). Wilder noted his need to clarify his values, increase his self-awareness, and bolster his sense of vision. For the 4 years Wilder was in office, Virginia ranked first in the nation in state governmental efficiency.

Participants in leadership training can use journaling, as Wilder does, to help identify and analyze their call to leadership. The journaling allows leaders to examine their values and create strategies to protect their core sense of self. Wilder's mental journal included his decisions on how to manage issues of race in the public that he believed were designed to negate his call to lead. He recognized that his personal path to leadership was not linear but framed by numerous experiences constructed in a racially conservative cultural environment.

Race, culture, gender, and language differences are major factors in America's history of leadership, organization, and conflict. Each person who seeks to answer her internal call to lead may encounter responses and reactions similar to those described by Wilder, and she must decide how to manage a variety of challenges to her leadership strategically based on reactions to her identifiable characteristics. These negative reactions have the potential to determine how one's leadership role is defined, evaluated, performed, stymied, or legitimated. Similarly, these identifiable characteristics have the potential to influence the organizational vision that a leader creates, the extent to which the leader is able to develop a broad cadre of followers, and the degree to which the leader is able to pressure for change. However, does gender, age, language spoken, ethnicity, or sexual orientation affect one's opportunity to become an effective leader? When a leader seeks to improve the life quality of specific groups or communities, does that endanger his leadership or the societal perception of him as a leader? Does American culture expect its leaders to address controversial differences in race, ethnicity, or culture as Truman did in integrating the United States military or as Lyndon Johnson did in signing a civil rights bill? Does a leader jeopardize his standing if he addresses issues of social justice? Must leaders of color moderate their political views as Wilder did in order to succeed (Edds & Duke, 1990)? How does a leader reconcile and maintain her own sense of identity and values when reactions to her identifiable characteristics are so negative? Here, too, the use of a personal journal can be helpful for increasing self-awareness, motivation, and desire for leadership.

Services for dependent children have historically been reflective of these internal and external dilemmas about race, culture, and ethnicity. These race, culture, and ethnic dilemmas are reflected by their absence in the initial policy proposed by an American president to improve services for children. President Theodore Roosevelt's administration was not able to exercise leadership in matters of race, culture, and ethnicity. A brief analysis of his administration helps to place race and leadership in perspective. Further, in Figure 10.1, social policies that were developed from 1910 to 2010 for children and families are juxtaposed with antidiscrimination and diversity policies developed over the same period. These parallel policies hold important considerations for emerging leaders to recognize, assess, and understand. As part of the context here on historical precedents, it is important for leaders to study the processes that led to the content in the policies proposed by President Roosevelt and by President Obama in the 21st century.

RACE, CULTURE, ETHNICITY, AND DEPENDENT CHILDREN

At the start of the 20th century, three related factors—race, culture, and ethnicity—were instrumental in determining who ascribes importance and meaning to selected social problems and who would lead the populace toward their prospective solutions. Existing cultural values and beliefs tended to attribute causation of many social ills to individual, racial, and ethnic group behavior, and the prevailing

Children and Families Milestones		Antidiscrimination and Diversity Milestones
Legislation (H.R. 618 & S. 938) introduced for 100th anniversary of White House Conferences on Children (2009)	**2010s**	Clarification of Federal Employment Protection Act (H.R. 2232) introduced (2007) *Gratz v. Bollinger*—a federal judge ruled that the use of race as a factor in admission was constitutional (2000). Upheld in 2003.
The Children's Bureau's Improving Child Welfare Outcomes through Systems of Care demonstration initiative commenced (2003)	**2000s**	Diversity management and inclusion programs become integral in workplace practices and policies 1990s–2000s
Child and Adolescent Service System Program initiated by National Institute of Mental Health and U.S. Department of Health and Human Services to help states in planning and designing systems of care (1984)	**1990s**	The Family and Medical Leave Act of 1993 (PL 103-3) Civil Rights Act of 1991 (PL 102-166) The Americans with Disabilities Act of 1990 (PL 101-336)
Adoption Assistance and Child Welfare Act of 1980 (PL 96-272)	**1980s**	Landmark Supreme Court Case limits affirmative action—*Regents of the University of California v. Bakke* (1978)
Individuals with Disabilities Education Act of 1975 (PL 94-142)	**1970s**	The Voting Rights Act of 1965 (PL 89-110) Age Discrimination in Employment Act of 1967 (PL 90-202)
Child Abuse Prevention and Treatment Act of 1974 (PL 93-247) President Kennedy's Community Mental Health Centers Act (PL 88-164) (1963)	**1960s**	U.S. Equal Employment Opportunity Commission (EEOC) formed (1965) Civil Rights Act of 1964 (PL 88-352)
Joint Commission on Mental Illness and Health's report released Joint Commission on Mental Illness and Health created (1955)	**1950s**	The U.S. Civil Rights Act of 1957 (PL 85-315) *Brown v. Board of Education*—racial discrimination in public schools ruled unconstitutional by U.S. Supreme Court (1954)
	1940s	United Nations' Universal Declaration of Human Rights (1948) Fair Employment Act of 1941 (Executive Order 8802)—first law to prohibit employment discrimination in the United States
President Franklin D. Roosevelt "New Deal" creates federal economic and social program (1933)	**1930s**	
The Child Welfare League of America established (1920)	**1920s**	U.S. Department of Labor created (1913)
First White House Conference on Children convened by President Theodore Roosevelt in 1909. Seven conferences were held until 1970.	**1910s**	The National Association for the Advancement of Colored People (NAACP) is founded (1909)

Figure 10.1.   Two parallel paths of historic milestones.

leadership devised public policies that were congruent with the cultural values and beliefs, albeit narrow and fractious. Segregation by race, age, class, gender, diagnosis, and behavior was a dominant cultural theme that undergirded many of the policies and practices proposed by governors and state legislators in their interpretation of the 10th Amendment to the Constitution. In addition, a willingness to maintain and protect states' rights and federalism dominated the period and was a chief criterion for selecting and evaluating individual and organizational leadership (Boyd, 2006; Davis, 2008). Children, racial minorities, women, and the poor were vulnerable, lacked access to promised civil rights, protection under the law, political power, or adequate participation in leadership decisions at all levels. Mainline service organizations operated as racial and ethnic silos with minimal input from the population of families, children, and communities they served or those that sorely needed their services. Rothman (1970) described this as a period in history in which Americans continued to assume their society and values were at risk. In response to these assumptions that the society was disintegrating, the states proposed an institutional-based versus a community-based solution to dependency and neglect. As a result, institutionalization of dependent and neglected children became the primary public policy approach.

A dependent child or youth was defined in the early years of the 20th century as a child or youth who was neglected, orphaned, disabled, ill, deformed, vagrant, delinquent, criminal, or who was financially dependent on the community. Rarely was race, ethnicity, or language seen as increasing these risks as these populations were not eligible for services in mainline social service organizations. Philosophically, dependency of Caucasian children and adults was viewed as a substantive threat to the viability of the American social order and its Puritanical emphasis on individualism, individual responsibility, and work, as it had been in England (Day, 1989; Pumphrey & Pumphrey, 1961). The families of dependent children and youth were viewed as inadequate rather than vulnerable, justifying action by the state to institute custody proceedings against them (McRoy, 2004).

Throughout much of the twentieth century, the primary public policy solution chosen in the United States for managing dependent children and youth was placement in a government operated institution for an indeterminate period of time. Only minimal credence was placed in community-based strategies designed to assist families. However, some variation was allowed in the type of institutional placement of a dependent child or youth based on whether their presenting problem was emotional disturbance, retardation, delinquency, vagrancy, a serious criminal offense, parental neglect or abandonment (McRoy, 2004). Policy makers in the 1900s assumed that institutionalization would immediately curb the inordinate and disturbing increase in rates of dependency, homelessness, delinquency, and vagrancy of children and youth (Rothman, 1970). State and local governmental leaders passed legislation to create orphanages, asylums, correctional facilities, and long-term foster care organizations for dependent and delinquent children, whose numbers continued to increase, particularly in low-income areas within large cities.

By the midpoint of the 20th century, state institutions for children and youth were ubiquitous, overcrowded, overutilized, and a source of friction between the states and the federal government and a host of social justice advocates. In addition, the overrepresentation of black and brown children in the child welfare system had become a crisis without a clear process for change (Brown & Bailey-Etta, 1997; Lawrence-Webb, 1997; Matheson, 1996; Turner-Hogan & Sau-Fong, 1988).

The White House Conferences were envisioned in 1909 by President Roosevelt as the public recognized the dismal condition of many American children and the failure of fragmented services, provided by the states, to alleviate either these conditions or their causes. Members of Roosevelt's administration believed that it was necessary to transform the existing approach to service delivery by state-based organizations as well as the philosophical and theoretical assumptions that supported the status quo. Furthermore, participants in the first White House Conference sought to replace long-term governmental policies and practices viewed as harmful to the emotional and physical well-being of vulnerable children and their families (Child Welfare League of America, 2009). The conference leaders called for efforts to empower families, children, communities, and organizations, although racial and ethnic disparities were excluded from consideration or meaningful participation.

Although considerable progress has been made over the past 100 years toward Roosevelt's transformative vision of meeting the needs of children, the path to transformation has not been linear, racially equitable, or consistently sensitive to cultural diversity or resulting disparities. Perverse beliefs and practices are entrenched in public policies and in American values that circumscribe the distribution of effective prevention, coordination, and collaboration, while maintaining high levels of preventable risk, trauma, and disparities (Annie E. Casey Foundation, 2009; McRoy, 2004). Near the close of this first decade of the 21st century, numerous questions remain unanswered about how to transform fragmented services and practices to meet the needs of vulnerable and displaced children, families, communities, and organizations—across racial and ethnic lines. Culture and leadership questions are paramount.

CULTURE AND THE REMOVAL OF CHILDREN

Welfare laws in America have been based on a series of philosophical assumptions and legal theories that have attributed poverty, neglect, or disability to individual weaknesses or defects in character, morals, or values and only rarely to broad socioeconomic conditions outside the control of the individual (McRoy, 2004; Pumphrey & Pumphrey, 1961).

The first White House Conference on Children and Youth in 1909 represented a significant departure/fracture in the policy relationships forged for decades between the federal and state governments (Child Welfare League of America, 2009). The conference forced a reexamination of the underlying cultural assumptions about individual responsibility that had been a primary theoretical stance of the states. Inherent in the existing approach to services for children and youth was an assumption that "lower class culture and income" were causal factors in producing dependent and delinquent behavior in children and youth. A policy allowing removal of children from such environments was consistent with these cultural assumptions and the promises to improve the lives of children but also to increase public safety while lowering costs.

Prior to the White House Conference, state government leaders exercised almost total monopolistic power over social services policies, practices, and organizations for their populations. The federal stance in most of these social policy areas was usually distal and laissez faire, although the states' monopolistic power was sporadically challenged by Supreme Court decisions and federal legislation (*Brown v. Board of Education,* 1954; Civil Rights Act of 1964 [PL 88-352], 1965, 1968; *McCulloch v. Maryland,* 1819; *Olmstead v. L.C.,* 1999; *Wyatt v. Stickney,* 1974). Each of these new federal laws and judicial decisions weakened/decreased the exclusive role of the state to decide the conditions under which American children lived without respect to any national standards, values, or new social science findings (Street Law, 2006). However, the White House Conference focused national attention on the condition of dependent children and youth and the poorly conceptualized cultural assumptions about causation, problem identification, solutions, and goals utilized as the basis of services provided by the states.

President Roosevelt attempted to transform public practices by eliminating the twin problems of dependent youth and the overutilization of public institutions for children, although this was immediately seen as interference in the affairs of state government. Obviously, the changes he proposed could not be successfully implemented without fundamental alterations in the day-to-day operations of state governments, thus potentially shifting the long-term balance of federalism toward Washington (Boyd, 2006; Davis, 2008). Roosevelt saw the problems of dependent children and youth as national policy issues and not merely issues under the traditional aegis of states' rights.

President Roosevelt successfully redefined the child welfare problem for American children as overuse of institutionalization and the application of punitive policies aimed at poor families, particularly widowed mothers. Based on his reinterpretation of the problem, he introduced a number of new hypotheses about causes and several policy goals to resolve the redefined problem. Roosevelt believed that ascribing dependency to individuals was an ill-conceived policy direction, albeit congruent with American values, culture, and the states' interest in the maintenance of its institutional-based remedy for children from poor families. Although his proposal was not a formal system of care for children, Roosevelt's leadership supported a totally new vision based on the leadership of new federal agencies, organizations, and advocates.

The number of children in out-of-home placements in 1909 clearly supported Roosevelt's concerns. Research findings showed that "an estimated 170,000 children were living in out-of-home care (approximately 95,000 in orphanages and institutions for the developmentally disabled; 50,000 in foster care, and 25,000 in juvenile correctional facilities)" (Curtis, Dale, & Kendall, 1999, p. 4). Part of the explanation for the large number of Caucasian children in out-of-home care was the subtle encouragement for parents in distress or economic need to give up custody of their children to the state or county government (McRoy, 2004). Rather than provide a range of supportive services for families, poverty was increasingly seen as a proxy for relinquishment of parental rights. However, removing the children did not eliminate the family's poverty or the plight of single or widowed mothers. Subsequent development of Aid to Families with Dependent Children within the Social Security Act would be a response to some of these needs.

The 1909 White House Conference on Children attracted over 200 people interested in changing the underlying conditions within the states that lead directly to dependency and institutionalization of children and youth. The participants did not accept the prevailing theory that saw poverty as a valid or morally acceptable reason to remove children from the care of their parents. The participants shared Roosevelt's stated goals to transform the state systems responsible for the care of children and the promulgation of polices and regulations that supported out-of-home care. The conference participants made a number of policy and service recommendations to the president to change the dismal conditions that children and youth and their families faced in the states (Child Welfare League of America, 2009). These recommendations included increasing the emphasis on mechanisms to strengthen families and home environments and establishing a state foster care system with regulated federal inspections and health care. However, the most significant recommendation was the proposal to create a federal agency that would oversee the condition of American children at all levels within the states (Child Welfare League of America, 2009). Subsequently, Roosevelt asked the congress to pass legislation creating the Federal Children's Bureau. The conference also proposed the creation of widow pensions, adoptions, and small cottages or group facilities to replace large institutions. Many of these policy recommendations were converted to public laws and became the grist for future conferences and disputes over federalism throughout the next 70 years (Boyd, 2006; Child Welfare League of America, 2009; Davis, 2008).

Although Roosevelt provided the leadership and vision to begin transformation of services for children, his administration failed to address a number of critical issues reflected in long-term disparities created by race, ethnicity, and region: The Roosevelt administration did not include children and families of color in its vision of well-being, nor were leaders from these communities included in the White House Conference and the concerted push to transform national policy. However, the 1900 census of population showed that populations of color represented close to 9.3 million or 12% of the population of the United States with significant increases in the number of vulnerable children. Of this number, close to 9 million were people of African descent, 266,000 Native Americans, 119,000 of Chinese descent, and 86,000 of Japanese descent (Merriam, 1901). The census of 1900 also showed that children of color were far less likely to be either in school most of the year or as literate, compared to Caucasians. For example, 30% of African American children ages 10–14 attended school for less than 6 months of the year compared to 28% of Native Americans and 22% of Asian children, whereas only 6.2% of Caucasian children attended school less than 6 months of the year (Merriam, 1902). Children of color in 1900–1910 were far more likely to live in poverty, receive less schooling, live in rented substandard dwellings, and have a range of life-threatening illnesses than Caucasian children of the same age (Merriam, 1901). The disparities in well-being, life chances, and quality of life characterized the majority of children of color from 1900 to 1910 with minimal abatement up through the 1960s (U.S. Department of Commerce, 1975, 1978).

Roosevelt's vision was unclear on how culture and race intersected in the design and delivery of future federal services or policies for dependent children and youth. While race was used to exclude African American children from welfare support in the Southern states, President Roosevelt's administration was uncertain how to involve populations of color as leaders or build collaborative organizations that advocated for and provided services to dependent children and youth. Roosevelt's administration was equally uncertain about the policy direction that was needed to meet the needs of an increasingly larger number of dependent children and youth from African American, Native American, Hispanic, or Asian American families whose economic vulnerability and continued discrimination increased their risk of institutional or out-of-home placement. Would attention to race and ethnicity in the new vision require the dismantling of racial restrictions in the South? The policy recommendations that emerged from the White House Conference on Children simultaneously reduced the emphasis on poverty as a short-term proxy for removing Caucasian children from their homes while ushering in race, ethnicity, language, single parenting, and morality as new proxies. This rapidly increased the number of children of color in out-of-home placements while their single parents were unable to obtain governmental support under existing laws. These racial and moral proxies greatly influenced the direction and tenor of public policies and legal challenges throughout the 20th century.

SYSTEMS OF CARE AS A NEW VISION

In the post-Roosevelt era, the United States created a number of public policies, programs, and services designed to reduce and prevent vulnerability and reduce risk in children and their families (Matheson, 1996; Mental Health Amendments, 1965, 1967; Mental Retardation Facilities and Community Mental Health Centers Construction Act of 1963 [PL 88-164]). President Kennedy's community mental health challenge, like Roosevelt's, was to reduce the utilization of large state institutions as the primary source of care for emotionally disturbed children and adolescents (Kennedy, 1961). The dilemma was to find ways to integrate services for children and families across the broad spectrum of separate agencies, organizations, and disparate systems in which they were found. Governor Wilder faced similar issues as the first African American governor of Virginia. Wilder used studies and reports on the increasing cost of out-of-home placements to build a collaborative network that helped pass Virginia's Comprehensive Services Act for At Risk Youth and Families. His staff documented that costs were increasing by 22% per year and that his state agencies were unwittingly serving the same 5,000 children and youth rather than the assumed 15,000. Based on these findings, his leadership strategy involved developing a coalition of public and private agencies along with low-income families to petition the legislature. Wilder also used his leadership position to merge eight separate funding streams to support the new legislation.

The need for such a broad-scale approach has been documented and facilitated by the Annie E. Casey Foundation and its 20 years of data collection (2000, 2009). The Casey Foundation used a set of 10 indicators to determine the overall level of well-being of children and the level that their well-being improved (O'Hare & Lamb, 2009). The Casey Foundation studies have compared and contrasted the 50 states on these 10 measures and ranked them over the past 20 years. The Casey Foundation concluded that there remains a discrepancy between what states know about the conditions of children and their actual progress toward changing these conditions, despite overwhelming and consistent data about the need. A variety of historic factors tend toward the maintenance of the status quo rather than the introduction and support of innovation or transformation. For example, one key finding is the continued barriers that disproportionately face children and families of color. These barriers start at birth with higher than expected frequencies of infant mortality and continue through high school dropout rates, accidents, emotional illness, unemployment, lower family incomes, disabled parents, and early pregnancies. The Casey Foundation concluded that major barriers in American society continue to impede the progress and success of racial minority children and their families. These barriers to children of color are most pronounced in, although not confined to, the southern states and Mississippi, in particular. Although Mississippi has achieved remarkable 10% improvement in the well being of its children of color (O'Hare & Lamb, 2009), it remains last in almost all of the ten indicators of child well-being (Annie E. Casey Foundation, 2009). There is a clear relationship between child well-being and geography. Of the 10 states that rank consistently at the bottom of child well-being, only 2 are not located in the South with large populations of African American children (Annie E. Casey Foundation, 2009). Of the top 25 states in child well-being, only 1 Southern state, Virginia, is included.

In 2000, there were close to 800,000 children and youth in the child welfare system in the United States. Close to 60% were children and youth of color

(McRoy, 2004). In specific cities and states the proportion of children of color in the child welfare system significantly exceeds their proportion of the population. McRoy finds that the rates in the largest cities in New York, Michigan, California, Texas, North Carolina, Pennsylvania, Illinois, and Virginia are disproportionately children of color.

The continued data on the slow pace of changes in the well-being of children and the disproportionate impoverished condition of children of color in the United States have been the basis for proposing new federal legislation. The overall philosophical intent of these newer public policies has been to create collaborative systems of care for children that would replace the fragmented services and racial bias that had characterized the states' long-term approach to children. Systems of care were first defined in the Child and Adolescent Service System Program (CASSP) in 1983. CASSP sought to coordinate the range of disconnected services that children and families needed in their own communities rather than through institutional placements (Pires, 2002).

Systems of care seek to coordinate services in the community in what is termed the least restrictive environment. Systems of care recognize that children and adolescents and their families require a wide array of services without constraints imposed by their auspices. The most critical aspect of a system of care is the involvement of families as key leaders in the creation of the system and its maintenance. In addition, systems of care value cultural competence and the development of systems that anticipate and respond to racial, ethnic, and linguistic differences of the U.S. population (Pires, 2002; Stroul, 1996). As with other approaches to the needs of children and adolescents, systems of care must also grapple with questions about the significant changes in culture, race, ethnicity, and leadership that characterize child-serving systems and the nation as a whole. How does culture influence participation in systems of care? How do parents of color emerge as leaders within systems of care? How does a system of care increase the participation of people of color in the effort to increase child well-being (Davis, 1982)? These are essential questions that determine not only the relevancy of the system of care model but the effectiveness of its services for these populations.

MODELS OF CULTURAL DIVERSITY AND INCLUSION IN HUMAN SERVICE ORGANIZATIONS

Historically, the pattern and frequency of active voluntary participation and leadership in human service and mental health organizations have been differentiated by race, ethnicity, language, social class, and other cultural characteristics (Davis, 1982). Few conceptual models have emerged to give leaders of color guidance in how to gain and lead in the voluntary sector. For example, populations of color and women are found less frequently in executive leadership and voluntary advocacy positions in human service organizations than other populations

(Halpern, 2006; Kunreuther, 2003; Teegarden, 2004). Halpern's analysis of prior studies revealed that "the nonprofit sector is approximately 82% White, 10% African American, 5% Latino, 3% Other, and 1% Asian or Pacific Islander" (2006, p. 7). In addition, "84% of executives are Caucasian only, 42% of the nonprofits that they lead serve primarily white communities, and U.S. communities are becoming more diverse" (Teegarden, 2004, p. 2). At the same time, human service organizations have sought to change the demographic landscape of its volunteers, boards, and workforce (Mor Barak & Travis, 2009). However, Grogan and Gusmano (2007) indicated that once populations of color become involved in voluntary organizations they often remain silent and less involved in the policy setting or advocacy agenda. They propose that this "public silence" lessens the opportunity of leaders of color to change the direction and content of public policy. In our experience, voluntary participation in communities of color has traditionally taken place in religious and civil rights organizations rather than in more heterogeneous settings where community policies are established (Davis, 1977, 1982).

The impetus for increasing leadership, voluntary participation, and workforce diversity has been driven by organizations' interest in better reflecting the diversity of its client base (Hardina, Middleton, Montana, & Simpson, 2008; Mor Barak & Travis, 2009) and the corresponding charge to engage in culturally competent practices (Nybell & Gray, 2004). Mor Barak and Travis pointed out that human service organizations' desire to increase the representation of different cultural groups, particularly those protected by federal Equal Employment Opportunity laws, is a reactive form of diversity management. This is due to organizations' focus on recruiting, hiring, and maintaining racially and ethnically diverse employees as well as other minority groups (e.g., women). On the other hand, organizations' proactive efforts to promote inclusion center on accepting and valuing diversity as well as effectively providing opportunities for both workers and volunteers from different cultures and identity groups to involve themselves in critical organizational processes (Mor Barak & Travis, 2009). This is exemplified in the following statement by (Pless & Maak, 2004):

> Following an inclusionary approach, differences are recognized, valued and engaged. Different voices are understood as being legitimate and as opening up new vistas; they are heard and integrated in decision making and problem solving processes; they have an active role in shaping culture and fostering creativity and innovation; and eventually in adding value to the company's performance. (2004, p. 130)

How do inclusive organizations distinguish themselves from other types of organizations in terms of board representation, executive leaders, staff, and volunteers? (See Figure 10.2 for three differing models of cultural diversity and inclusion.) Cox's (1991, 2001) classic model of organizational diversity demonstrates an ideal in which inclusion can blossom (Mor Barak, 2005). As such, *multicultural organizations* are heterogeneous, are absent of prejudice and discrimination, and demonstrate limited intergroup conflict (Cox, 1991, 2001). In Hyde's examination

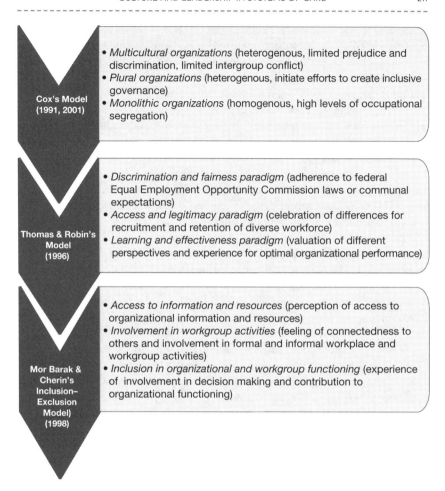

Figure 10.2.   Models of cultural diversity and inclusion.

of multicultural organizational development in human services, the following statement exemplifies Cox's ideal:

> A fully realized multicultural agency is premised on a broader definition of diversity, a reconfiguration of power and privilege, and a commitment to social justice. It strives to create one culture premised on the strengths of various groups (for example, race, socioeconomic status, gender) and perspectives within the organization. (2004, p. 8)

Multicultural organizations differ from both plural and monolithic organizations (Cox, 1991). Simply stated, *plural organizations* can be considered in process. These organizations have a heterogeneous demographic composition and initiate efforts to create inclusive governance, volunteer, and work culture. *Monolithic* organizations, on the other hand, are highly homogenous and have high levels of segregation across all sectors—boards, volunteers, and staff (Cox, 1991). Thomas and Robin's (1996) model also depicts the dimensions of diversity management and inclusion in organizational settings. At one level, organizations operating within a *discrimination-and-fairness paradigm* seek to diversify their workforce to be in compliance with federal Equal Employment Opportunity laws or communal expectations in regard to volunteers. Even though this paradigm focuses on increasing demographic diversity within organizations, intergroup conflicts do not necessarily get addressed and assimilation is valued. Next, the *access-and-legitimacy* paradigm focuses on celebrating differences to attract and retain diverse customers to increase one's competitive advantage. The last paradigm—*learning-and-effectiveness*—focuses on diversity as a tool to enhance organizational effectiveness. The basic premise of the learning-and-effectiveness paradigm is that different ideas and perspectives are valued and optimized to inform key organizational processes and outputs.

Mor Barak and Cherin's (1998) inclusion–exclusion model reflects the continuum of an individual's, group's, or community's perception regarding the extent to which they feel part of vital organizational processes. These include access to information and resources, involvement in workgroup activities, and inclusion in organizational and workgroup decision making. Thus, the focus of the inclusion–exclusion model is on an employee's, group's, or community's contribution, rather than specific demographic attributes.

Effective leadership is critical to an organization's ability to create a culture of inclusion. Effective leaders help set and inspire a vision, influence others to act, foster collaboration, promote problem solving, and drive constructive change (Holosko, 2009; Kouzes & Posner, 1987). In a system of care model, leaders are charged with working collaboratively across racial, ethnic, language, and class lines to create a robust and flexible system that aims to address the needs of diverse children and families. Central to these efforts are functional partnerships in which diverse stakeholders from across the community have voice and are involved in decision making and policy. This requires leaders to work within and among organizations to align individuals with diverse backgrounds and experiences to action by bridging differences and promoting inclusion. The inability to bridge these differences is a distinguishing feature of Roosevelt's approach, which differs from the system of care model and principles created by Pires (2002) and Stroul (1996).

CHALLENGES OF CULTURAL
DIVERSITY IN COLLABORATIVE ORGANIZATIONS

Human service organizations that operate within a system of care framework are challenged to cultivate optimal outcomes for the well-being of the diverse children, families, and communities that they serve. Creating an inclusive, multicultural environment within and among multiagency partnerships can help facilitate the accomplishment of communitywide service-oriented goals, as well as foster collaboration and innovation. Yet, a dynamic set of challenges from multiple sources can thwart organizations' inclusion efforts and overwhelm the vision of their leaders. As already noted, unresolved disputes over federalism, states' rights, finance, interpretations of the Constitution, or racial proxies can act as substantive barriers to leaders and organizations. The slow pace of change noted in the Southern states, where a significant proportion of children at risk are African American, may be based on these historical racial precedents that frustrate and delay social change (Annie E. Casey Foundation, 2009).

Internal and External Environmental Constraints

From a macro perspective, the environment in which human services operate can impede the development of multicultural, inclusive organizations (Hyde, 2004). These challenges are enhanced in a collaborative partnership as individual organizations grapple with factors such as funding constraints, political pressures, and changing demographics. Researchers have also found that within organizations, stressful, non-supportive working conditions can hinder efforts to create multicultural, inclusive work organizations (Hyde, 2004). Human service workers have reported such stressors as high and demanding workloads, lack of work–family balance, limited time with clients due to paperwork and travel time (American Public Human Services Association, 2005), as well as low pay, risk of violence, staff shortages, administrative burdens, inadequate supervision, and inadequate training (U.S. General Accounting Office [GAO], 2003). Managers and administrators, although not on the frontlines, also experience stressors. As David S. Liederman, the past executive director of the Child Welfare League of America said:

> Running a national human services organization is a tough job. You have to keep one eye on the mission and the other on the bottom line. You have to provide high-quality services to your members, work collaboratively with your board, and keep staff morale high. You have to criss-cross the country, keynoting conferences, addressing leadership gatherings, and attending annual meetings. You have to meet the press, inspire the troops, and work with colleagues in other national organizations. And you have to remember everybody's name! You have responsibilities to yourself, to your organization, to your members, to the human services field, and to the nation at large. (1995)

Narrow Conceptualizations of Organization Change Toward Inclusion and Multiculturalism

Compellingly, Hyde (2004) found that how an organization and its members conceptualize change can hinder multicultural organizational development, thereby affecting the potential of organizational inclusion. As such,

> Systems change is not for the fainthearted . . . when we decide to undertake systems change, we risk incurring the wrath of the relatively powerful who benefit from the status quo and that of the relatively powerless who fear that their position in the social system, no matter how unsatisfactory, will be jeopardized. (Ramsey & Latting, 2005, p. 277)

Further, change efforts that are "quick fixes" or short-term solutions to valuing, ensuring, and managing diversity (Hyde, 2004) may be considered reactive rather than proactive (Mor Barak & Travis, 2009). Hyde stated that these efforts can also undermine an organization's efforts due to a lack of integrating an inclusive vision into organizational operations, practices, and processes. Similarly, Halpern (2006) declared that organizations shift the commonly accepted ideal of addressing cross-cultural differences in short-term diversity trainings or educational initiatives. According to Halpern, retooling organizational cultures to be truly inclusive requires attitudinal shifts, and effective leadership is central to this process.

Differences in Power and Privilege

Individuals' personal and professional diversity characteristics may be categorized based on their dominant and nondominant group status according to societal norms (Calvert & Ramsey, 1996). In the United States, men, Caucasians, Christians, and heterosexuals are all normatively dominant group members based on personal diversity characteristics (Calvert & Ramsey, 1996). These characteristics are often valued as desirable traits in leaders of voluntary organizations or as leaders of governmental organizations. Similarly with regard to work-related characteristics (such as educational levels, managerial ranks, and agency tenure) one's nondominant group status can also create dynamics that increase people's positions of power or influence based on their membership in a dominant group. Thus, social group membership offers advantages over other social groups based on the dominant status of that group (Mor Barak, 2005). For example, less financially stable organizations may defer to others when confronted with organizations that have more financial resources, thereby relinquishing their ability to participate in decision-making and change efforts. As a result, individuals or organizations that have nondominant group distinctions may remain silent rather than fully participate, which may undermine the basic premise of working within a collaborative, multiagency partnership (Grogan & Gusamano, 2007). Within this collaborative paradigm, emerging leaders of color have both the task of managing the organization's operations or board activities while also managing the racial, ethnic, or cultural environment. These emerging leaders of color also may find that they often represent the minority on boards, commissions, collaborative ventures, or in the workplace. In some instances, the position of minority leader of a majority organization may result in the community's distancing itself from the organization and the minority leader or staff, resulting in cultural isolation. Thus, considering the history of systems of care models, organizational leaders would be remiss not to consider how power and privilege may continue to play out among collaborative organizations.

The Ideal of Colorblindness

The ideal of a colorblind society is a major impediment to inclusion, voluntary participation, emerging leadership models, and multiculturalism. In organizational settings, individuals may consider diversity from the viewpoint that "we are all the same" and therefore visualize a colorblind society, organization, or movement. Colorblindness is the general assumption that if race or racism is not discussed then it is not a concern (Norton, Sommers, Apfelbaum, Pura, & Ariely, 2006). The concept of assimilation shares a similar perspective to the ideal of colorblindness in its focus on a "melting pot" culture in which the Caucasian majority power structure is the given (Wolsko & Judd, 2006). Apfelbaum, Sommers, and Norton defined *strategic colorblindness* as the "avoidance of talking about race— or even acknowledging racial difference—in an effort to avoid the appearance of bias" (2008, p. 918). Apfelbaum et al. further contend that "many individuals who exhibit colorblindness are not 'racists' seeking to hide bias but rather relatively well-intentioned individuals who genuinely believe that colorblindness is a culturally sensitive approach to intergroup conflict" (p. 930). However, researchers have contended that more problems can occur as individuals seek to build strong intergroup relationships through the lens of colorblindness. First, efforts to create an inclusive environment can be hampered because issues of power and privilege are not addressed (Ferber, 2007; Mor Barak & Travis, 2009). In addition, based on the principle of recognition, individuals desire to be recognized for their own contribution *and* their cultural background, or experience gets overlooked (Pless & Maak, 2004). Further, holding a colorblindness perspective actually can generate greater racial bias (Richeson & Nussbaum, 2004). Thus, in building effective cross-cultural partnership and relationships, leadership should consider fostering inclusiveness without stifling what makes an individual group or community unique.

Establishing Trust

Finally, organizations can face considerable challenges in establishing trust among stakeholders. In any given collaborative relationship among individuals from different cultural backgrounds, trust among key stakeholders is assumed (Pless & Maak, 2005), but trust needs to be developed, nurtured, and not taken for granted. When trust is damaged, it can "uproot the interpersonal relations" (Rajagopal & Rajagopal, 2009, p. 245). As trust is established, partners, allies, and other stakeholders can create a participative exchange by engaging and facilitating the participation of different others' and nondominant groups (Pless & Maak, 2005).

RECOMMENDATIONS

To foster inclusion among collaborative organizations in multiethnic, multiracial partnerships, all leaders are advised to take a two-pronged approach. This approach involves the following:

• Taking stock on intra- and interorganizational processes and practices

• Developing interpersonal skills for effective cross-cultural communication

Although this chapter focuses on diversity from a discrete perspective (in the focus on racial and ethnic differences), the following recommendations are geared toward creating inclusion among different others—regardless of one's membership in a dominant or nondominant group.

Taking Stock of Inclusive Organizational Practices

The context and environment in which work organizations function may either bolster or encumber their ability to build and sustain collaborative, multiagency partnerships as the characteristics of the population change. As such, leaders are encouraged to assess the extent to which the organization's formal and informal policies and practices are inclusive and culturally competent. When working within a system of care framework, this is particularly significant, as an organization may have its own established ways of functioning and hold different assumptions that may differ from its counterparts, the community, and the target populations.

The historical and contextual circumstances that frame the systems of care model can help provide additional perspective to shape organizations' assessment of their processes and practices. Accordingly,

> Quality assessment and planning activities clarify why [multicultural, cross-cultural, and cultural competent development] is undertaken; determine the scope of what needs to happen and the level of commitment and available resources; facilitate input and participation from various stakeholders; suggest intervention strategies; and send a message that this is a serious organizational undertaking. (Hyde, 2004, p. 13)

Thus, by continuously and systemically taking stock of one's policies and practices, inclusion and cultural competence become part of the fabric of an organization. As such, key questions for leaders to address include the following:

- What is our vision of multiculturalism, diversity, competence, and inclusion?

- How can we ensure that we hold true to our vision and values of inclusion?

- Are our processes and practices consistent with this vision?

Finally, a key part of surveying organizational processes and practices involves examining how one's organization relates to its community and stakeholders (Hyde, 2004). Thus, additional questions emerge:

- Are we practicing, modeling, and advocating for inclusion among our partners and allies?

- Do our service activities help to facilitate our efforts to be culturally competent and inclusive?

- Are we engaging in culturally competent practices with our clients that are consistent with our vision of inclusion?

- Are we leveraging the diverse perspectives of our stakeholders—from workers, board members, clients, funders—to build effective systems of care?

Accordingly, leadership plays an important role in ensuring that inclusive practices are central to an organization's functioning. Leaders at all organizational levels can encourage learning among different others, facilitate dialogue around controversial issues—such as racism or oppression—advocate for research-informed training to help bridge differences, and attempt to secure funding for inclusive and culturally competent services and trainings (Argyris, 1980; Hyde, 2004). To also ensure that nondominant groups are brought to the forefront of top executive positions within nonprofit and other human service organizations, leaders can create opportunities for mentoring, recruiting, and retaining well-qualified team members (Halpern, 2006) who share a vision of inclusive, culturally competent practices within a system of care framework.

Leaders are also responsible for establishing, holding, and cultivating a vision of inclusiveness that empowers others. Organizationally based empowerment is at its best when the leadership is shared and its members are afforded opportunities to develop skills and influence organizational processes (Zimmerman, 1990). This is the essence of the systems of care perspective that seeks to foster effective partnerships that address the mental health needs of children and their families.

Effective Cross-Cultural Communication Among Diverse Groups

Good communication is a fundamental imperative for organizations to build effective and productive collaborative partnerships and alliances (Barclay & Kerr, 2006). Although the focus on good communication may appear a given, the ability to communicate well with others warrants great skill that requires cultivation. In addition, a "black box" factor exists as leaders are charged to communicate well to effectively build collaborative partnerships; however, the drivers or skills to communication effectively are unknown or assumed. Although seemingly deceptively simple, the skills discussed in this chapter offer organizational leaders specific, actionable, and trainable methods that help foster inclusion and bridging differences.

Scholars and practitioners have toted a host of interpersonal skills that foster effective intergroup communication (Figure 10.3) including mindfulness, empathy, capacity to deal with personal anxiety, productive management of the unknown, constructive expression of self and ideas, and participative decision making (Ensari & Miller, 2006; Gudykunst, 2008; Pless & Maak, 2004). Why are these specific skills important? First, mindfulness, one's ability to draw novel distinctions (Langer & Moldoveanu, 2000), provides opportunity for individuals to move beyond interpreting others' behaviors based on one's own experience or frames of reference (Gudykunst, 2004). In interpersonal communications, being mindful involves seeking clarification from others in discussion as well as asking for clarification when further understanding is needed (Gudykunst, 2004). Hence, mindfulness may help individuals cultivate an ability to "walk in another's shoes." Langer and Moldoveanu (2000) also stated that mindfulness creates opportunity for greater sensitivity, openness toward different others, and enhanced awareness

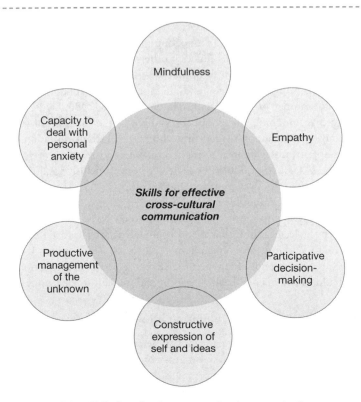

Figure 10.3. Skills for effective cross-cultural communication among collaborative partnerships.

of various perspectives. Journaling (as discussed in the beginning of the chapter) is an example of a tool that helps create a space for mindfulness, where leaders can realize their vision as well as impediments to that vision.

One's ability to handle the unknown (or ambiguity) and anxiety are skills that are beneficial in working with others (Gudykunst, 2004). For example, ambiguity about one's role can be a great source of organizational stress (Langer & Moldoveanu, 2000; Rizzo, House, & Lirtzman, 1970). In this instance, individuals maybe unclear about work-related expectations (House & Rizzo, 1972; Rizzo, House, & Lirtzman, 1970) or unaware of others' experiences or perspectives (Gudykunst, 2004). Similarly, one's own anxiety about a situation may cause difficulties in effective communication (Gudykunst, 2004). The skill involved in managing anxiety focuses on how an individual interprets others' behaviors and actions. Often individuals may make judgments by overgeneralizing, focusing negatives, jumping to misguided conclusions or assumptions, dramatizing problems, labeling and blaming, or simply getting caught up in what *should be* rather than what *is*. As a result, individuals' ability to empathize is a critical skill for effective intercultural communication (Ensari & Miller, 2006; Gudykunst, 2008;

Pless & Maak, 2004). Through empathy, individuals can engage in taking perspective, which involves considering others' feelings, needs, perspectives, and experiences. Taking perspective helps individuals acknowledge rather than dismiss group differences (Ramsey & Latting, 2005) and personalize others to "disconfirm the negative stereotypes of members of out group distinctions . . . and thereby, reduce intergroup conflict" (Ensari & Miller, 2006, p. 593).

Finally, the capacity to speak up and constructively express oneself and ideas as well as the ability to facilitate participative decision making in cross-racial and cross-ethnic settings are critical skills for all stakeholders—leaders, aspiring leaders, and consumers alike—that can foster inclusion among collaborative, multiagency partnerships. Cultivating an ability to constructively break the silence is vital to intra- and interorganizational learning and innovation. By gaining these communicative skills, individual leaders may also have a greater opportunity to feel engaged and committed to their alliances with other organizations. Despite the potential benefits of breaking the silence, some leaders of color may feel that their ideas and input may be overlooked or dismissed and not make a difference. Some may fear isolation from partners, allies, or constituents if they stress agendas that match the needs of their own racial and ethnic community. Therefore, engaging in *constructive communicative behaviors*—and having that voice heard and heeded—can result in real or perceived benefits.

Facilitating participation in decision making can help create organizational empowerment (Laschinger, Sabiston, & Kutszcher, 1997; Parker & Price, 1994; Zimmerman, 1995). The facilitation of participative decision making involves more than simply asking for input (Carroll, 1994). Organizational leaders must restructure their policies and practices to generate and maintain consumer, community, and worker empowerment (Bowen & Lawler, 1995) and to provide opportunities for meaningful input into decision making (Bednar, 2003). For example, Bowen and Lawler (1995) found that implementing empowerment-based practices that increase autonomy in performing tasks, addressing problems, and handling mistakes can, in turn, contribute to participation in decision making. Thus, there are direct implications for developing skills in facilitating participative decision making within and among multiagency partnerships.

LESSONS LEARNED

A clear lesson that 21st-century leaders must learn is the tremendous effects that social, political, and historical expectations and legal precedents have on them and their organizations. In all too many instances, these expectations and precedents are deeply rooted in the culture and are designed to maintain and sustain the status quo by slowing down the pace and the extensiveness of change. Change is staunchly resisted because it is inconsistent with the past. This was as true at the turn of the century when Roosevelt assumed the presidency as it is today as Barack Obama and his administration seek to change the American health care system. Roosevelt found his administration awash in a leadership battle with state governmental leaders that did not see the value or need for change in the conditions under which many American children and their families suffered. There were numerous reasons for the position held by the states, not the least of which was the ongoing fear of federal government takeover of state functions inconsistent with their interpretation of the Constitution. Similar views are being expressed currently about impending changes in national health insurance (Cannon, 2009). Leaders must anticipate resistance to change and measure carefully their pace, depth, and strategies as a means of counteracting and blunting resistance that will be offered.

A corresponding lesson here is that leaders must identify workable strategies that will increase the chances that their transformative visions will be adopted, supported, and pursued. To lessen the constraints imposed by historical precedents, child welfare advocates during the Roosevelt era designed a two-pronged strategy to have the president be seen as the face of national leadership on these issues. Using his bully pulpit, the president could command attention throughout the nation to this cause and his vision. Their second strategic move was to convene the first White House Conference on Children and Youth as a national platform to expose the broad dimensions and extensive scope of the problem. This latter strategy included bringing hundreds of highly motivated advocates to the geographic center of American democracy where their story would resonate with national and international media. Advocates would have access to the congress and to leaders of national organizations. Governor Wilder used several of these leadership strategies to move the Comprehensive Services Act for At Risk Youth and Families through the Virginia legislature.

Roosevelt's character, history, and stature were instrumental in the success of this first effort to change conditions for children. However, when Governor Wilder sought to close a children's psychiatric hospital during a recession, he did not heed the Roosevelt strategy. The hospital was located in a small county where the governor assumed there would be minimal opposition to the closure. Although the governor's reasons for closing the facility were fiscally sound, his staff did not anticipate the level of resistance that would be exerted to save the jobs and the economic impact on this small county. The opposition was extensive and unrelenting for months. As a result, the governor had to rescind his closure plan and his leadership suffered as he sought another political office (Edds & Duke, 1990).

A third lesson for leaders is to determine how to raise and discuss potentially volatile issues that have been hidden or that have previously brought about opposing positions (Apfelbaum, Sommers, & Norton, 2008). The Roosevelt administration was able to raise the overall issue of child well-being but unable to publicly address the underlying racial discrepancies where the scope, magnitude, and implications were more severe than in the white population, so these issues were not raised, nor were advocates from minority communities part of the overall national transformative effort. The failure to raise these issues was a political genuflection to the Southern racial ethos but ignored the plight of children of color and their families that languished for decades to come (Annie E. Casey Foundation, 2009; Brown & Bailey-Etta, 1997; Lawrence-Webb, 1997; Matheson, 1996; O'Hare & Lamb, 2009; Turner-Hogan & Sau-Fong, 1988; U.S. Department of Commerce, 1975). A key impediment to resolving these issues was the inability of the Roosevelt administration to wade comfortably into the labyrinth of race, culture, and ethnicity. The administration lacked the language and communication skills to manage the reactions and responses to this level of direct attention to race and ethnicity (Barclay & Kerr, 2006). This inability may have reinforced the resistance in the South to racial justice, necessitating lengthy legislative efforts and numerous Supreme Court decisions, followed by further resistance. Governor Wilder had a successful history of engaging the public on many of these issues, but he based his proposed legislation for children on the issue of escalating costs to the state rather than the obvious racial disparity. His knowledge of race and policy helped him conclude that a strategy showing financial savings had a better than average chance of success.

In the recent presidential race, candidate Obama found that he, too, had to exercise leadership on issues of race and ethnicity lest his candidacy fail. Although the internal strategy of the Obama team appears to have been to make race differences secondary to his political platform objectives, numerous issues forced the candidate to address the issues more frontally (Wolffe, 2009). Obama's presentation on race was one of the most significant public statements by any presidential candidate on race in the history of American politics, and it appears to have increased his stature, trustworthiness, and confidence as a leader. Throughout the first 9 months of the Obama presidency, race remained a latent issue that undergirded and fueled opposition to his policies, at least as interpreted by former President Carter and others (Phillips, 2009). The leadership lesson for the Obama administration is the value of using effective language to communicate with audiences, groups, communities, and nations about thorny issues in the public arena (Grogan & Gusamano, 2007; Wolffe, 2009).

Another important lesson for leaders is to learn how to develop goals and vision that incorporate culture, race, and ethnicity. Many programs and services espouse diversity but lack a culturally competent means of incorporating their goals (Mor Barak & Travis, 2009). Far too often, goals, vision, strategies, staffing, and participation continue to reflect the traditional population of decision makers. However, population forecasts conclude that the United States will be a minority-majority nation by the year 2030. Increasingly, the demand for services, positions, opportunities, and participation will come disproportionately from populations of color. Thus, new models of service, standards, and tools based on cultural competence will need to be devised and implemented in university training programs (Abe-Kim & Takeuchi, 1996; Betancourt, Green, Carillo, & Ananeh-Firempong, 2003; Brisbane, 1998; Center for Mental Health Services, 2000; Davis-Chambers, 1998; Fleming & King, 1997; Hernandez & Isaacs, 1998; Lopez, 1997; Pumariega & Balderrama, 1997; Whaley & Davis, 2007). The movement toward application of evidence-based practices is an example. Although these models have been researched principally on Anglo populations, it is expected that the knowledge and skills gained are universally applicable to all groups (U.S. Department of Health and Human Services, 2001). Leadership in the 21st century must insist that clinical samples include diverse populations of consumers, researchers, and policy makers. There must also be substantive efforts to adapt evidence-based practices to ensure a better fit with diverse populations.

Leadership for people of color is based on each of these lessons as well as others. Leaders of color, based on mutual experiences, must retain an important connection to their racial, ethnic, or cultural community while balancing their connection to their organization's values and interest. It seems a truism that these leaders of color often lead lives of dualism (Dubois, 1908/1991; Ifill, 2009) in which they have multiple attachments, responsibilities, ties, and commitments that risk bifurcating their identity and marginalizing their contributions to social change. Leaders who are able to creatively manage the dualism increase their opportunities and those of their organizations and communities.

REFERENCES

Abe-Kim, J., & Takeuchi, D.T. (1996). Cultural competence and quality of care: Issues in mental health service delivery in managed care. *Clinical Psychology: Science and Practice, 3,* 273–295.

Age Discrimination in Employment Act of 1967 PL 90-202.

American Public Human Services Association. (2005). *Report from 2004 Child Welfare Workforce Survey: State agency findings* [Electronic version]. Washington, DC: Author. Accessed August 4, 2009, from http://www.aphsa.org/Home/Doc/Workforce%20Report%202005.pdf

Annie E. Casey Foundation. (2000). *2000 Kids count data book: State profiles of child well-being.* Baltimore: Author.

Annie E. Casey Foundation. (2009). *2009 Kids count data book: State profiles of child well-being.* Baltimore: Author.

Apfelbaum, E.P., Sommers, S.R., & Norton, M.I. (2008). Seeing race and seeming racist? Evaluating strategic colorblindness in social interaction. *Journal of Personality and Social Psychology, 95,* 918–932.

Argyris, C. (1980). Making the undiscussable and its undiscussability discussable. *Administrative Review,* 205–213.

Barclay, G., & Kerr, C. (2006). Collaborative working across children's services: Where are we now? *Educational and Child Psychology, 23,* 35–46.

Bednar, S. (2003). Elements of satisfying organizational climates in child welfare agencies. *Families in Society: Journal of Contemporary Human Services, 84,* 7–12.

Betancourt, H., Green, A.R., Carillo, J.E., & Ananeh-Firempong, O. (2003). Defining cultural competence: A practical framework for addressing racial/ethnic disparities in health and health care. *Public Health Reports, 118,* 293–302.

Bowen, F., & Blackmon, K. (2003). Spirals of silence: The dynamic effects of diversity on organizational voice. *Journal of Management Studies, 40,* 1393–1417.

Boyd, E. (2006). *American federalism,1776 to 1997: Significant events.* Washington, DC: U.S. Government Printing Office. Retrieved August 3, 2009, from http://usinfo.state.gov.usa/infousa/politics/states/federal.htm

Brisbane, F.L. (1998). *Cultural competence for health care professionals working with African American communities: Theory and practice* (Vol. 7). Rockville, MD: Center for Substance Abuse Prevention.

Brown, A.W., & Bailey-Etta, B. (1997). An out of home care system in crisis: Implications for African American children in the child welfare system. *Child Welfare, 76,* 65–84.

Brown v. Board of Education. 347 U.S. 483 (1954).

Calvert, L.M., & Ramsey, V.J. (1996). Speaking as female and white: A non-dominant/dominant group standpoint. *Organization, 3,* 468–485.

Cannon, M.F. (2009). *Fannie Med? Why a "public option" is hazardous to your health* (Rep. No. 642). Washington DC: The Cato Institute.

Carroll, A. (1994). *What's behind the "E" word: Myths about empowerment and why you need it.* Retrieved July 9, 2006, from http://www.interactiondesign.com

Center for Mental Health Services. (2000). *Cultural competence standards in managed care mental health services: Four underserved/underrepresented racial/ethnic groups.* Rockville, MD: U.S. Government Printing Office.

Child Welfare League of America. (2009). *The history of White House Conferences on Children and Youth* Arlington, VA: Author.

Civil Rights Act of 1957. PL 85-315.

Civil Rights Act of 1964. PL 88-352, 78 Stat. 241.

Civil Rights Act of 1965. PL 89-110, 79 Stat. 437.

Civil Rights Act of 1968. PL 90-284, 82 Stat. 73.

Civil Rights Act of 1991. PL 102-166.

Clarification of Federal Employment Protections Act of 2007. HR 2232.

Community Mental Health Centers Act of 1963. PL 88-164.

Cox, T.H., Jr. (1991). The multicultural organization. *Executive, 5,* 34–47.

Cox, T.H., Jr. (2001). *Creating the multicultural organization: A strategy for capturing the power of diversity.* San Francisco: Jossey-Bass.

Curtis, P., Dale, G., & Kendall, J. (1999). *The foster care crisis: Translating research into policy and practice.* Lincoln: University of Nebraska Press.

Davis, K. (1977, Spring). Blacks and voluntary action: A review of the research literature. *Journal of Voluntary Action Leadership,* 17–21.

Davis, K. (1982). An alternative theory of race and voluntary participation. *Journal of Voluntary Action Scholars, 11,* 18–21.

Davis, K. (2008). New Freedom, new federalism, and states rights. In I. Colby (Ed.), *The comprehensive handbook of social work and social welfare* (pp. 145–176). Hoboken, NJ: John Wiley & Sons.

Davis-Chambers, E. (1998). *Cultural competence performance measures.* New York: New York State Office of Mental Health, The Research Foundation.

Day, P.J. (1989). *A new history of social welfare.* Englewood Cliffs, NJ: Prentice Hall.

Dubois, W.E.B. (1991). Conservation of the races. In H. Brotz (Ed.), *Negro social and political thought 1850–1920.* New York: Basic Books. (Originally published in 1908)

Edds, M., & Duke, P. (1990). *Claiming the dream: The victorious campaign of Douglas Wilder of Virginia.* Chapel Hill, NC: Algonquin.

Ensari, N.K., & Miller, N. (2006). The application of the personalization model in diversity management. *Group Processes and Intergroup Relations, 9,* 589–602.

Fair Employment Act of 1941. Executive Order 8802.

Family and Medical Leave Act of 1993. PL 103-3.

Fleming, C.M., & King, J. (1997). *Cultural competence guidelines in managed care mental health services for Native American populations* Boulder, CO: Western Interstate Commission for Higher Education Mental Health Program.

Gratz v. Bollinger, 539 U.S. 244 (2003).

Grogan, C., & Gusamano, M. (2007). *Healthy voices, unhealthy silence: Advocacy and health policy for the poor.* Washington, DC: Georgetown University Press.

Gudykunst, W.W. (2008). *Bridging differences: Effective intergroup communication* (4th ed.). Newbury Park, CA: Sage.

Halpern, R.P. (2006). *Workforce Issues in the nonprofit sector: Generational leadership change and diversity.* Kansas City, MO: American Humanics.

Hardina, D., Middleton, J., Montana, S., & Simpson, R.A. (2008). *An empowering approach to managing social service organizations.* New York: Springer.

Hernandez, M., & Isaacs, M.R. (1998). *Promoting cultural competence in children's mental health services.* Baltimore: Paul H. Brookes Publishing Co.

Holosko, M.J. (2009). Social work leadership: Identifying core attributes. *Journal of Human Behavior in the Social Environment, 19,* 448–459.

House, R.J., & Rizzo, J.R.(1972). Role conflict and ambiguity as critical variables in a model of organizational behavior. *Organizational Behavior and Human Performance, 7,* 467–505.

Hyde, C.E. (2004). Multicutural development in human services agencies: Challenges and solutions. *Social Work, 49,* 7–16.

Ifill, G. (2009). *The breakthrough: Politics and race in the age of Obama.* New York: Doubleday.

Individuals with Disabilities Education Act of 1975. PL 94-142.

Kennedy, J.F. (1961). Letter to Secretary Ribicoff concerning the role of the federal government in the field of mental health. Washington, DC: The American Presidency Project. Retrieved August 5, 2009, from http://www.presidency.ucsb.edu/ws/print.php?pid=8469

Kouzes, J.M., & Posner, B.Z. (1987). *The leadership challenge: How to get extraordinary things done in organizations.* San Francisco: Jossey-Bass.

Kunreuther, F. (2003). The changing of the guard: What generational differences tell us about social-change organizations. *Non-Profit and Voluntary Sector Quarterly, 32,* 450–457.

Langer, E.J., & Moldoveanu, M. (2000). The construct of mindfulness. *Journal of Social Issues, 56,* 1–9.

Laschinger, H.K.S., Sabiston, J.A., & Kutszcher, L. (1997). Empowerment and staff nurse decision involvement in nursing work environments: Testing Kanter's theory of structural power in organizations. *Research in Nursing & Health, 20,* 341–352.

Lawrence-Webb, C. (1997). African American children in the modern child welfare system: A legacy of the Flemming rule. *Child Welfare, 36,* 9–30.

Liederman, D.S. (1995). Introduction: Challenges for leaders of national human services organizations. In L. Ginsberg & P.R. Keys (Eds.). New Management in Human Services, 2nd edition (pp. 37–63). Washington, DC: NASW Press. Retrieved January 15, 2010, from http://www.naswpress.org/publications/bestbuys/inside/new-mgmt-chapter.html

Lopez, S.R. (1997). *Cultural competence in psychotherapy: A guide for clinicians and their supervisors.* In C.E. Watkins Jr. (Ed.). *Handbook of Psychotherapy Supervision* (pp. 570–588). New York: John Wiley & Sons, Inc.

Matheson, L. (1996). The politics of the Indian child welfare act. *Social Work, 41,* 232–235.

McCulloch v. Maryland, 17 U.S. 316 (1819).

McRoy, R. (2004). The color of child welfare. In K. Davis & T. Bent-Goodley (Eds.), *The color of social policy* (pp. 37–63). Alexandria, VA: Council on Social Work Education Press.

Mental Health Amendments of 1967, PL 90-31, 81 Stat. 79.

Mental Retardation Facilities and Community Mental Health Centers Construction Act Amendments of 1965. PL 89-105, 79 Stat. 427.

Merriam, W.C. (1901). *Twelfth census of the United States—1900.* Washington DC: U.S. Department of the Interior.

Merriam, W.C. (1902). *Abstract of the twelfth census of the United States.* Washington DC: U.S. Government Printing Office.

Mor Barak, M.E. (2005). *Managing diversity: Toward a globally inclusive workplace.* Newbury Park, CA: Sage.

Mor Barak, M.E., & Cherin, D.A. (1998). A tool to expand organizational understanding of workforce diversity. *Administration in Social Work, 22,* 47–64.

Mor Barak, M.E., & Travis, D.J. (2009). Diversity and organizational performance. In Y. Hasenfeld (Ed.), *Human services as complex organizations* (pp. 341–378). Newbury Park, CA: Sage.

Norton, M.I., Sommers, S.R., Apfelbaum, E.P., Pura, N., & Ariely, D. (2006). Color blindness and interracial interaction: Playing the political correctness game. *Psychological Science, 17,* 949–953.

Nybell, L.M., & Gray, S.S. (2004). Race, place, space: Meanings of cultural competence in three child welfare agencies. *Social Work, 49,* 17–27.

O'Hare, W.P., & Lamb, V.L. (2009). *Ranking states on improvements in child well-being since 2000.* Baltimore: Annie E. Casey Foundation.

Olmstead v. L.C. (98-536) 527 U.S. 581 (1999).

Parker, L.E., & Price, R.H. (1994). Empowered managers and empowered workers: The effects of managerial support and managerial perceived control on workers' sense of control over decision making. *Human Relations, 47,* 911–917.

Phillips, K. (2009). Carter's racism charge sparks war of words. *New York Times Politics and Government Blog.* Retrieved August 3, 2009, from http://thecaucus.blogs.nytimes.com/2009/09/16/carters-racism-charge-sparks-war-of-words/?scp=1-b&sq=&st=nyt

Pires, S. (2002). *Building systems of care—A primer.* Washington, DC: National Technical Assistance Center for Children's Mental Health, Georgetown University Child Development Center.

Pless, N., & Maak, T. (2004). Building an inclusive diversity culture: Principles, processes and practice. *Journal of Business Ethics, 54,* 129–147.

Pumariega, A.J., & Balderrama, H.H. (1997). *Cultural competence guidelines in managed care mental health services for Latino populations.* Boulder, CO: Western Interstate Commission for Higher Education Mental Health Program.

Pumphrey, R.E., & Pumphrey, M.W. (1961). *Heritage of American social work.* New York: Columbia University Press.

Rajagopal, L., & Rajagopal, A. (2009). Trust and cross-cultural dissimilarities in corporate environment. *Team Performance Management, 12,* 237–252.

Ramsey, V.J., & Latting, J.K. (2005). A typology of intergroup competencies. *Journal of Applied Behavioral Science, 41,* 265.

Regents of the University of California v. Bakke, 438 U.S. 265 (1978).

Richeson, J.A., & Nussbaum, R.J. (2004). The impact of multiculturalism versus colorblindness on racial bias. *Journal of Experimental Social Psychology, 40,* 417–423.

Rizzo, J.R., House, R.J., & Lirtzman, S.I. (1970). Role conflict and ambiguity in complex organizations. *Administrative Science Quarterly, 15,* 150–163.

Rothman, D. (1970). *The discovery of the asylum.* Boston: Little, Brown.

Street Law. (2006). *Powers of the federal government.* Silver Spring, MD: Street Law and the Supreme Court Historical Society. Retrieved August 5, 2009, from http:// www.landmarkcases.org

Stroul, B. (1996). *Children's mental health: Creating systems of care in a changing society.* Baltimore: Paul H. Brookes Publishing Co.

Teegarden, P.H. (2004). *Change ahead: Nonprofit executive leadership and transitions survey 2004.* Baltimore: Annie E. Casey Foundation.

The Adoption Assistance and Child Welfare Act of 1980. PL 96-272.

The Americans with Disabilities Act of 1990. PL 101-33.

The Child Abuse Prevention and Treatment Act of 1974. PL 93-247.

The Voting Rights Act of 1965. PL 89-110.

Thomas, D.A., & Robin, J. (1996). Making differences matter: A new paradigm for managing diversity. *Harvard Business Review, 74,* 70–90.

Turner-Hogan, P., & Sau-Fong, S. (1988). Minority children and the child welfare system: An historical perspective. *Social Work, 33,* 493–497.

U.S. Department of Commerce. (1975). *Historical statistics of the United States: Colonial times to 1970.* Washington, DC: Bureau of the Census.

U.S. Department of Commerce. (1978). *The social and economic status of the black population in the United States: An historical view, 1790–1978* (Series P-23 ed., Vol. 80). Washington DC: Bureau of the Census.

U.S. Department of Health and Human Services. (2001). *Mental health: Culture, race, and ethnicity: A supplement to Mental Health: A report of the Surgeon General.* Rockville, MD: U.S. Department of Health and Human Services, Substance Abuse and Mental Health Services Administration, Center for Mental Health Services.

Whaley, A.L., & Davis, K. (2007). Cultural competence and evidence based practice in mental health services: A complementary perspective. *American Psychologist, 62,* 563–574.

Wolffe, R. (2009). *Renegade: The making of a president.* New York: Crown.

Wolsko, C.P.B., & Judd, C.M. (2006). Considering the Tower of Babel: Correlates of assimilation and multiculturalism among ethnic minority and majority groups in the United States. *Social Justice Research, 19,* 277–306.

Wyatt v. Stickney, 344 F. Supp. 373 (Ala.1971).

Zimmerman, M.A. (1990). Taking aim on empowerment research: On the distinction between individual and psychological conceptions. *American Journal of Community Psychology, 18,* 169–177.

Index

Page numbers followed by *f* indicate figures; those followed by *t* indicate tables.